THE EMOTIONAL BODY

A Method for Physical Self-Regulation

Laura Bond

The Emotional Body
A Method for Physical Self-Regulation
© 2017 Pure Expressions, LLC
www.emotionalbody.co

Book Design by Erifily Nikolakopoulou
Figure and Facial Illustration Designs by Meghan Theye
Chart and Diagram Designs by Laura Bond and Erifily Nikolakopoulou

ISBN 978-0692046111
Printed in the USA

Second Edition 2018

This book development project was made possible by Hatchfund.org, a nonprofit organization devoted to assisting artists with raising start-up funding for their projects. Hatchfund helped us raise enough money to front the book design, editing and publishing costs. Between the months of January and March of 2017, The Emotional Body project received support from sixty-two generous financial donors from all over the United States, and from Australia, Brazil, Canada, Great Britain, Hong Kong, New Zealand and Switzerland!

We are so grateful to all those who donated funds toward the development of this book project and made our campaign successful!

We also want to extend a special thank-you to our major donors who went above and beyond in financial generosity, bringing our book development fundraising campaign up to a very high level of success.

A Special Thanks To:
Dan, Cheryl & Trinity Facciponti
George M. Bond Sr.
David C. Farmer
Patricia & Anthony Facciponti
Lorna Pearson-Hall

Table of Contents

Acknowledgments

I am extremely grateful to our Asheville writers group, who faithfully and tirelessly read, reread, critiqued, and encouraged the writing of this book. Barbara Marlowe, Bonita Osley, and Lavinia Plonka, thank you so much for your dedication to this book's development. It would not have been written without your support!

Additionally, I would never consider writing a book without running every single word by my editor, Stephanie Schlie, whom I have come to trust for her honest appraisal of my writing and for her advice on each chapter's clarity.

UNC Asheville has consistently supported my research on Alba Emoting and my development of teaching practices for the emotional effector patterns. The university granted me two sabbaticals, which I dedicated to researching and writing about the emotional effector patterns, and any time I have proposed a new course that incorporated these physical emotion regulation methods, it was approved and welcomed as a valuable contribution to the university curriculum. These were important opportunities for me to explore ways to teach the emotion patterns as they relate to various topics and fields, and they were invaluable experiences for my students as they learned more about their emotions and how they affect every aspect of their lives. I am so blessed to work for a university that values this work and supports its development!

My family and close friends have been a steadfast foundation and my greatest source of encouragement over the years. They are the ones who never failed to ask about how the emotion studies work was coming along while cheering me on to finish the book. My husband, George, adopted the mantra, "It's all about the book right now" as he tiptoed around the house and kept the dog quiet while I wrote for hours on end. The support, love, and encouragement of my family and friends were the battery power that kept me going day after day, pushing to reach the finish line. The blessings my family and friends constantly bring to my life cannot be expressed clearly enough in words and seem only to be captured fully in expressions of loving gratitude.

This book and the development of this physical approach to emotion regulation would not be possible without the original researchers who discovered the emotional effector patterns and the many teachers and somatic practitioners who have influenced the creation of this particular style of teaching the emotion patterns, called Emotional Body. I believe that humanity will be forever grateful for the discoveries made in the early 1970s by the original researchers of the emotional effector patterns: Susana Bloch, a full professor of neurophysiology at the University of Chile; and Guy Santibáñez, her colleague in the Medical School's Department of Physiology and the Department of Psychology. Later on, their colleague Pedro Orthous, professor of dramatic art from the Department of Drama, joined them to develop an approach, called the BOS Method, for using the patterns for emotion regulation. I am particularly grateful for the instruction and guidance I received from Susana Bloch and for her dedication to providing as a gift to humanity her own approach to teaching the emotional effector patterns, Alba Emoting.

The development of the Emotional Body teaching approach would not have been possible without constant collaborations with guild-certified Feldenkrais instructors Lavinia Plonka, Odette Guimond, and Jessica Beck. These three women, using Moshe Feldenkrais's philosophy of somatic education, were highly influential in my development of this approach. I will be forever grateful to these instructors for their encouragement, generosity, and intellect.

The Emotional Body was also influenced by the voice research and developments of Jo Estill. I want to thank my Estill Voice Training instructors, Julie Fortney and Kerrie Obert, for their encouragement to learn Estill Voice and to make connections between Estill and the emotional effector patterns.

I am also grateful to the many teachers I have worked with and observed over the years, both in the United States and in Chile. I believe great teachers and teaching methods are born from gleaning the best from the best, yet adopting a unique teaching style, and strengthening it with continuous reading, research, and a quest for adapting to the needs of the learner. If all teachers did this, then in theory each new generation of teachers would become better than the last. I hope that I have honored the teachers of my past by adopting some semblance of the best of their best practices while also sharing new knowledge, ideas, and methods to move the work ever forward. I encourage those that I have taught to do the same as they evolve and find their own approaches.

Finally, I want to thank all those whom I have taught over the years, for you have truly been the ultimate research collaborators in the development of this style of teaching the emotional effector patterns. Each workshop and course was an opportunity to strengthen teaching theories and practices and try new ones. Many of you who have returned to my emotion regulation courses over the years have commented on how the lessons have evolved, allowing you to learn something new and go deeper into the study of emotional fluency. That evolution certainly would not have been possible without all of you! Thank you for your willingness to participate in the development of The Emotional Body while you learned about your own!

Acknowledging Trademarks

The following methods referred to in this book are trademarked, and this book acknowledges their trademark here. Throughout the rest of the book the trademark is implied by this reference.

Alba Emoting™

Emotional Body™

Estill Voice Craft™

Feldenkrais Method®

Forward

This book emerged out of a persistent need to explore and examine the instruction of the emotional effector patterns, first discovered in scientific research in the early 1970s. Teaching methods for applying the patterns began development in the mid 1980s, and a small group of first-generation teachers trained by one of the original researchers of the emotional effector patterns emerged between 1990 and 2010. I was one of those teachers.

Between 1999 and 2003, I trained for over seventy hours in three different workshops, including one with teacher Nancy Loitz and two in which one of the original researchers, Susana Bloch, was a companion instructor with other teachers like Mauricio Gonzalez and Roxane Rix. Then, I served as a teaching assistant for two additional workshops led by Roxane Rix. With this training experience, I gained an excellent understanding of the emotional effector patterns and their application to performance, but I wanted to learn more about their potential for personal use and professional practice as well as how others were teaching the method.

In October 2005, I spent a sabbatical with Susana Bloch in Chile, where she and I designed a full month's private teacher training course for my studies of the emotional effector patterns and Alba Emoting, which is Susana Bloch's own system of teaching the emotional effector patterns. She helped me refine my practice of the emotion patterns, observed me teaching others, and then had me work with her on designing, planning, and teaching Alba Emoting workshops. She also arranged for me to meet with and observe the teaching of other Chilean teachers.

One particular teacher, Sergio Lara, who is a psychologist, psychotherapist, and master teacher of Alba Emoting, had created a body/mind center in Santiago called the Alba Institute. The center offered courses and private sessions in yoga, meditation, therapy, and Alba Emoting. The interior of the building supported a calm and centering atmosphere, designed with cool comforting colors, water fountains, and sacred spaces in each room. The center had a respectful, caring, and grounded feel to it. I spent the day observing classes and talking with the teachers and students. The students in the classes were from various professions, and most were taking the courses for personal emotion regulation development. The lessons I observed were gentle, gradual, and exploratory. This was a very different approach to teaching the patterns than I had seen in the past, particularly with performers. Participants at the Alba Institute were encouraged to use the emotion patterns as a means for self-discovery, to promote meaningful discussions about emotions, and to help them increase their ability to feel emotions in themselves as well as see their subtle expressions in others. These teachers also understood the difference between teaching the originally researched emotional effector patterns and developing specific styles of teaching the patterns, as with the Alba Emoting system. It was a liberating experience, and afterwards I had many conversations with Sergio about teaching the emotional effector patterns. I knew this experience would influence my own future developments as a teacher of the patterns, and I will be forever grateful for Sergio's generosity in sharing his approach and philosophy of teaching this method.

As I departed from my month-long study in Chile, Susana Bloch encouraged me to find my own style of teaching the emotional effector patterns and stressed that further exploration of vocal and physical expressions of the patterns was needed. She mentioned various somatic practices I might look into to enhance my work on the patterns and my teaching, and she asked me to look into vocal research and its relationship to the emotional effector patterns. Susana Bloch encouraged me to write about Alba Emoting as much as possible and to help spread the teachings of the emotional effector patterns.

After she had granted me the highest level of teaching certification in Alba Emoting available at the time, I returned to the states and realized I had found my research and teaching mission: to further develop the instruction of Alba Emoting and the emotional effector patterns and to help them become more approachable and available to the general public as physical methods for emotion regulation.

To fulfill this mission, I have sought the advice and expertise of professionals in various fields, intending to enhance my knowledge and understanding of our complex bodies and become a better instructor of physical emotion regulation. To my delight, throughout the last decade, all whom I approached responded with hearty acceptance and gave with great generosity.

Upon my return from Chile, guild-certified Feldenkrais teacher Lavinia Plonka and I decided to collaborate and create a somatic emotion regulation learning retreat in Mexico. In March 2007, eighteen people from various backgrounds attended our weeklong workshop in the picturesque beachfront village of Puerto Morelos. This collaboration prompted many exciting new developments in my teaching. I will always remember one of our participants, Feldenkrais teacher Odette Guimond, who casually said, "There must be a Feldenkrais way of teaching Alba." Her insightful statement fueled my search for many years after that to find a "Feldenkrais way." For several years, Odette attended more of my workshops and then invited me to teach in her home city of Montreal, Canada. Meanwhile, Lavinia Plonka and I developed regular workshops in Asheville, North Carolina. Throughout these years, I learned so much more about somatic sensing and the need to develop an instructional style based on clear and specific instructions. I started to develop a teaching style that built upon gradual steps of development and gave more personal space to the individual to explore their experiences of the patterns while learning about their own emotional body.

Additionally, the Feldenkrais teachers' understanding of human anatomy and physiology encouraged me to delve further into this information so that I could speak from a clearer knowledge of the body's functions when teaching the emotion patterns. I found myself becoming a happy research geek, poring through scientific journals, reports, and articles whenever possible, filing away interesting facts and keeping notes on important and influential research.

I also trained in the Estill Voice technique to explore a part of the emotion patterns that was still unresolved: vocal expression. Interestingly enough, there are many similarities between the emotional effector patterns and the scientific discoveries made by Jo Estill on the voice. After five years of study, practice, and then working as a teaching assistant in Estill Voice, I not only became a master teacher of Estill Voice but also made some important discoveries about the relationship between the expressive voice and the emotion patterns.

As my teaching style became more gentle, gradual, and universally approachable, I began teaching the emotional effector patterns to various groups. I taught the patterns to Live Strong classes at the YMCA, where cancer survivors learned the benefits of certain emotions that could help them reclaim healthier and more optimistic emotional states as they bravely persevered to live stronger, healthier lives. I designed a workshop for ontological coaches and helped them make connections between the emotion patterns and their life coaching practices. I shared the lessons of the emotion patterns with public speakers, somatic practitioners, teachers, college freshmen, caregivers, therapists, and even scuba divers. Each group was able to see how learning these emotional effector patterns could help them better understand themselves as well as how the patterns might apply to vocations or avocations. Teaching these groups also helped me continue to develop methods for reaching diverse populations and sharing the patterns with them while recognizing the patterns' universal ability for physical self-regulation of emotion. Each year, I applied these newfound developments and insights to my teaching as I taught the patterns to hundreds of people and shared my pedagogy in training more than a dozen new teachers.

Another Mexico workshop participant, Jessica Beck, who was becoming certified in both Alba Emoting and Feldenkrais, was particularly attracted to the Asheville workshops. Even though she had studied with many other Alba Emoting teachers, each summer she returned to Asheville. One day, she said, "You know, nobody else is teaching the emotional effector patterns quite the way you do. Your teaching approach is truly unique and detailed. You need to write about this and publish it." In this moment, Jessica's words reinforced something that I was beginning to believe internally but now knew was clear to those attending our workshops. After ten years of study and development, and with a constant focus on teaching pedagogy, I had developed a new and different approach to teaching and exploring the emotional effector patterns. I had created the Emotional Body approach to teaching the emotional effector patterns discovered in the 1970s.

The Emotional Body isn't the Alba Emoting system of teaching because Susana Bloch says the style of teaching Alba Emoting must first be learned in big strong ways and at high levels. Instead, the Emotional Body is a very gentle and gradual learning style, focused on developing somatic sensing skills and reinforcing a subtle and low-intensity approach to adopting the emotional effector patterns. This method also uses the new labeling system I created for the patterns, which removes the limitations of emotionally charged words, allowing the individual to complete their own subjective interpretation of the emotions or feelings evoked. The Emotional Body also focuses on exploring subtle movements of the muscles in the vocal tract, face, and posture to help the learner recognize how chronic low-level emotions could be carried over into their daily lives through very subtle behaviors and habits. The Emotional Body focuses on developing emotional fluency, with lessons on recognizing subtle differences between mixed emotions and entanglements, while also providing a lexicon of emotion words that relate back to the basic emotion patterns. Additionally, the Emotional Body offers many new exercises, research findings, and lessons developed through years of workshop refinement and exploration.

The Emotional Body is a new and unique approach to physical emotion regulation and developing emotional fluency. Emotional Body lessons incorporate the original emotional effector patterns discovered in scientific research and developed by the BOS team. The instructional style is influenced by the teachings of Moshe Feldenkrais and Jo Estill and informed by seventeen years of researching emotion studies and then developing my own style of teaching the emotional effector patterns.

Many people who finish our Emotional Body workshops say that they feel inspired, elated, and forever changed. They express gratitude in learning so much about themselves and their newfound ability to understand emotional expression and how it can exist within their daily behaviors. They leave our workshops feeling they have more control of their emotions and a new respect for the expressions of others. They say learning this technique is truly a gift to their lives. I hope you find similar discoveries as you explore this book and get to know your emotional body!

-Laura Bond

Preface

E motions are emotional. This statement may seem obvious, but it is important to recognize that the topic of emotions and their relationship to your life will naturally evoke a variety of emotions.

We are sensitive about emotions. Even though this book reveals methods developed out of extensive scientific research, the topic of emotion and how it relates to our lives can be personally sensitive. Each society and culture establishes universally understood boundaries for emotions, including their usefulness and appropriateness. Various professions support specific philosophies concerning emotions, their capacity to serve or hinder human development, and their limits of use within particular fields. Each person holds their own beliefs about emotions and their expressive capabilities, reinforced by a lifetime of experiences.

We have emotions about emotions. Although human bodies begin with the same basic biological components designed to create and express emotions, as we mature and interact with our surroundings, emotions become highly individualized and complex. We evaluate our behavior. We can get upset over how we react to a moment or become frustrated by our own emotional limitations or habits. Our own psychological analysis can go on long past the actual emotional event. Some emotional events can manifest into complex psychological states from neuroses to serious trauma. Additionally, extreme life experiences, imbalances in chemicals and hormones, or uncommon neurological activities can create exceptional emotional challenges in some individuals. Stepping into the psychological underpinnings and socially constructed waters of emotions, which flow with deep personal and professional philosophies and practices, is entering into a complicated area that is best left to social scientists, clinical therapists, and psychologists.

Therefore, the methods supported in this book focus on the physical and physiological aspects of emotions rather than the psychological. The goal is to provide an evidence-supported somatic (body-centered) method for emotional awareness and regulation. The exercises and methods introduced here are intended as tools for somatic sensing, self-discovery, and physical self-regulation of emotions. This book is not intended as a substitute for therapeutic care or guidance from specialists.

The Emotional Body provides step-by-step lessons designed to build your understanding of basic emotion theory and the physical regulation of emotion. Stories shared help contextualize this information, centering on low-to-moderately intense emotional situations, providing potentially universal themes. Exploratory exercises guide you through gradual levels of self-discovery and the development of new tools for physical emotion regulation.

The information and lessons in this book will certainly influence your understanding of emotion and may improve your personal expressive capabilities. The book also provides valuable tools to use within fields such as mental and medical health, somatic education, business and communication, public presentation, and performance.

Many people have described the process of learning this method as "exhilarating," "enlightening," and "demystifying the mysterious world of emotions." They find this newfound knowledge to be "life-changing" and "personally empowering." Let the book spark your curiosity. Try the exercises that feel approachable. Allow yourself to gain a fresh new perspective on your expressive capabilities and their potential to enrich your life. Give your beliefs, philosophies, and preconceived notions about emotions a vacation, just long enough to absorb and consider this method as another way of looking at, experiencing, and expressing emotions.

An Invitation for Humanity

Learn about the possibility of entering and leaving emotional states with precision. Improve your awareness of what happens with your own emotions and learn to recognize them better in others. You could then become a better administrator or master of your emotions, not for the sake of control or manipulation, but in order to communicate better and thus be happier.[1]

- Susana Bloch

---

1. Susana Bloch, *The Alba of Emotions: Managing Emotions through Breathing* (Santiago: Grafhika, 2006), 108.

Meet Your Emotional Body

We are emotional bodies. We were born with bodies primed and ready to express our needs through emotions. Newborns don't have the ability to speak or gesture to convey their needs, and so basic emotions are preprogrammed communication functions in the human brain, providing genetic tools for surviving and living.[1] A baby's emotions are communicated through a cry or grimace when uncomfortable, hungry, lonely, or feeling threatened. The baby smiles or displays a serene look when comfortable, satiated, or feeling close and safe. As we mature, our communication of these feelings becomes more complex, and yet these inherent basic emotions stay with us our entire lives, influencing all that we feel, think, do, and say.

All the basic emotions are hardwired in the brain at birth, yet each emerges as the brain develops. We begin life shifting between two polar states of positive and negative affects (emotions). As we sense and then communicate physical disturbances or body needs, we go between the polarities of content/discontent, comfortable/uncomfortable, safe/distressed, and satiated/hungry.[2] The baby is

---

1. J. Panksepp, "Affective Consciousness: Core Emotional Feelings in Animals and Humans," *Consciousness and Cognition* 14 (2005): 30–80.

2. M. Lewis and L. Michalson, Children's Emotions and Moods: Developmental Theory and Measurement (New York: Plenum Press, 1983),139-155.

content and looks serene, discontent and begins to grimace. The baby is hungry, becomes uncomfortable, and cries until the discomfort stops after feeding, and then smiles. The emotional expressions are very simple at this point of human development because the basic survival needs are quite simple.

Gradually, we differentiate raw survival states into specific emotions like joy, sadness, anger, interest, tenderness, distress, contentment, sensuality, and fear. Generally, by the time we reach eight months old, all basic emotions have emerged and are actively used from moment to moment.[3]

When teaching emotion regulation, I often use pictures and videos of babies to demonstrate the basic emotions. We delight in the animated simplicity of their expressions and discuss how emotions become much more complex and challenging to interpret as we mature.

I explain, "As you practice this method, you may feel as if you are going back to your baby state, and it may feel strangely animated, like the expressions we see in clowns." Life was simple when we were babies, and babies' expressions may seem foreign to us now as adults. Yet their universality is clear and actually quite mesmerizing.

When my granddaughter was born, I had the opportunity to hold her at just 20 minutes old. Holding her, I was part of a group of adoring adults who were all transfixed by her face, which was already expressing so much of what she was feeling through tiny microexpressions. That moment demonstrated the incredible power of basic emotions and their ability to draw adult attention. A few weeks later I saw her again, and nearly all the basic emotions had clearly emerged.

Young children are just as transfixed by basic emotional expressions. They can clearly interpret them, often more than adults. Since verbal language takes much longer to develop, children rely on emotions as their primary source of information for their needs and social interactions.

Once, I was sharing a short video on the emotional effector patterns with my sister-in-law, and my three-year-old nephew joined us. While the video revealed pictures of babies, and adults demonstrating the emotion patterns, my young nephew promptly called out each of the emotions displayed, more accurately than his own mother: "Oh, he's sad." "Why is that man angry?" "She is happy!" He paused temporarily as an adult was expressing

3. C.E. Izard and C. Malatesta, "Perspectives On Emotional Development I: Differential Emotions Theory of Early Emotional Development," in *Handbook of Infant Development*, 2nd ed., ed J. Osofsky (New York: Wiley, 1987), 494-554.

sensuality, and then after a moment he said, "I think she likes her clothes."

Basic Emotions

Basic emotions are primal, instinctive reactions. They originate deep in the brain with the primary role of communicating survival information to the entire body. They can bypass the thinking part of our brains to deliver the fastest life-sustaining action by connecting directly to our reflexes and immediately activating the whole body.[4]

Emotions are complex functions. They incorporate muscle tension and movement, hormone release, cardiovascular changes, facial expression, visual and physical attention, and cognition (thinking).[5] A basic emotion emerges when a change in our state of being is needed for a situation. If we are in danger, fear emerges immediately in our reflexes, making us flee. If we feel the need to defend, anger rises in us and provides us with energy and defensive posturing for the fight. If we are in need of social connection, tender or sensual emotions arise, assisting with social bonding.

Feelings are subjective interpretations of bodily sensations. These can include those associated with emotions, as well as descriptors of body comfort or discomfort, social conditions, and motivations.[6] A person could be sad or angry (basic emotions) but also feel tired, cold, or sick (body discomfort). Someone could feel neglected or appreciated (social conditions) or motivated to take a trip, take a nap, or go out to dinner (motivations). Feelings might describe interpretations of personal conditions or motivations, whereas basic emotions are universal biological functions.

Emotions are constantly triggered by everything we encounter. Although emotion theorists have argued over centuries about where emotion begins and how it is triggered,[7] most scientists now agree emotions can be triggered by thoughts, actions, physiological changes, and the senses as well as through external stimuli, like environmental influences, social situations, noises, etc. Basically, emotions are triggered by anything we think, feel, sense, do, or come into contact with.[8]

---

4. J. Panksepp, "The Periconscious Substrates of Consciousness: Affective States and the Evolutionary Origins of the SELF," *Journal of Consciousness Studies* 5 (1977): 566–582.

5. Barbara L. Fredrickson and Michael A. Cohn, "Positive Emotions," in *Handbook of Emotions*, 3rd ed., eds. Michael Lewis, Jeannette M. Haviland-Jones, and Lisa Feldman Barrett (New York: Guilford Press, 2008), 778.

6. J. Panksepp, "At the Interface of Affective, Behavioral and Cognitive Neurosciences: Decoding the Emotional Feelings of the Brain," *Brain and Cognition* 52 (2003), 4-14.

7. G. Myers, "William James's Theory of Emotion," *Transactions of the Charles S. Peirce Society* 5, no. 2 (1969): 67–89, http://0-www.jstor.org.wncln.wncln.org/stable/40319566.

8. Lewis, "The Emergence of Human Emotions," *Handbook of Emotions*, 3rd ed., ed. Michael Lewis, Jeannette M. Haviland-Jones, and Lisa Feldman Barrett (New York: Guilford Press, 2008), 308.

Emotion Triggers

1. **Physiology** – illness, hormone shifts or imbalances, heart rate changes, etc.
2. **Actions** – movements, facial expressions, and breath patterns
3. **Thoughts** – beliefs, memories, imaginings, interpersonal and intrapersonal encoding
4. **Senses** – smell, hearing, touch, taste, sight
5. **Environment** – weather, space, animals, location/proximity
6. **Social Situations** – relationships, culture, community, work environment
7. **Events** – special occasions, significant life-altering events, rights of passage, moments of trauma

Emotions inform our bodies about a need for change. They function as an ongoing information superhighway for our bodies. Through sensing, feeling, and thinking, our bodies are constantly evaluating the ability to survive. Positive emotions inform us that we are successfully surviving and thriving, sending messages that all is well and to keep going about our activities. Negative emotions inform us that our survival is threatened and ongoing actions may harm us.[9] This is an ongoing, reciprocal process of sending and receiving messages as we move around, use our senses, and think. We are continuously oscillating between emotional states in different degrees of intensity,[10] and so the assumption is if we are awake, we are in some level of an emotional state.[11]

Negative Emotions (*Anger, Fear, Sadness*)
Survival oriented; meant for immediate and short-term application to life-threatening situations

Positive Emotions (*Tenderness/Care, Sensuality, Joy*)
Signal social safety and promising prospects for survival and meaningful community attachments; meant for long-term application to sustain life

The Emotional Body

We are our bodies, and our bodies are holistic representations of all that we think, sense, feel, and do. Contrary to many popular beliefs around mind-body connection or disconnection, there is not a division between the head and the rest of the body. The term *mind-body connection* refers to the brain's continuous monitoring of the entire body and how the bodily state dynamically influences brain function. The entire body, from head to foot, is constantly engaged in reciprocal neurological

---

9. M. Cabanac, "Pleasure: The Common Currency," *Journal of Theoretical Biology* 155 (1992), 173–200.

10. Susana Bloch, *The Alba of Emotions: Managing Emotions through Breathing* (Santiago: Grafhika, 2006), 31.

11. Michael Lewis, "The Emergence of Human Emotions," *Handbook of Emotions*, 3rd ed., eds. Michael Lewis, Jeannette M. Haviland-Jones, and Lisa Feldman Barrett (New York: Guilford Press, 2008), 308.

activity regulating all aspects of our survival, including breathing, digestion, muscle activation, thoughts, and emotions.[12]

Your body is the sum of your whole self. The notion of a mind-body disconnect is being abandoned by the great majority of scientists, particularly in regard to emotions.[13] All sensory and motor experience is accompanied by emotional discharge of some sort, and our habitual posture is the result of our emotional experience. The entire body, inside and out, is experiencing persistently recurring emotional states that become habitual and essentially create an individual's character.[14] Throughout this book, when the term *body* is used, it is referring to the whole and completely connected self.

Emotional Awareness

We can be emotional and not know it. Our bodies are constantly shifting emotional states, so it is possible, and quite common, to be in an emotional state and not recognize it.[15] Since the neocortex (thinking part of the brain) is not essential for generating basic emotions, we can enter emotional states, and even express them to others through our actions, yet not recognize an emotional event has occurred.

Our days are filled with countless emotional state shifts. They emerge through our posture, movement, gestures, breath, voice, facial expressions, and words. Meanwhile, they simultaneously affect our brain activity, thoughts, hormones, vagal tone, and the entire cardiovascular system. All of this is happening at once, inside and out, on varying levels of intensity, and constantly throughout our days. Can you see how we might not always be aware of our emotions?

Our emotions can be denied and repressed. We may choose to ignore an emotional state, not wanting to give it attention or expose to others how we are really feeling. More often than we realize, we may deny the very existence of an emotion, claiming we are not angry, happy, hurt, attracted, sad, afraid, or feeling guilty—even if we are. Defense mechanisms, including denial and repression, actually serve as important functions at times, preventing an individual from experiencing emotions that they deem unacceptable or risky. In fact, children as young as two and a half years old develop the ability to mask their emotions as well as to consciously use them to get what they want or to get out of a situation they perceive as threatening.[16]

---

12. Stephen W. Porges, *The Polyvagal Theory: Neurophysiological Foundations of Emotions, Attachment, Communication, Self-regulation* (New York: Norton & Company, 2011), 248.

13. Susana Bloch, *The Alba of Emotions: Managing Emotions through Breathing* (Santiago: Grafhika, 2006), 39.

14. Moshe Feldenkrais, *Body & Mature Behavior: A Study of Anxiety, Sex, Gratification & Learning* (New York: International Universities Press, 1949), 127–128

15. Ibid.

16. Michael Lewis, "The Emergence of Human Emotions," *Handbook of Emotions*, 3rd ed., eds. Michael Lewis, Jeannette M. Haviland-Jones, and Lisa Feldman Barrett (New York: Guilford Press, 2008), 314.

Emotions can be unconscious reactions. Basic emotional states originate deep in our survival instincts. There are times when a certain emotion is needed because a threat to our physical or social survival is detected; then, a basic emotion will temporarily override clear thinking and reason.[17] These unconscious emotional reactions can be as big as an overriding fight-or-flight response when we feel physically threatened or a bold action in a social environment that serves the need for acceptance or inclusion. Our unconscious emotional tactics may also come in the form of small acts, like slips of the tongue, or nonverbal vocal expressions, like sighs, groans, chuckles, and growls. This unintentional behavior can reveal unconscious emotions that are felt but not fully expressed.[18]

My husband recently went through a very challenging time. He lost his job due to a corporate cut and at the same time needed extensive foot surgery that meant he could not put any weight on his foot for up to three months. The slightest misstep, trip, or fall could put him right back into another surgery, and more months of no activity. Additionally, we were both dealing with the worry of having lost half of our household income for an indefinite amount of time until he was back on his feet and employed again.

I immediately found myself in a position as his full time caregiver, safety advisor, and driver as well as cheerleader and morale booster, all while trying to maintain my busy professional demands. Having a generally upbeat and positive demeanor, I did not think it would be difficult to maintain a cheery disposition as I took on this new role. However, I soon found myself sighing a great deal, usually when alone, but then the sighing became more prominent and began to slip out when talking to my husband. At first I thought, "I'm just tired and feeling overwhelmed. I need to rest when he rests and that will solve it." But after a few days attempting that strategy, the sighs persisted, now seemingly beyond my control and becoming apparent to my convalescing husband. This was not good. Although I kept apologizing for my behavior, I knew I had to address it soon or it would affect us both.

Then, it dawned on me: "I'm worrying constantly about my husband's condition and emotional well-being. My body knows it and needs to express it, even though I am consciously working hard to mask the worry with optimism." I knew that if I did not address this worry in a constructive way, it would keep trying to surface and would eventually become destructive to our situation.

I shared my worries with a supportive impartial group of peers and was

17. J. Panksepp, "The Periconscious Substrates of Consciousness: Affective States and the Evolutionary Origins of the SELF," *Journal of Consciousness Studies* 5 (1998): 566–582.

18. S. Freud, *The Psychopathology of Everyday Life,* trans. A. Tyson (New York: Norton, 1960), 74-139. (Original work published 1901)

surprised by how quickly the tears and sobs of worry, sadness, and fear all came to the surface. While finally admitting to how I was really feeling, my body trembled and released months of suppression. I did not try to hold it back, but permitted it to flow out of me as much as it needed, knowing I was in a safe place to let this happen. Then, after a short time of feeling numb from such a dynamic release, I was amazed at how good I felt. I promised myself to keep the communication going with this group so they could support me while I supported another. Soon, I was back to my truly cheery self again, and the sighs were gone.

Even after almost twenty years of studying and teaching emotion awareness and regulation, I still find myself in awe of the powerful overriding effect that our basic emotions can have on our lives.

Did you know...?

There can be some high costs to emotional suppression over long periods of time. Emotional suppression can affect our ability to remember information received from others[19] and to communicate effectively. It also has an impact on our comfort and ease with loved ones.[20] Defense mechanisms sometimes used by suppressors can create a negative emotional balance between couples and cause enough stress within the relationship to affect their overall health and deplete their immune systems.[21]

Emotionally Unaware

We can be unaware of our emotions, "not seeing the forest for the trees." The complexity of our emotional body makes it quite possible to be in and out of awareness from moment to moment. We might even be in an emotional state and not understand how to articulate what is happening or know how to express it clearly. Emotions can be subtle changes in our physiology or hormone levels, which cause us to feel a little different or affect our behavior unusually and without our understanding.[22] Our lack of emotional awareness does not mean

---

19. J.J. Gross, and O.P. John, "Individual Differences in Two Emotion Regulation Processes: Implications for Affect, Relationships, and Well-Being," *Journal of Personality and Social Psychology 85* (2003): 348-362.

20. E.A. Butler, B. Egloff, F.W. Wilhelm, N.C. Smith, E.A. Erickson, and J.J. Gross, "The Social Consequences of Expressive Suppression," *Emotion 3* (2003): 48–67.

21. T. Loving, K. Heffner, J. Kiecolt-Glaser, R. Glaser, and W. Malarkey, "Stress Hormone Changes and Marital Conflict: Spouses' Relative Power Makes a Difference," *Journal of Marriage and Family 66*, no. 3 (2004): 595–612, http://0-www.jstor.org.wncln.wncln.org/stable/3600215.

22. M. Lewis, (2005, October 17). "Early Individual Differences in Coping with Stress: Emotional Behavior, HPA and ANS Reactivity," (Paper presented at the New York Academy of Sciences, Psychology Section, New York, October 17, 2005)

these emotions are not affecting us; it merely means we are not aware of how they affect us and those around us. Emotions can impact our health, our actions, our communications, our perspective and perception of the world, and our relationships with others.

Emotions Affect Our Health

Anger, fear, and sadness tend to fall under the label of negative emotions because, when overused, they become detrimental to our well-being. The *negative emotions* are biologically designed for immediate and short-term application to life-threatening situations. In short-term use, these emotions are very important for our survival and serve to appropriately mark the importance of serious losses. However, if we do not shift back to a positive emotional state (joy, tenderness, sensuality), or if our life-threatening situation persists and we are required to sustain some level of a negative emotional state, then our health and well-being is seriously affected.[23]

The negative emotions are stressful. They elevate stress hormones and require heightened attention from our autonomic nervous system (ANS), which is responsible for controlling organ functions, including those of the respiratory system, heart, stomach, and digestive tract. With our ANS focused on sustaining negative emotion levels, it is diverted away from regulating organ functions. Prolonged negative emotion levels have direct implications for diseases, including heart disease, arthritis, diabetes, immune disorders, and even acne[24] or the common cold.[25] Extreme levels or prolonged use of negative emotions affects our mental and social well-being as well as our mortality. Overuse or misuse of negative emotions contributes to the development of anxiety disorders, eating disorders, depression, and sexual dysfunction as well as issues with self-injury, suicide, aggression, and violence to others.[26]

Tenderness, sensuality, and joy are called *positive emotions* because they affirm our well-being. Sustaining prolonged levels of positive emotion improves immune function, decreases pain levels, and increases our longevity. Positive emotions send reinforcing messages throughout our bodies, telling us we are socially safe and have promising prospects for survival and meaningful community attachments. Sustaining positive emotions prompts us to engage in our environment, partake in

---

23. J.K. Kiecolt-Glaser, L. McGuire, T.F. Robles, and R. Glaser, "Emotions, Morbidity, and Mortality," *Annual Review of Psychology* 53 (2002): 83–107.

24. Ted A. Grossbart and Carl Sherman, *Skin Deep: A Mind-Body Program for Healthy Skin* (New Mexico: Health Press NA Inc. (2009): 20-25.

25. Nathan S. Consedine, "Health-Promoting and Health-Damaging Effects of Emotions: The View from Developmental Functionalism," *Handbook of Emotions*, 3rd ed., eds. Michael Lewis, Jeannette M. Haviland-Jones, and Lisa Feldman Barrett (New York: Guilford Press, 2008), 676–678.

26. J.K. Kiecolt-Glaser, L. McGuire, T.F. Robles, and R. Glaser, "Emotions, Morbidity, and Mortality," *Annual Review of Psychology* 53 (2002): 83–107.

social activities, play, commit to meaningful relationships, and essentially become more socially integrated.[27]

Positive emotions encourage us to thrive and to savor the world around us. Moderated by opioid receptors and natural dopamine produced in our brains, they activate our natural desire "to want" and "to like." Sustained positive emotions actually encourage us to seek knowledge, become more flexible and resilient, and produce novel and creative thoughts.[28] Positive emotions broaden our scope of attention, which provides us with more information and greater processing and reasoning strategies. This, in turn, improves our outcome expectancy and overall outlook on our potential and the world around us.[29]

Attempting to maintain high levels of positive emotions at all times and in all situations is not necessarily the answer to achieving emotional well-being. Cultivating positive emotions as a general backdrop to our lives, while still reacting to short-term emotionally meaningful events either negatively or positively as needed, is considered more beneficial and healthy. [30]

Emotions Affect Our Perspective
Emotions act as a lens through which we see and perceive. Although emotions can emerge as reactions to our surroundings, they also motivate, organize, and guide our perceptions, thoughts, and actions.[31] Emotions actually influence what we see and how we assign meaning to what we see. We can walk the same path, see the same landscape, and interact with the same people; however, depending on the emotional state we are in, our experience and perception of the event will vary dramatically.

Negative emotions narrow our vision. They act like binoculars on a specific area of focus, which is first perceived as a threat. People passing by look more suspicious, the environment feels more threatening, and the objects around us can be perceived only as obstacles, getting in our way. When we are in life-threatening situations, this acute focus is essential to our survival.[32] Even when survival is not an immediate issue, the negative emotions will limit our visual scope, keep us from interacting

27. Barbara L. Fredrickson and Michael A. Cohn, "Positive Emotions," in *Handbook of Emotions*, 3rd ed., eds. Michael Lewis, Jeannette M. Haviland-Jones, and Lisa Feldman Barrett (New York: Guilford Press, 2008), 777–783.

28. Ibid.

30. A.M. Isen, K.A. Daubman, and G.P Nowicki, "Positive Affect Facilitates Creative Problem Solving," *Journal of Personality and Social Psychology*, 52 (1987): 112–113.

30. Barbara L. Fredrickson and Michael A. Cohn, "Positive Emotions," in *Handbook of Emotions*, 3rd ed., eds. Michael Lewis, Jeannette M. Haviland-Jones, and Lisa Feldman Barrett (New York: Guilford Press, 2008), 781.

31. C.E. Izard, *The Psychology of Emotions* (New York: Plenum Press, 1991), 14.

32. Barbara L. Fredrickson and Michael A. Cohn, "Positive Emotions," in *Handbook of Emotions*, 3rd ed., eds. Michael Lewis, Jeannette M. Haviland-Jones, and Lisa Feldman Barrett (New York: Guilford Press, 2008), 777–783.

with others, and cause us to miss or dismiss a large percentage of our surroundings.

Positive emotions broaden our vision. Positive emotional states engage our eyes in visual search patterns, increasing our peripheral stimuli and allowing us to take in more information about our surroundings.[33] This increased information seeking and broad visual perspective can eventually provide us with a global view of our world. As a result, perceptions of our environment become optimistic, open, and contemplative. We tend to listen more and carefully consider information. We welcome challenging, new, and creative ideas. We are more receptive, flexible, and inclusive of others. Positive emotions create a feeling of contentment, which then prompts self-insight and may encourage us to savor our surroundings.[34]

Positive emotions are far more durable and beneficial in the long term than negative emotions. The personal resources gained through a positive emotion's broad view and optimistic perspective are long lasting and provide benefits well beyond the brief initiation of the emotional state. They cultivate long-term personal transformation, enriching our lives and supporting our potential to be more creative, knowledgeable, resilient, socially integrated, and healthy individuals.[35]

Many years ago I tried a new exercise with one of my emotion study classes. The students had a clear sense of basic emotions: how to evoke them, experience them on various levels, and use them for actions and interactions. However, they were working in a studio environment and not yet aware of how each of these emotions would influence their vision, hearing, thoughts, and perceptions of their surroundings. So I took them outside, stood them all in a big circle, and asked each individual to depart the circle, walk a path of their own choosing, and then return to the circle. After their paths were selected, I then directed them to walk their paths again, and again, but each time embodying a different emotional state for their journey.

As students chose positive emotions for their journey, hands reached out and touched flowers, bushes, trees, and benches along their paths. Bare feet spread toes and sensed the changing terrain. Heads turned and tilted in response to new sounds of birds, planes, and distant voices. They smelled the branches of an evergreen, openly received a shifting breeze, or burst into laughter as they reacted to a sight or sound. At a point when all the students were applying positive emotions to their journeys, they appeared

33. H.A. Wadlinger and D.M. Isaacowitz, "Positive Mood Broadens Visual Attention to Positive Stimuli," *Motivation and Emotion* 30, no. 1, (2006): 87–99. http://doi.org/10.1007/s11031-006-9021-1.

34. Barbara L. Fredrickson and Michael A. Cohn, "Positive Emotions," in *Handbook of Emotions*, 3rd ed., eds. Michael Lewis, Jeannette M. Haviland-Jones, and Lisa Feldman Barrett (New York: Guilford Press, 2008), 777–783.

35. Ibid.

as a homogenized group in harmony with their surroundings.

Then, when the group applied various negative emotions to their walk, suddenly there was a tumultuous and disconnected array of individual perspectives. Some sobbed quietly while touching a leaf or dragged feet slowly along the path, looking at the ground the entire time. Others moved quickly through open spaces and hid under the protective tree coverings or behind bushes, keeping their distance from others. Some stomped along, angrily pushing away branches and shoving past people who moved too slowly. These emotive views created a group in discord with each other and their environment.

The group returned to the circle and we talked about their experiences. One student shared his experience with the emotional lens of Tenderness: "I could not believe how beautiful this garden looked and felt! I walk through here all the time and have never really noticed all the plants, the stepping-stones, or the sundial over there. When I walked, I felt light and loving everything and anything in front of me." The student then shared his experience of the same path in Sadness: "When I walked the same path, I didn't even notice half the things I saw before, and the things I did notice, I didn't care about, because all my focus was on me and inside myself!" The student continued with a third experience using Joy: "Again, I didn't notice the things I saw in the first two walks. This time my focus of attention was further outside the garden. I could hear and see more things beyond this place, and the same path was once again a whole new experience of delight, joy, and laughter. Funny, I assumed I would feel differently with each pattern, but I had no idea that changing my emotional state would completely change WHAT I would see."

The rest of the group exploded with concurrences of similar experiences, and more stories were shared of individual interpretations using an emotional lens. They all agreed that emotion transformed and influenced how they felt, what they thought, how they interacted, what they sensed, what they saw, and where they chose to place their attention. Exciting personal discoveries were made that day on how emotion affects far more than how we feel and can actually alter our focus, our attention, and what we perceive through hearing, smell, and touch. This has become a favorite exercise I now use with nearly every workshop or class on emotional embodiment and self-regulation.

Emotions and Social Bonding

We are hard-wired to connect with other humans. Social bonding is actually a physiological survival need, communicated through strong neural pathways.

Natural opioids are released into our systems when we are gregarious, playful, and engaged in meaningful social interactions. Raised opioid levels create an organic addiction to social attachments,[36] to the point where we go through a powerful separation distress phase, due to opiate withdrawal, when we lose meaningful social attachments. This may explain why lonely, disenfranchised individuals can be attracted to opiate drugs.[37] Additionally, since high opioid levels make us more confident and dominant,[38] it is also possible that individuals will take bold actions to maintain social attachments.

We get emotional about social situations. The strong emotions and chemicals driving social bonding and acceptance can override clear thinking in the moment. This may result in emotional behavior considered dysregulated for a particular social interaction. Angry or crying outbursts are not tolerated in most public or social situations. Poorly regulated negative emotions, like anger, in addition to creating conduct problems, can also result in peer rejection.[39] Anger's function is to overcome obstacles that get in our way either physically, mentally, or socially. If anger is not regulated within certain social situations, it actually repels others and diminishes potential for bonding.[40] Although disengaging emotions, like anger, fear, sadness, and disgust, do have the power to distance us from others, this is not always negative. Sometimes, these emotions provide distance from those who may cause harm or appear unsupportive.[41] However, when social bonds are broken, absent, or disrupted, including when we lose a loved one, our health is at risk.[42]

Positive emotions can act as "social glue." When we consciously use positive emotions to form and maintain meaningful social relationships, we can build long-lasting networks of social support.[43] Such conditions actually enhance our capacity to heal ourselves, maintain health, and reverse illness.

---

36. J. Panksepp, *Affective Neuroscience: The Foundations of Human and Animal Emotions* (New York: Oxford University Press, 1998), 261- 279.

37. E.J. Khantzian, "Understanding Addictive Vulnerability: An Evolving Psychodynamic Perspective," *Neuro Psychoanalysis* 5 (2003): 5–56.

38. J. Panksepp, J. Jalowiec, F.G. DeEskinazi, and P. Bishop, "Opiates and Play Dominance in Juvenile Rats," *Behavioral Neuroscience* 99 (1985): 441–453.

39. N. Eisenberg, R.A. Fabes, I.K. Guthrie, and M. Reiser, "Dispositional Emotionality and Regulation: Their Role in Predicting the Quality of Social Functioning," *Journal of Personality and Social Psychology* 78 (2000): 136–157.

40. A.A. Marsh, N. Ambady, and R.E. Kleck, "The Effects of Fear and Anger Facial Expressions on Approach and Avoidance-related Behaviors," *Emotion*, 5 (2005): 119–124.

41. Ibid.

42. Stephen W. Porges, *The Polyvagal Theory: Neurophysiological Foundations of Emotions, Attachment, Communication, Self-regulation* (New York: Norton & Company, 2011), 295.

43. Agneta H. Fischer and Antony S.R. Manstead, "Social Functions of Emotions," in *Handbook of Emotions*, 3rd ed., eds. Michael Lewis, Jeannette M. Haviland-Jones, and Lisa Feldman Barrett. (New York: Guilford Press, 2008), 456–461.

Did you know...?

When a person socially disengages, prompted by emotions of shame, embarrassment, or depression, the body experiences diminished levels of serotonin and dopamine, considered the "happiness and contentment hormones."[44]

Yet when a person engages in joyful social play, these hormone levels increase[45] while also fueling brain development, building enduring intellectual resources, and increasing creative thinking capabilities.[46]

Secure social situations encourage us to share emotions more freely. When we are among loved ones or within an intimate relationship, we tend to share our emotions more freely as a means of bonding to those we care about and who we know care about us. Within relationships, positive emotions connect us with others on more meaningful levels while negative emotions provide cues to loved ones that we need support, want changes, or feel uncomfortable with a specific situation.[47]

When we were in our late twenties, my younger brother and I were helping our parents paint an upstairs bedroom. As we stood casually talking during a break, suddenly a bright flash of blue light filled the room, followed by a tremendous bang. Within the initial light flash, my body instinctively jumped up and back about two feet as I screamed and pulled my arms in toward my body and leaned back, as if trying to pull myself as far away from the source of the light as possible in one quick movement. My eyes popped wide open, and I froze in fear while trying to determine what happened. In the same instant, my brother instinctively jumped about two feet forward, at an angle, landing with his body between me and the source of the light flash. He pulled his chest up and forward, and as he emitted a growling sound, his hands fisted in front of him and he narrowed his eyes on the source of

44. J. Panksepp, G. Yates, S. Ikemoto, and E. Nelson, "Simple Ethological Models of Depression: Social-Isolation Induced "Despair" in Chicks and Mice," in *Animal Models in Pyschopharmacology*, ed. B. Olivier, J. Mos, & J. L. Slangen (Basel: Birkhauser-Verlag, 1991), 161-181.

45. J. Panksepp, *Affective Neuroscience: The Foundations of Human and Animal Emotions* (New York: Oxford University Press, 1998), 261-279.

46. L.R. Sherrod and J.L. Singer, "The Development of Make-believe Play," in *Sports, Games and Play*, ed. J. Goldstein (Hillsdale, NJ: Erlbaum, 1989), 1–38.

47. Agneta H. Fischer and Antony S.R. Manstead, "Social Functions of Emotions," in *Handbook of Emotions*, 3rd ed., eds. Michael Lewis, Jeannette M. Haviland-Jones, and Lisa Feldman Barrett (New York: Guilford Press, 2008), 456–461.

the flash, as if daring it to try to penetrate him. We both froze in this stance for about ten seconds, and then our mother called up from downstairs, "Is everyone okay? The electrical transformer on the telephone pole outside just blew up." As soon as we understood the source of the explosion and realized there was no longer a threat, we started laughing and joked with each other about our very different reactions to the explosion.

In that instant, it was clear that my brother's instinctive reaction to potential bodily harm was to fight and protect whereas mine was definitely to flee the situation. We had already established a familial relationship that supported these roles, and our individual bodies knew within less than a second what was the best reaction to the situation.

Did you know…?

Our beliefs about emotions, and whether they are fixed or malleable states in our lives, actually affect our emotional well-being. If we think our emotions are fixed, then we tend to believe that our personality, intelligence, and even our emotional competency does not change. We think we don't really have the ability to shift and regulate emotional states; instead, we tend to believe emotions are uncontrollable reactions to what happens in our lives. However, if we think that emotions are malleable, we believe that our personalities, abilities, intelligence, and social competency are influenced by our emotions and their regulation.

In a study conducted at the University of California, Berkeley, researchers determined those who believe emotions are malleable tend to experience greater levels of positive emotions, fewer negative emotions, and higher levels of social adjustment and feelings of well-being. Additionally, those who believe emotions are malleable experience less depression and feelings of loneliness.[48]

Emotional Intelligence

Emotions are tools we use every day, either consciously or unconsciously. Emotional intelligence is our conscious use of emotions, aligned with our goals and the social standards of certain situations or cultures.

48. M. Tamir, O.P. John, S. Srivastava, and J.J. Gross, "Implicit Theories of Emotion: Affective and Social Outcomes Across a Major Life Transition," *Journal of Personality and Social Psychology* 92 (2007): 731–744.

Someone with strong emotional intelligence can...
- *Perceive* and *express* emotions accurately
- Understand and *express* emotions appropriately for the situation
- *Regulate* emotions in order to foster personal growth and successfully manage situations with others[49]

Notice how much of emotional intelligence requires heightened bodily awareness and clear embodiment of emotions (marked in italics in the above definition). Perceiving emotions requires sensing them in your body. Expressing emotions accurately relies on a clear understanding of basic emotions and how they are expressed as well as an awareness of your habitual embodiment of these emotions. Regulating emotion requires the physical ability to shift into a different emotional state, to manage a situation in a different way.

Physical Self-Regulation of Emotion

Emotion Regulation is how we use emotions to support our lives. If we are regulating our emotions, we are consciously choosing which emotions we have, when we have them, and how we experience and express them.[50] If emotions were a car, taking you on a journey through your life, emotion regulation would be like being in the driver seat of emotions, rather than in the passenger seat. You are more in control of the twists and turns of the journey. You decide which path to take in each situation, rather than sit by and be a passive observer of the journey.

Generally, acceptable emotion-regulation practices make negative emotion use more beneficial and short-lived while promoting positive emotions for long-term regular use.[51] When emotions are poorly matched for the situation, are of an inappropriate intensity level, or are generally not serving us well, then they are dysregulated. Successful self-regulation of emotion requires sensing when dysregulation occurs and having the ability to shift into a different emotional state or intensity level that is better suited for the situation. Continuing with the car analogy, it is like adjusting to the twists and turns in the road by decreasing speed, shifting gears, or hitting the breaks.

Physical self-regulation of emotion requires developing deep and detailed somatic sensing skills and a knowledge of how these translate into emotional expression.

Somatic is a term that relates to the body. The word *soma* comes from the Greek

---

49. J.D. Mayer and P. Salovey, "What Is Emotional Intelligence?" in *Emotional Development and Emotional Intelligence*, eds. P. Salovey and D.J. Sluyter (New York: Basic Books, 1997), 3–31.

50. J.J. Gross, (1998). "The Emerging Field of Emotion Regulation: An Integrative Review," *Review of General Psychology 2* (1998): 271–299.

51. J.D. Mayer and P. Salovey, "What Is Emotional Intelligence?" in *Emotional Development and Emotional Intelligence*, eds. P. Salovey and D.J. Sluyter (New York: Basic Books, 1997), 3–31.

word for body, and *somatic sensing* is physically "tuning into" many aspects of our bodies using all our senses (sight, smell, taste, sound, touch, and movement). Touch and movement sensing includes awareness of minute movements of muscles, skin temperature, pulse, breathing patterns, and any feelings like tingling, looseness or tightness of certain areas, resistance or ease of movement, or overall physical attitudes or intentions with movement. In addition to somatic sensing skills, physical self-regulation requires an understanding of how these sensations translate with respect to emotions. Learning how emotions emerge and express in and through our bodies is an essential element in achieving somatic self-regulation of emotion.

Few people have developed a heightened sense of bodily awareness and physical emotion self-regulation. Unfortunately, for far too many years, emotion has been addressed primarily from a purely psychological point of view. The perpetuation of a mind-body disconnect has caused us to live almost exclusively in our heads. However, with somatic sensing education and training, we can learn to more accurately recognize what we are feeling and express it clearly to others.[52]

Emotion regulation is a learned skill. It is first taught to us by our parents or guardians and then reinforced by community and cultural standards. These early emotion regulation lessons are acquired through trial and error. Children first read the body language of adults for reinforcement. When adults smile and clap hands enthusiastically at a child's behavior, it is reinforced. When adults frown at them, children sense their behavior is not meeting approval. Once language is understood, children receive more lessons in emotion regulation as adults articulate acceptable and unacceptable behaviors understood within the family, community, and culture. Childhood emotion regulation experiences have a strong impact on our future abilities to self-regulate our emotions.[53]

Did you know...?

Studies have shown that parents who reinforce positive emotions and discourage overuse of negative emotions raise children who show high quality social functioning, or social competence. However, parents who reinforce emotion regulation through harsh parenting methods, particularly when dealing with a child's anger, contribute to greater levels of anger in the child as

52. Susana Bloch, *The Alba of Emotions: Managing Emotions through Breathing* (Santiago: Grafhika, 2006), 32.

53. C.Z. Malatesta and J.M. Haviland, "Learning Display Rules: The Socialization of Emotion Expression in Infancy," *Child Development* 53 (1982): 991–1003.

well as to the development of aggression and conduct problems over time.[54] When parents instead respond to a toddler's anger with calm neutrality or cheerful displays, the result is a child who shows interest in the environment, exhibits more positive emotions, and displays competent and empathetic behavior.[55]

As we grow up, individualized emotion self-regulation methods are developed instinctively through personal exploration. Here are some examples of common instinctive practices for physical self-regulation of emotion[56]:

- Reading a room full of people and "acting accordingly" in the ways our culture has deemed as appropriate behavior

- Using more positive emotional behavior to establish and maintain social connections or advance professionally

- Suppressing emotions in attempts to avoid negative thoughts, feelings, or interactions

- Using physical practices or activities to soothe ourselves or help us feel calm, centered, optimistic, or regenerated. Such activities might include conscious deep breathing, dancing, eating desirable foods, exercising, getting a massage, interacting with nature, playing joyfully, listening to music, meditating, singing, engaging in sports, walking, or practicing yoga.

The instinctive self-regulation methods listed here do not necessarily require much skill in somatic sensing or an understanding of emotion physiology, but they can help us successfully maneuver social situations. Many of the physical practices mentioned in the last bullet item may also naturally stimulate various areas of the vagus nerve. The vagus nerve is the longest cranial nerve, and it has the most extensive distribution of all the cranial nerves, stretching from the brainstem down to the abdomen. The nerve's sensory fibers come in contact with many major organs in the body. Stimulating this nerve can provide high vagal tone and may serve as a form of self-regulation of emotion by making us feel more calm and content.[57]

---

54. S.E. Fine, C.J. Trentacosta, C.E. Ixard, A.J. Mostow, and J.L. Campbell, "Anger Perception, Caregivers' Use of Physical Discipline, and Aggression in Children at Risk," *Social Development* 13 (2004), 213–228.

55. C.Z. Malatesta and J.M. Haviland, "Learning Display Rules: The Socialization of Emotion Expression in Infancy," *Child Development* 53 (1982): 991–1003.

56. Peter Salovey, Brian T. Detweiler-Bedell, Jerusha B. Detweiler-Bedell, and John D. Mayer, "Emotional Intelligence," in *Handbook of Emotions*, 3rd ed., eds. Michael Lewis, Jeannette M. Haviland-Jones, and Lisa Feldman Barrett (New York: Guilford Press, 2008), 533–543.

57. Stephen W. Porges, *The Polyvagal Theory: Neurophysiological Foundations of Emotions, Attachment, Communication, Self-regulation* (New York: Norton & Company, 2011), 142–143.

The success of physical modes of self-regulation depends on understanding how the activities are conducted. For example, a person could sing, dance, or walk sadly; or someone might meditate with such concentration that they evoke low-level anger; or an individual could believe they are playing joyfully, but their play actually has elements of fear, sarcasm, or jealousy. A person who has not developed a clear sense of emotions and how they are expressed through breath, face, and posture could participate in these activities and still evoke negative emotions. In such cases, the activity could become an emotionally dysregulating action.

Somatic Psychology

Somatic psychology methods emerged as emotion regulation was receiving an unprecedented amount of focused scientific research.[58] Somatic psychology and somatic psychotherapy practices focus on bodily experiences and acknowledge the importance of examining and supporting holistic practices. The original meaning of psychology comes from the Ancient Greek word psyche, meaning "breath, soul, and mind." *Somatic psychology* then, literally translates to "the study of body, breath, soul, and mind," which forms a holistic approach to analysis and therapy and provides tools for somatic self-regulation.

Some schools of somatic psychology use extrinsic methods, meaning that emotion regulation is assisted by someone or something else. Extrinsic practices may have a trained professional guide a client through self-regulation or use hands-on methods for helping a person release chronic tensions associated with negative emotions and trauma. Conversely, intrinsic methods of emotion regulation are when emotion is self-regulated. With intrinsic methods, a person learns to sense when, how, and where emotion emerges in the body and then acquires skills for self-regulating these emotions. Intrinsic emotion-regulation methods are also used by many practitioners of somatic psychology, in which trained therapists provide lessons on how to sense emotions, and clients gain tools for self-regulating emotions without external guidance.[59]

The *Emotional Body* provides an intrinsic physical method for both somatic sensing and aligning sensations with emotional expression. The exercises in this book assist you with breaking down bodily sensations into emotional expression terms and provide specific tools for choosing and constructing new expressive patterns. By learning how your body expresses the basic emotion patterns you will increase your ability to recognize emotions in yourself and others, to regulate emotional expression, and to shift from undesirable emotional states to more desirable ones.

---

58. J.J. Gross, "The Emerging Field of Emotion Regulation: An integrative Review," *Review of General Psychology 2* (1998): 271–299.

59. J.J. Gross and R.A. Thompson, "Emotion Regulation: Conceptual Foundations," in *Handbook of Emotion Regulation*, ed. J.J. Gross (New York: Guilford Press, 2007), 3–24.

Did you know…?

When we consciously sustain positive emotions, either through conscious self-regulation practices or by engaging in loving and nurturing relationships, we actually increase our levels of oxytocin (a healthy neuropeptide). Studies have shown that the emotion of tender love and the consistent exchanges of actions often associated with this emotion—like hugging, caressing, and loving touch—produce high levels of oxytocin, which induces states of relaxation, low blood pressure, and increased feelings of trust.[60] The nurturing act of breastfeeding also produces oxytocin, which provides the added benefits of social-emotional reinforcement, feelings of trust and social sensitivity, and an inhibition of separation distress.[61]

Get to Know Your Emotional Body

By learning more about emotions and developing skills for sensing how they emerge and express through your body, you can become more adept at self-regulating emotions.[62] Learning the physical methods for emotion regulation covered in this book will provide you with valuable tools that will influence many different aspects of your life.

Once you practice and apply the methods in this book, you will find you can

- Self-regulate your emotions with greater ease and success
- Create regular and sustained states of calm and contentment
- Decrease overuse of emotions that are damaging to yourself and others
- Discover new levels in your expressive capabilities
- Embody, express, regulate, and release emotions easily
- Practice emotion regulation without relying on subjective contexts
- Acquire a better understanding of yourself and others
- Develop more options for responding to the actions of others

Read on. Practice the exercises in this book. And enjoy the journey of getting to know your emotional body while discovering new levels in your expressive capabilities!

---

60. Barbara L. Fredrickson, Positivity: *Top-notch Research Reveals the Upward Spiral that will Change Your Life* (New York: Three Rivers Press, 2009), 94.

61. J. Panksepp, *Affective Neuroscience: The Foundations of Human and Animal Emotions* (New York: Oxford University Press, 1998), 261-279.

62. Tanja Wranik, Lisa Feldman Barrett, and Peter Salovey, "Intelligent Emotion Regulation: Is Knowledge Power?" *Handbook of Emotion Regulation*, ed. J.J. Gross (New York: Guilford Press, 2007), 393–403.

Basic Emotions 2

How Many Basic Emotions?

Scientists disagree on the number of basic emotions. The research on basic emotions is often conducted through the lens of various branches of science. The results are quite varied. In fact, the number of basic emotions discovered can range from as few as four to as many as nine. Many of these studies identify more negative emotions than positive emotions, with some reporting only one positive emotion.

Each emotion's distinctly different role in survival may be the reason that negative emotions get more attention than positive ones. For example, anger is clearly aligned with a fight (or protect) response. Fear ignites an urge to flee. Sadness is directly associated with personal loss of control or social attachment needs. During urgent situations, a negative emotion often demands intense and focused use of the entire body, resulting in the short-lived activation of one strong basic emotion. Due to this fact, negative emotions may be more clearly identified by study participants reporting their emotional experiences as well as by the scientists conducting the studies.[1]

Positive emotions have a very different role in survival than negative ones. Positive emotions make us feel good and are meant for long-term use. Tenderness is associated with nurturing and caring for others. Sensuality allows us to savor our surroundings as well as to invite and engage in intimacy. Joy fulfills our need to play and celebrate life. Since positive emotions initiate a broader range of thoughts and actions, people often experience multiple positive emotions at once or quickly move from one to the other without even realizing it. For example, we can be in the midst of joyously

---

1. Barbara Fredrickson and Michael A. Cohn, "Positive Emotions," in *Handbook of Emotions*, 3rd ed., eds. Michael Lewis, Jeannette M. Haviland-Jones, and Lisa Feldman Barrett (New York: Guilford Press, 2008), 777–783.

celebrating while also savoring the moment; we can be exchanging brief looks or touches of intimacy with a romantic partner while giving hugs of tender love to others around us. With so many subtle shifts possible within a moment, positive emotions are less cognitively distinct and we have a hard time describing how we are feeling in these moments. Likewise, scientists and their study participants may not have been able to clearly distinguish between the subtleties of different positive emotions, so many studies in the past may have missed these distinctions and neglected to report on more than one positive emotional state, often labeling any positive emotion as either *joy* or *happiness*.[2]

Studies conducted by Dr. Jaak Panksepp, as well as the Chilean research team led by Susana Bloch, clearly identified several positive emotions. Conducted within the neuroscience field, these studies took precise neurological activity readings and recorded observations of actions, gestures, breathing, and facial expressions in order to distinguish between the basic emotions.

Dr. Jaak Panksepp was a renowned neuroscientist and psychobiologist who, in the 1990s, coined the term *affective neuroscience*, the name for the newly developing field studying neural mechanisms of emotion.[3] With research goals similar to Susana Bloch's, Dr. Panksepp has dedicated his professional career to the identification and scientific support of basic emotions. His research was primarily conducted on animals, and he related the neurological findings to all mammals, including humans.[4]

In the 1960s and '70s, Susana Bloch was a full professor of neurophysiology who specialized in brain function and its relationship between biology and psychology. Her initial research was with animals. In the early 1970s, after a full career in brain research of animals, she proposed a shift. While developing psychology courses for the theater school of her university, she changed the focus of her research to how the brain functions with human emotions. From that point on, she and her colleague, Guy Santibáñez-H from the Medical School's department of Physiology and Psychology, made remarkable discoveries on physiological activity and emotions.[5] They also collaborated with Pedro Orthous, professor of Dramatic Art from the Drama department to bring the scientific discoveries of the emotional effector patterns into a physical emotion regulation method they called the BOS method (using an acronym derived from the initials of their last names).[6] For the remainder of this chapter and

---

2. Ibid.

3. J. Panksepp, "A Critical Role for Affective Neuroscience in Resolving What is Basic about Basic Emotions", *Psychological Review* (1992): 99.

4. J. Panksepp, *Affective Neuroscience: The Foundations of Human and Animal Emotions* (New York: Oxford University Press, 1998), 9-23.

5. G. Santibáñez-H and S. Bloch, "A Qualitative Analysis of Emotional Effector Patterns and their Feedback," *Integrative Psychological and Behavioral Science* 21 (1986): 108–116.

6. Susana Bloch, Pedro Orthous, and Guy Santibáñez-H, "Effector Patterns of Basic Emotions: A Psychophysiological Method for Training Actors," *Journal of Social Biological Structure* 10 (January 1987) 1–19.

this book, the patterns discovered in their research will be referred to as the *emotional effector patterns* (or *emotion patterns* for short), and the first method developed for instructing the patterns to others will be referred to as the *BOS method* (or *BOS* for short).

Interestingly enough, both Panksepp's and the BOS team's final conclusions on the number of basic emotions were quite similar. With the exception of Panksepp's identifying *seeking* as a basic emotion, their conclusions match nearly one to one.

BOS[7]	Panksepp[8]
Joy	Play
Anger	Rage
Sadness	Grief
Fear	Fear
Tenderness	Care
Sexual Love	Lust
	Seeking

Additionally, within their research on emotions, the BOS team went beyond the act of systematically identifying the basic emotions. They proceeded to develop a method for physically evoking each of the basic emotions by instructing people on how to replicate the breathing and muscular patterns identified in their research. This extended research and development was highly successful, and as a result, the BOS team created the foundations for a reliable and scientifically based method for physical self-regulation of emotions. The BOS method is the foundation for the basic emotions addressed in The *Emotional Body* and the technique for their embodiment and regulation that is shared throughout the book.

The BOS Research Team Findings

In 1970, the BOS team worked to identify a clear link between breathing and emotional shifts.[9] The team conducted research on emotions, monitoring the respiration rates as well as the heart rates, arterial pressure, and muscle tone of subjects reliving emotional states while under hypnosis.[10] They wanted to

---

7. Ibid, 131–141.

8. J. Panksepp, "Affective Consciousness: Core Emotional Feelings in Animals and Humans." *Consciousness and Cognition* 14 (2005): 30–80.

9. Susana Bloch, *The Alba of Emotions: Managing Emotions through Breathing* (Santiago: Grafhika, 2006), 113–124.

10. G. Santibáñez-H and S. Bloch, "A Qualitative Analysis of Emotional Effector Patterns and their Feedback," *Integrative Psychological and Behavioral Science* 21 (1986): 108–116.

measure as many physiological changes occurring during basic emotional states to see if specific universal patterns could be identified. The team based their research on the five basic emotions identified by 19th century philosopher William James and physician Carl Lange—known for the James-Lange theory of emotion, which hypothesizes that physiological arousals initiate emotions.[11] The BOS team's initial plans intentions were to identify two positive emotions: joy and love. However, as their research progressed, it became evident that there were two kinds of love that were subjectively, physiologically, and behaviorally different. They identified the difference between *sexual love* and *tenderness*.[12]

The team's clear identification of the physiological differences between two forms of love was a critical distinction for science and for humanity. Susana Bloch acknowledges that very few researchers include these forms of love (tenderness and sexual love) in their lists of basic emotions, but her own research supports their universal biological roots. She stresses that without these two forms of love, our very survival would be under threat. Without sexual love, we would not mate and our species would become extinct. Without tenderness, we would not form and maintain the social bonds necessary for our health and well-being.[13]

The BOS team, along with many other scientists, agree with the Darwinian perspective that each basic emotion not only has a specific, direct one-to-one correspondence to an internal state or function but is also itself a physical and mental functional state of the entire organism. According to this perspective, the basic emotions make up the essential relating code that allows all human beings to adjust to diverse situations. These emotions perpetually run through our life functions, even when situations are complex. In fact, basic emotional coding is at the root of our abilities to adjust to and manage every situation.[14]

Susana Bloch continued research on the emotional effector patterns throughout the 1970s and 1980s. While acknowledging that the scientifically discovered emotional effector patterns were published and available for anyone to read about and explore, she also recognized the need to develop specific approaches and tenets for teaching the emotion patterns. She proceeded to move beyond the BOS method for teaching the patterns and refined and trademarked her own system for instructing people to physically evoke emotions using the emotional effector patterns. Her system for teaching the patterns is called *Alba Emoting*, derived from the Spanish word for dawn (*alba*) and the English word for expressing emotion (*emoting*).[15]

11. C. Golightly, "The James-Lange Theory: A Logical Post-Mortem," *Philosophy of Science* 20, no. 4 (1953): 286–299.

12. Susana Bloch, *The Alba of Emotions: Managing Emotions through Breathing* (Santiago: Grafhika, 2006), 49–55.

13. Ibid.

14. Michael Lewis, "The Emergence of Human Emotions," *Handbook of Emotions*, 3rd eds., eds. Michael Lewis, Jeannette M. Haviland-Jones, and Lisa Feldman Barrett. (New York: Guilford Press, 2008), 308.

15. Susana Bloch, *The Alba of Emotions: Managing Emotions through Breathing* (Santiago: Grafhika, 2006), 25–55

The Alba Emoting method of teaching includes instruction on the emotional effector patterns, neutral, and Step Out as well as the incorporation of three tenets for instructional practice: *style*, *ethic*, and *aesthetic*.[16] In general terms, the *style* of teaching Alba Emoting includes starting emotion pattern application with the breathing part of the pattern and initially applying each pattern with high intensity. The learner is given the space to experience the effects of the pattern without concern for perfecting the application. Eventually, the individual's system adopts a resonance with the imposed emotion pattern, and the emotion adapts into a less mechanical and personal style of expression. The *ethic* of Alba Emoting is meant to ensure that an instructor has a mature and spiritual approach to the philosophy of life and is using the patterns not as a tool for negative manipulation of people but for the good of humanity. Finally, the *aesthetic* tenet is a reminder that the emotional effector patterns are biological patterns that essentially serve as an approach to reconnecting with nature. Therefore, it is recommended that some semblance of nature is present when teaching the emotional effector patterns as a visual reminder of their roots.[17]

Since developing this method in the late 1980s, Susana Bloch has trained a small number of trusted instructors to teach the emotion patterns and use the Alba Emoting method of instruction. The teachers she personally certified continue to share the benefits of these scientifically supported patterns and to honor the foundations of Alba Emoting while also gradually developing their own approaches to teaching the emotional effector patterns. At the time of this book's development, teachers of Alba Emoting in both Chile and the United States are in the process of forming organizations to support the ongoing development, dissemination, and instruction of these patterns. The United States organization currently calls Alba Emoting the *Alba Method*.

Mixed Emotions

Basic emotions eventually mix with each other to create new, or secondary, emotions. Once babies mature enough to move and interact more with others and to eat foods beyond their mothers' milk, new emotions emerge to express their feelings, such as disgust, pride, shame, embarrassment, envy, guilt, and shyness.[18] The terms used for these new emotions vary greatly among scientists. Some call the basic emotions *primary* and refer to the new emotions as *secondary*. The *Emotional Body* uses the term *emotional mixes* to align with the theory that life begins with basic emotions and, as humans socialize and engage with their environment, those original basic emotions mix to create new emotions. Mixed

16. Susana Bloch, interviewed (video recorded) by Laura Facciponti at Susana Bloch's house in Cachagua, Chile on October 5, 2005.

17. Ibid.

18. Michael Lewis, "The Emergence of Human Emotions," *Handbook of Emotions*, 3rd ed., eds. Michael Lewis, Jeannette M. Haviland-Jones, and Lisa Feldman Barrett (New York: Guilford Press, 2008), 304–317.

emotions become the majority of the emotions expressed in our mature adult behavior, with pure basic emotions emerging in rare and very clearly identified moments of expression. Consider the metaphor of color mixing to understand how our emotional mixes are produced—much like a painter's palette where primary colors are mixed to create new and exciting hues. This is similar to our emotional expression. We move back and forth between using the primaries and the mixes.[19]

As we create these emotional mixes, we each develop our own unique emotional palette. Although we can easily recognize many of the mixed emotions there will be subtle differences in the ways two people express them. Let's return to the metaphor of mixing paint. Imagine that several individuals mixed the three primary colors (red, blue, yellow) to create new colors. Even though each person began with the exact same colors, the resulting new colors would have subtle differences. The new colors created could be identified as forms of purple, orange, green, or brown; however, they would vary slightly depending on how much of one primary color was mixed with another. If you put the painters' individually created purples next to each other, each would look slightly different from the others, some having more red tones and others more blue. The same is true for emotional mixes. If you ask a group of people to express a mixed emotion (like disgust), each person will have their own interpretation of how to express it, despite how easy the emotion may be to identify.

This book is dedicated to instructing the embodiment of basic emotions, both by describing the patterns discovered in the initial research conducted by the BOS team and by providing instructions for their embodiment, regulation, and clearing. This process of emotional embodiment is actually a method for relearning what our bodies instinctively know; however, a lifetime of mixing emotions has taken us further and further away from the primary process emotions with which we started life. As Susana Bloch states, "The more we are disconnected from pure basic emotions, the more complicated [become] our inner states, to the point that frequently we lose the capacity to identify them in ourselves and in others."[20] Once we are reacquainted with the basic emotions, which are the fundamental structures from which mixed emotions are organized, emotional mixes become much easier to identify. Similar to the color mixing theory, once you know how to sense, see, and reproduce the primaries, any mixed emotional behavior can be deconstructed into the basic emotion components. Likewise, any mixed emotion can be consciously constructed by mixing those basics. Learning this method can provide you with advanced skills in self-regulation of emotion as well as the ability to more clearly read and understand the emotions expressed by others.

---

19. Susana Bloch, *The Alba of Emotions: Managing Emotions through Breathing* (Santiago: Grafhika, 2006), 63.

20. Ibid, 55.

Emotional Entanglements

An *emotional entanglement* is when a basic emotion other than the emotion an individual intends to express, intermingles with the intended emotion and creates an undesirable mixed emotional state. Entanglements feel like an inability to express one emotion without another one hijacking the situation. Susana Bloch referred to these as "emotional parasites"[21] that have attached themselves to a person's emotions and expressions.

An example of an emotional entanglement is when someone wants to express anger but ends up crying through their attempts to be serious and strong. In another situation, embedded fears might keep a person from receiving or expressing tender love or sensual touch. They may find their body is suddenly overtaken with tension, which effectively pulls them back from the affection they desire. In these cases, a person wants to express one emotion but can't without another one attaching itself, seemingly permanently. It's like a plant that wants to grow and bloom but can't because the weeds entangled around its base grow up the stem and hold the plant back from its potential. Entanglements are formed by life experiences, in which a person has received messages or lived situations that strongly associate these emotions with each other. The result is dual expressive states, where a person finds that one emotion cannot be expressed without the other.

Someone who has entangled emotions might think, "I want to address the group seriously about something that is important to me, but I keep getting teary-eyed and my voice quivers," or "Every time I try to speak tender words of love and caring, I get choked up, so I remain silent and I fear I appear cold and uncaring," or "I feel as if I have been taken for granted and I want to stand up for myself, but every time I try to confront the situation I weaken, pull back, and fail to speak up."

It can feel as if these entanglements are permanent parts of our personalities and that we must live with these limitations. However, this is simply untrue. They can be "un-entangled." With the Emotional Body practice, you can begin to sense exactly when and where another emotion creeps in and tries to attach itself to the other. Through gradual repetitive practice, the associated emotion becomes detached from its host, and the two become their own independent emotions again. The emotion patterns are like individual keys to open the door to each basic emotion. With practice, the feelings associated with each basic emotion become more precise, and the "parasite emotions" start to disappear.[22]

Learning the Emotional Body method of emotion regulation not only provides reliable tools for sensing and controlling emotions; it also helps us free up

---

21. Ibid, 65.

22. Ibid.

emotions that have been held back or entangled. It is an incredibly liberating moment to experience, and to witness, when an entangled emotion is finally released from the weeds holding it back and we are liberated from a lifetime of frustration and worry over this confined aspect of our expressive capabilities. Our feelings and expressions become much clearer to us and to others.

In every workshop I teach, emotional entanglements are addressed, and I advise participants as follows on their potential discovery during the workshop:

> *If you are not aware of personal entanglements now, you will most likely discover at least one during the course of the workshop. Try not to judge the entanglement or get caught up in why that entanglement exists. See if you can allow its discovery to be an aha moment, where you treat it more as a physical curiosity, inviting somatic exploration. This way you can remain in the somatic sensing state rather than get caught up in cognitive interpretations or personal histories.*

These instructions seem to help participants let go of their worries about their personal emotional histories as well as lifetimes of baggage potentially tied to entanglements. By doing so, their attention remains on the physical sensations and movements within the patterns, and they are better able to make the physical adjustments to clear the entanglement.

Most are able to embrace the physical exploratory process and gradually clear an entanglement, providing them with incredible feelings of release and freedom.

For example, a workshop participant who was a single mother had low-level sadness entangled in much of her body language and a strong entanglement of sadness in her tenderness, to the point where she could not express a tender loving smile without tearing up and then sobbing. Once this was discovered, she asked if I would help her un-entangle the sadness. By slowly building the tenderness pattern one component at a time, we were able to find exactly where the sadness pattern entered. It snuck in just as she was moving the muscles around her mouth to form a smile. Her chin would start to quiver, then her forehead pinched to engage a very sad smile, and soon the tears were flowing. She and I worked together, slowly and patiently repeating the muscle movements around the mouth, and each time the chin quiver started, I instructed her to try to override the quiver by engaging more of the muscles that form the smile, and to try to release the muscles in the chin. Each time we were able to take the tenderness pattern a little further before sadness attempted to hijack the tenderness. Eventually, she

was able to recondition her entangled tenderness into a pure state.
Throughout the rest of the workshop, she worked on this pattern, and
pure tenderness grew exponentially within her expressive capabilities.
In addition, her habitual facial expressions and body language, initially
fraught with subtle low-level sadness entanglements, were absolutely
transformed in a matter of days.

Emotional Intensity

Emotions have varying levels of intensity, with the high levels tending to get the most attention, often creating misunderstandings about emotions. People often connect the word "emotion" only with high levels of intense expressive behavior. Subsequently, the positive emotions get overlooked and may not be considered emotions at all, most likely due to their tendency for use over longer periods of time and at low levels. I will never forget a time when I was facilitating a workshop where only the positive emotion patterns were taught. Even after two hours of discussion on emotion and the opportunity to experience the positive emotion patterns, a participant asked, "When are we going to get to do the emotion patterns?" The question spoke volumes about the misunderstandings around positive emotions as well as emotional intensity.

The basic emotions can appear in very low levels, or low arousal, where they are barely detected by us or not detected at all. Low levels of emotional arousal might be caused by subtle hormone shifts affecting our behavior. Throughout a single day, our attention moves from one thing to the next, often without our conscious attention. Reactions to our own thoughts or to the words or actions of others can result in tiny microexpressions on our faces and in our body language. These low level arousals can happen by the thousands throughout one day, and most might be undetected, or simply overlooked, as our attention is on other things.

Mid, or moderate, emotional arousal or intensity might be more noticeable. These can be moments when you laugh at something someone said or did or are surprised by someone's behavior. They can be brief moments in the day when you remember something that made you angry or when the conditions around you make you feel frustrated. Mid-level emotional arousal can be the little sympathetic or caring moments shared with loved ones or coworkers. The little stories we tell throughout our day to share experiences can be peppered with a large collection of mid-level emotions. Although these mid-level intensities are a little more noticeable, they may still happen by the hundreds throughout one day.

Then there are the high, or maximal-level, emotions that appear in more obvious degrees and are rarely overlooked by us or by others. These are the moments where we lose our temper, make a snide or hurtful remark, or express frustration in an exasperated flurry of words and actions. These are the times when we double over with laughter and hysterics or when we burst into tears and sob over a loss. These are the memorable flirtations that result in new love or in making love, or the fearful moments that have us shaking at the knees and looking for an escape. High intensity emotional experiences often mark important moments in our day, our week, or even our whole lives. They have the potential to mark our emotional memories with indelible ink.

Emotional Intensity Levels

Low/Minimal – barely perceptible expressions, subtly expressed by the entire body; low intensity levels in the breathing and muscles

Mid/Moderate – noticeable and common-level expressions of the entire body; moderate intensity levels in the breathing and muscles

High/Maximal – large, obvious, and overwhelming expressions of the entire body; high intensity levels in the breathing and muscles

Understanding emotional intensity levels is important for your practice with the emotion patterns. You will start your practice on a mid or moderate level of intensity, which allows you to sense the emotion emerging but not at such a high level that you lose a sense of refinement or control. Gradually, after practicing the patterns for some time at a moderate level, then you can start to explore them on higher and lower levels. This will also help you understand emotional intensity in all its possible manifestations throughout your days.

While teaching a college class in film acting, I was coaching an actor before a scene shoot. The actor was familiar with the Emotional Body method and he was excited to see how this method translated from his stage acting practice to film acting. He recognized that film acting, particularly in close-up shots, requires extremely low-level use of the emotion patterns so that the expressions are not too big for the camera. He was working on reducing his expressive level just before he was due on the set for filming.

The student director of the project was watching his rehearsal and kept stopping him and instructing, "Deliver this text with no emotion at all." The actor was confused about how to deliver the text with absolutely no emotion, so he tried a few takes using various low-level emotional choices, hoping that was what the director was looking for in his delivery. However, the director kept insisting, "No. I really don't want to see any emotion at all."

I finally pulled the actor aside and instructed him, "If the director really • *wants no emotion, I think you should show him what no emotion truly is. Use the neutral pattern and deliver the entire text while staying in*

*neutral. This will mean that your voice will be monotone with no expressive intonation, you will have no gestures, facial expressions, and will simply stand with your body relaxed, symmetrical, and softly staring at the camera." The actor returned to his rehearsal spot and began his text as I instructed. He looked and sounded like a robot reciting text. The director looked at him, speechless. Finally he said, "What was that?" The actor calmly replied, "That was a delivery with the closest I can humanly come to speaking with no emotion. Is that what you wanted?" The director started laughing, more so at himself than the actor, "No! Wow! Definitely **not** what I am looking for in this scene."*

I stepped in again, but this time I talked to both actor and director: "Perhaps we could talk a bit about what it is you are really looking for, and without using the phrase 'no emotion.' Then maybe we will be more successful in providing a performance that aligns with your vision." We engaged in a brief question-and-answer session about the director's vision for the moment and soon enough discovered that the director was trying to get the actor to express only low-level positive emotions. It was a classic situation where low-level positive emotions are overlooked, and only negative emotions are considered emotional. The actor finally knew what to do and was able to quickly provide a performance that made both director and actor happy.

A New Language for the Basic Emotion Patterns

Using verbal language to describe emotions is extremely challenging. Many scientists believe assigning a singular word, like *sadness* or *joy*, to describe primary process emotions is inaccurate and confines our perceptions of the multiple functions emotions have for our bodies. If we truly understand that emotions are motivational states with distinct biological characteristics, then there really is not a one-to-one correspondence between emotion words and emotional states. Additionally, two different emotion words do not imply two biologically different emotional experiences.[23] For example, feeling disappointed, gloomy, sad, sullen, downcast, or cheerless does not mean that each of these feelings has a different biological component simply because there is a different verbal distinction for the feeling. Our bodies will most likely interpret all of these words as one basic emotion, which we have called "sadness" so far in this chapter, since that is the dominant basic emotion in all these words. Likewise, feeling amused, lighthearted, happy, or spirited does not create different physiological signals within our bodies for each word, and most likely is interpreted by our physiology as one basic emotion, which we have named "joy" so far in this chapter.

Consider the color analogy for emotion. Our eyes see color and work with the

23. Michelle N. Shiota and Dacher Keltner, "What Do Emotion Words Represent?" *Psychological Inquiry* 16, no. 2 (2005): 32–37.

brain to interpret its meaning. However, the encoding structures in our retinas respond to only three wavelength ranges associated with the primary colors.[24] The physiological structures of color record only elements of red, blue, and yellow— and yet, we have countless words for the myriad shades of color in our world, like the giant box of crayons full of unique names for subtle shade variations. Likewise with emotion, our bodies only understand the basic emotions, and everything we experience is interpreted by a simple basic-emotion coding system. This is true even though humans have created an array of words to describe the feelings associated with those basic emotions as well as the limitless mixes they can create. The words we create for feelings are our attempts to understand and describe those physical sensations. If we don't have a word for something we are experiencing, it does not mean it does not exist and is not happening in the body. We just don't have the verbal capacity to describe it. For example, Tahitians do not have a word for sadness, but they still experience it.[25]

Generally accepted words for the basic emotions, like *sadness* and *joy*, have been used throughout this chapter as a means of establishing a common understanding of the basic emotions. It is important to understand basic emotion concepts before starting your practice of this method. Likewise, the terms *positive emotions* and *negative emotions* have been used due to their common application to discussing the effects of emotions on our bodies and in social situations. However, in my teaching practice, I prefer not to use words that may restrict our experiences with and understanding of emotions. With this in mind, throughout the rest of the book, I will use sparingly terms like *positive* and *negative* as well as the emotion words often associate with the basic emotions, like *joy* or *sadness*.

Individual perceptions of emotional experiences can be constrained by the vocabulary available to describe them. If we take away subjective words for the emotion patterns, which are laden with personal emotional interpretations, then we are much better prepared to use our senses to determine what is going on in our bodies. If emotion words were continually used while learning somatic sensing skills, you would find yourself limited by your interpretations of these words as well as your life experiences with the feelings they represent. If emotion pattern instruction used emotion words, you would most likely envision your subjective experiences with the words and embody your own habituated patterns rather than reveal the original biological patterns with which you were born. Practicing in this way, led by the subjectivity of emotional language, would only perpetuate personal habits and hold back your opportunity to re-establish primary emotional expression and then expand your emotionally expressive vocabulary.

---

24. Ibid.

25. R. Levy, *The Tahitians* (Chicago: University of Chicago Press, 1973), 288 – 313.

In 2008, I was invited to teach a workshop at a college in Georgia, where a group of theater students wanted to learn the method as an acting tool. Up until this point in my teaching, I was using the basic emotion words assigned by Susana Bloch for each of the patterns.

A typical Alba teaching practice was to resist using the emotion word for each pattern as long as possible, allowing people to have at least their first experience with the pattern free from the verbal limitations and potentially leading language of emotion words. However, once more patterns were introduced, it became very challenging to resist using the emotion word. Recognizing the need for less leading language while teaching, I would use short descriptions like, "Now let's start the intense nose-breathing pattern" or "Let's go back to the soft mouth-breathing pattern." However, these descriptions only focused on one aspect of the pattern. Additionally, the use of phrases like these certainly became cumbersome to say quickly and efficiently to a room full of students.

The host professor of my Georgia workshop was a very insightful individual, who often found herself caught up in analyzing the emotion words and their social and cultural implications. At one point in the workshop— after a brief discussion about how challenging it was to withhold emotion words while students were somatically sensing the patterns—the professor said, "Wouldn't it be great if you could create a different way of labeling the patterns so that no emotion words are used at all, allowing people to remain focused on their senses all the time and interpreting for themselves what the feelings mean to them?" It was one of those great aha moments in life. I knew she was right, but at the time I did not have an answer for how to do it.

Later, after the workshop was over, I was rereading Susana Bloch's book, The Alba of Emotions, *and realized that when she described the neutralizing pattern and its accompanying Step Out procedure (designed to help people release emotions), she referred to this pattern as a zero level: "This 'Step Out' exercise acts as a kind of 'reset' or back to 'zero level' of emotional excitement and allows the person to return to a neutral state."[26] I started thinking, "Numbers do not have any emotionally subjective implications. What if the Alba patterns were numbered, starting with neutral as zero?"*

Mathematical codes have long been associated with explanations of the building blocks of nature. Numbers also symbolize the potential for infinite combinations, much like how primary colors and emotions start with a simple few but create endless variations when combined. But, I didn't want

---

26. Susana Bloch, *The Alba of Emotions: Managing Emotions through Breathing* (Santiago: Grafhika, 2006), 151.

to simply number the patterns from one to six. How would I decide which would be one, two, three, and so on?

Then, I remembered a point I had brought up to Susana Bloch when I worked with her in Chile: "Have you ever thought about how the six basic patterns are cognate (related) pairs of two nose breathing, two mouth breathing, and two nose-mouth combinations? Isn't it interesting that each cognate pair has a positive and a negative emotion, as if we were biologically wired to move easily between the two polarities when breathing in a certain way?" Susana replied that she had not considered these ideas during her research, and it launched us into a very interesting conversation.

These questions have certainly influenced the way I teach the emotional effector patterns. From that moment on, I decided to number the patterns by their cognate pairs, as simply pair #1 (nose), pair #2 (mouth), and pair #3 (nose-mouth combination). I teach the pattern pairs in that order, starting with the nose breathing patterns because, in my experience, the nose breathing patterns are the most accessible for people to embody, possibly due to the fact that a higher majority of people are habitual nose breathers. I teach the nose-mouth combination patterns last, due to the complexity of the breathing pattern.

I never liked referring to emotions as positive or negative, believing that we need to access all the basic emotions, as long as they are used appropriately and in support of our well-being. In order to reduce judgments around negative or positive emotions, I decided to describe these polarities by a singular letter in the pattern label, using "a" for the emotions commonly considered positive and "b" for the negative.

And so, in 2008, I created a new labeling system for the emotional effector patterns, and I have used it consistently ever since. Once people learn the emotional effector patterns with these number-letter titles, they often express excitement over having a secret code or a new language for deconstructing and constructing universal emotional expression.

The Number-Letter Labels for the Patterns

The chart that follows illustrates the number-letter labels I developed and use in my teaching of emotional effector patterns. In this chart, I provide a single emotion word next to the pattern label to demonstrate how these patterns may fall within common interpretations of the basic emotions. However, from this point on, the patterns will be referred to by their number-letter label. This will help you focus on the somatic sensing process and allow you to form your own words for how the patterns make you feel.

0 Breath (Neutral & Balancing)	1 Nose Breathing	1a Tenderness 1b Anger
	2 Mouth Breathing	2a Sensuality 2b Fear
	3 Nose & Mouth Breathing	3a Joy 3b Sadness

The Three Parts of the Patterns

Each emotional effector pattern has three parts: (1) breathing pattern, (2) facial expression, and (3) postural attitude. All three aspects of each pattern were identified in the initial research conducted by the BOS team. The three parts work together to create one effector pattern, or biological code, that directly stimulates cells and organs. The resulting pattern creates a physical code that opens the door for one particular basic emotion to express throughout the entire body.

Voice: Possibly the Fourth Part of the Pattern

Vocalization and its relationship to the patterns was not part of the initial research in the BOS group or in the development of Alba Emoting. However, when I worked with Susana Bloch in Chile, she shared her interest in vocal patterns and her belief that vocalization could eventually be considered a fourth part of the pattern. After all, nonverbal vocal bursts are how infants communicate their needs and convey emotion. Vocalizations in infants are applied simultaneously with their embodied expressions of the basic emotions. As we mature, we continue to express and interpret emotions through non-verbalized sounds, and our nonverbal behavior (including vocal expression) has a much greater impact on others than the words we speak.[27]

Did you know...?

The neural circuits in our nervous system can react dramatically to sound, like sentries continuously evaluating potential risk through the senses, including our hearing. Our bodies tune into specific acoustic frequency bands in the environment and in the human voice.

---

27. G. Beattie, *Visible Thoughts: The New Psychology of Body Language* (New York: Routledge Press, 2003), 105-118.

> For example, a high-pitched voice evokes anxiety. A low, booming voice startles or frightens. Melodic mid-frequency voices evoke a sense of safety and calm.
>
> Likewise, music or sound effects in the same frequency band as the human voice—like violins, flutes, clarinets, oboes, and the French horn—do not elicit doom or urgency. Yet, music or sound effects that do not have the same frequency band as the human voice can alert our systems and evoke disturbing emotions. Low-pitched sounds, typically below the common human voice register, elicit a sense of danger and are associated with an approaching predator. High-pitched sounds, typically above the common human voice register— like a scream, baby cry, or siren—evoke a sense of urgent concern or empathy.[28]

Scientists have recently explored the relationship of sound and voice to emotion. For example, a recent study conducted across ten globalized cultures and compared with one remote village in Bhutan, revealed the universal and emotionally expressive qualities of vocal bursts. The study examined how emotions are distinguished by simply hearing a short (non-verbalized) vocal burst, like a sigh, growl, snort, or gasp. No visual information from the person producing the sound was provided during the study, so the focus of attention was purely on the sound of the voice. The vocal bursts most clearly identified with emotions were those that expressed anger, fear, sadness, or disgust. Not surprisingly, emotions like interest and serenity were moderately distinguishable, and other positive emotions like happiness, relief, and lust were not as clearly identifiable as their negative counterparts.[29] This recent study is an important development in examining the relationship between our voices and emotions, and Emotional Body instructors continue to examine how the voice sounds when we are expressing the basic emotions.

Although vocal expression is still in the exploratory stage in the emotional effector patterns, the lessons in this book include vocal exploration of the emotion patterns. This will help you understand the relationship between emotion and vocalization as well as your emotional response to sound. It will also better prepare you for speaking while in emotional states and recognizing how the patterns affect your speaking voice.

28. Stephen W. Porges, *The Polyvagal Theory: Neurophysiological Foundations of Emotions, Attachment, Communication, Self-Regulation* (New York: Norton & Company, 2011), 247–249.

29. Daniel T. Cordaro, Dacher Keltner, Sumjay Tshering, and Dorji Wangchuck, "The Voice Conveys Emotion in Ten Globalized Cultures and One Remote Village in Bhutan," *American Psychological Association*, 16 (2016): 117–128.

The Emotional Body Instructional Style

The goal when teaching the emotional effector patterns is to instruct a person on how to replicate these patterns. Their precise replication induces basic emotions. Instruction is also provided on how to clear the emotions back to a zero state and on how to regulate their intensity and use. The style of instruction for embodying the patterns varies greatly from one instructor to the next. This book contains the Emotional Body approach to teaching the patterns, which was developed over years of training, researching scientific journals on emotions, and teaching people from varying backgrounds and professions. It is also influenced by somatic education methods, like Feldenkrais.[1]

The Emotional Body is a course designed to take you through gradual and slow development of somatic sensing skills, starting with practicing the breathing patterns and facial muscle movements while lying on the floor. This allows you to focus your attention on the precise movements and the resulting sensations of initial pattern application. I have found that if you move too quickly through this process or attempt to immediately apply all three parts of the pattern at once, mixes and a lack of physical control ensue, keeping you from fully understanding the precise muscle movements in each pattern or from gaining control over all three aspects of the pattern. Once you have acquired a clear sense of these first exercises on the floor, you will gradually move to a sitting position, and then to standing, walking, and applying the patterns to activities.

---

1. The Feldenkrais Method is a form of somatic education that uses gentle movement and directed attention to improve movement and enhance human functioning. www.feldenkrais.com

The rest of this book is written in the order of the number-letter pattern labels. It concludes with a chapter on applications of the patterns to everyday life experiences and social interactions as well as to various professional practices. This book is designed around the process and gradual skill-building lessons I have used and thoroughly tested in my teaching over the years. The lessons build upon each other, slowly increasing levels of embodiment and somatic sensing activities, providing you with the opportunity to focus on specific areas of a pattern before attempting to embody the entire pattern.

Moving too quickly through the lessons or jumping to the end of a chapter for the description of the full pattern could result in a very generalized sense of the emotion patterns, leading you to miss the opportunity to explore the varying levels of emotional feelings associated with these primary states. Skipping steps in the learning process outlined by this book could also cause personal habitual mixes and entanglements to be embedded in your practice of the patterns.

With all this in mind, it is highly advisable to follow the book in the order it is written and at the pace recommended within the chapters.

Zero and Step Out

The first lesson provided is on how to release emotion and establish a state as close to neutrality as possible. The BOS team developed a neutral breath pattern and integrated it with a physical ritual of movements, called *Step Out*, designed to help rebalance and centralize the body into a physical state absent of any aspects associated with the emotion patterns. In the Emotional Body, neutral breath is called the *zero (0) pattern*, allowing you to establish your own word for how this rebalancing breath pattern feels. Many people have described the resulting state as calm, peaceful, or content. The zero pattern serves many functions in your practice of the Emotional Body and is used as a calming baseline or a comfortable and centered home base to return to before ending your practice sessions with the emotion patterns.

The most important first step in the Emotional Body course is to acquire a full understanding and practice of zero and Step Out before attempting to learn any of the emotion patterns. Make sure you take your time with the chapter on zero before continuing with the rest of the book.

Pattern Practice Learning Stages

When learning and practicing all the patterns, including zero, expect to go through three phases of development: (1) Robotic/Mechanical, (2) Induction, and (3) Integration.

Robotic/Mechanical:
The patterns are produced at a moderate intensity, with attention primarily on

the technical precision of the pattern while coordinating the various components of the breathing pattern and muscle movements. At this time, the pattern may feel stereotypical, childish or clown-like, oversized, and disingenuous.

Induction:

Once accurate technical production of the pattern is achieved, it induces a genuine and recognizable experience of emotion. The pattern initiates certain physiological responses, like changes in pulse rate, blood pressure, visual scope, and skin temperature. The induction may or may not stimulate memories and/or images. Once an induction occurs, a pattern merges with the organic experience, and subtle variations in the breathing and expressive intensity occur without losing the pattern's basic integrity. The appearance and experience of the emotion becomes genuine.

Integration:

Integrative pattern practice is when a pattern is physically mastered while regular and consistent inductions are also experienced. Inductions are achieved without using subjective images or triggers. The resulting expression looks and feels genuine and has no mixes or entanglements. The emotion tends to induce quickly and easily with very little effort or concerted application of the pattern, and yet the pattern is clearly evident in the resulting expression. At this point a person can, at will, control the intensity of the emotion, move from one emotion to another, and eventually mix emotions to create a greater and more mature vocabulary of expression.

The first two phases are not necessarily experienced in sequential order, and you will most likely move back and forth between these two phases throughout your initial exploration of the patterns. For example, during your first practice of the breathing and facial aspects of pattern 1b, you may feel an immediate induction, but then later when you apply the postural attitude, you may feel robotic or mechanical in its reproduction. However, the more you practice and refine the postural attitude, and align it with the breathing and facial aspects, gradually the entire pattern will create an induction. On the other hand, you may start your practice of pattern 1a and feel as if you are in the robotic/mechanical phase while applying all three parts of the pattern, until you get to the final chapter in this book where the patterns are applied to activities. An induction may finally occur because some refinements have been made in your practice of the pattern, because you managed to clear an entanglement, or because you reached a level of physical precision and understanding that simply took longer than other patterns that came more easily. Meanwhile, you may have had regular inductions with all the other patterns.

The learning phases you experience with each pattern are entirely individualized. Try not to judge yourself, worry about how this happened in your body, or overanalyze why one pattern seems more accessible than another. Getting caught up in asking questions about why emotional entanglements exist only places your attention on thinking and analyzing rather than on somatic sensing, releasing excessive tensions, and refining the patterns. You will have the best results learning and applying the the emotion patterns if you keep these guidelines in mind:

- Take your time with each exercise and allow your entire body to tune into your senses and feelings.

- Check all areas of the body for any habitual muscular tensions or emotional mixes not associated with the pattern you are practicing.

- Focus on refining all aspects of the pattern, conducting regular scans and reviews of the pattern's breathing, facial expression, and postural attitude.

- Trust the inductions will eventually emerge as you increase your detailed somatic sensing abilities and precise replication of the patterns.

- Recognize releasing entanglements is a long-term goal that could take weeks, months, or even years to achieve fully.

- Regularly practice the zero breath pattern and Step Out, with constant scans for emotional residue or entanglements keeping you from attaining a true state of tranquility and calm.

As your technical ease with the patterns increases, expressions of organic emotion will begin to flow freely in all kinds of circumstances, including interactions with other individuals, and in your daily posture, movement, and expressions. Eventually, you may reach the point where you can consciously make adjustments in order to change, clarify, intensify, or sustain an emotional state and then apply regular, advanced, physical emotion regulation methods in all areas of your life.

In 1999, during my first full training in Alba Emoting, I found I could easily induct in most of the patterns, except 1b (anger). When practicing 1b, I felt mechanical and forced. I did not experience an authentic induction with the emotion during the entire 32-hour workshop. In addition to my struggles connecting with and expressing true 1b, I had a strong entanglement of 3b (sadness) in most of the other patterns, and particularly in 1b.

I knew in my personal life that I struggled with expressing my anger. Most of the time I masked my anger with a smile, not allowing myself to truly express displeasure or disagreement. When I wanted to be taken seriously and stand up for myself, I was frustrated by the flow of tears accompanying my attempts to be strong, stern, or expressive of aggravation. As a woman serving in regular professional leadership roles, I knew I needed to clear this entanglement to ensure I was taken seriously and to lead with confidence and clarity.

Throughout the workshop, I worked to find where the 3b entanglement appeared in my practice of pattern 1b. Once I discovered the precise muscles of its engagement, which for me was in my forehead and the muscles around my eyebrows, I repeatedly practiced building the 1b pattern, paying close attention to those muscles, making sure they did not engage with a 3b pattern. Over time, I cleared the 3b entanglement from my 1b, as well as from all the other patterns. Yet, I still did not feel I had an induction in 1b.

During my second Alba Emoting workshop in 2001, I had the opportunity to study for the first time with Susana Bloch. I was determined to master the patterns during this workshop and finally experience an induction in 1b. During this workshop, I found that my postural attitude had elements of 2b (fear) entangled in it, specifically in the angle of my body—pulling up and back, rather than up and forward. In addition, I learned from Susana, who has a keen sense of the communications between the eyes and the brain, that my eyes were flashing microexpressions of 2b throughout my application of 1b. This was valuable feedback, helping me target two subtle areas of entanglements most likely responsible for my lack of induction. Over the course of this workshop, I practiced the 1b pattern regularly, and paid close attention to my posture and the muscles around my eyes.

All throughout this process, I was aware of the many reasons why I would have these entanglements. A host of personal life experiences, particularly in my childhood, had permanently merged all three negative emotions (anger, fear, and sadness) into a singular emotional expression. I always wanted to freely and bravely express my frustration and anger, but could not with entangled negative emotions subtly, or overtly, hijacking my expression. I was grateful the Alba Emoting teaching practices did not venture into why these were entangled, so I was able to put all my focus on how to physically examine where these emotional parasites emerged and pick them off one by one, as if they were leeches depleting my core emotional potential.

I eventually cleared this second entanglement in my 1b, and finally experienced inductions. It was an exhilarating experience to feel and express true 1b, free of its entanglements. This newfound clarity in my expressive vocabulary was empowering and gave me great confidence to try new things, take more chances, and pursue even more leadership roles in my life, knowing I had the ability to stand in my power when needed. Expelling these emotional parasites was truly a life-changing experience for me. It led me to access an important basic emotion, which propels my body forward, helping me feel brave, proud, powerful, and confident.

Articulating Your Emotional Experience

An emotional experience is when we have a conscious awareness of a shifting emotional state and can articulate how this shift feels. When a shift in our physiological state, or the sensation of an emotional experience, communicates with the neocortex (thinking, or rational, part of the brain), we establish a level of mental awareness and attempt to give meaning to the event. Our thoughts and words help us to interpret and evaluate what we are feeling and eventually to articulate how we feel to others.[2] This is an important process for achieving awareness and developing advanced skills in emotion regulation. Without attention and interpretation, we may not recognize that an emotional experience has occurred, even though we are in an emotional state.[3] For example, a person may exhibit signs of sadness or depression but only identify feeling tired. Another person may behave with anger and aggression but deny feeling or expressing their anger.

As you practice the exercises in this book, you will be asked to journal about your experiences and identify how each pattern made you feel. This process helps you develop skills in interpreting what you are sensing and then articulating these sensations with words. As your somatic sensing abilities grow and your pattern practice becomes more refined, so will the words you use to articulate your experiences. This process helps you increase emotional awareness and improve your ability to accurately express what you are feeling to others. Guiding questions are provided throughout the book to support your journal entries.

Things You Will Need for Your Practice

To practice the exercises in this book most effectively, you will need to put certain things into place. Here is a list of ideal supplies and conditions for your practice time.

• Practice the exercises in a quiet, private space with no music or disruptive sounds or activities nearby. It should be a place where you will not be interrupted and do not feel inhibited from fully engaging in the patterns and placing all your attention on your practice. If practicing at home while others are in the house, try scheduling a time in a room where your privacy will be respected.

• You will need to lie down on your back on the floor for many of the exercises. Have an exercise or yoga mat available for these times. Try not to place large pillows under your head, which cause you to change your posture dramatically, potentially leading to emotional mixes. If you need some soft support under

2. Michael Lewis, "The Emergence of Human Emotions," *Handbook of Emotions* 3rd ed., eds. Michael Lewis, Jeannette M. Haviland-Jones, and Lisa Feldman Barrett (New York: Guilford Press, 2008), 311.

3. Jaak Panksepp, "The Affective Brain and Core Consciousness: How Does Neural Activity Generate Emotional Feelings?" *Handbook of Emotions* 3rd ed., eds. Michael Lewis, Jeannette M. Haviland-Jones, and Lisa Feldman Barrett (New York: Guilford Press, 2008), 62.

your head, neck, or knees, try to use very small amounts of padding, just enough to support you but not so much as to influence big postural changes.

• Once the exercises progress to sitting position, it is ideal to use a fairly stiff straight-backed chair, similar to a dining table chair but without arms. This will provide you with a firm foundation and allow you to feel more of your muscle movements in the sitting posture. The lack of chair arms will also give you freedom of movement and expression with your arms. Do not use a chair with wheels or excessive cushioning.

• Eventually, you will practice the patterns while standing and walking, therefore an unobstructed space where you can walk at least six to ten paces is ideal.

• Keep a journal and writing instrument nearby (a computer is fine as well). Journaling should only be done after achieving a zero state to clear away emotion patterns.

• You will also want to have plenty of water to drink during your practice. Breathing exercises and pattern work can make you very thirsty. If possible, do not drink water while in an emotion pattern; wait to drink until after you have cleared to zero.

• A box of facial tissues is a good idea to have on hand. The nose breathing and nose-mouth patterns require a clear and unobstructed nasal passage. Some patterns can also elicit tears and clogged sinuses, requiring some time to clear and wipe away before fully achieving a zero state. Tissues can be used while in the emotion patterns, as well as during multiple applications of zero and Step Out, in order to help you return back to zero.

Important Recommendations for Learning and Practicing

(1) If you are learning these patterns on your own through the exercises in this book, recognizing this is your own self-guided exploration of the patterns with no feedback from an instructor, you may want to occasionally film your practice of the patterns and view them. This can help you evaluate your precision with the patterns and check for any entanglements.

(2) If you are learning these patterns in a group environment under the guidance of an instructor, make sure the instructor is a certified or experienced teacher. Ask about their teaching experience and certification level, history of teaching the method, and credentials. Conduct your own research on the internet for reliable sources listing credentialed teachers. This is not a method where a person can simply read a book and then teach to others. It takes years of training and

practice to learn how to guide a group of people through emotional inductions and to know how to conduct a room full of people in emotional states back to zero, all while safeguarding their health and well-being.

(3) Do not attempt to teach the emotion patterns to others. It is one thing to embark on your own personal learning of emotion patterns, but teaching others the patterns enters into a responsibility best left to experienced teachers or to clinical therapists and somatic psychologists. Understandably, you will be excited about what you are learning and want to share it with others. You may even feel as if demonstrating the patterns will help others understand the true benefits of this method, but I have learned over the years that it does not, and people don't really recognize the benefits of learning the patterns until they actually experience them while gradually increasing their somatic sensing abilities. By all means, talk about the method and share this book with others, but leave the teaching of the patterns to trained teachers.

(4) Children and young adults under the age of eighteen should not participate in a training or actively practice the emotion patterns unless this is a practice supported and guided by a clinical therapist. The brain pathways of children and young adults are still developing, and any technique designed to recondition organic pathways should not be used with children or young adults unless it is under the direct care of a clinical therapist or psychologist. Young adults can benefit from learning how postural attitudes, facial expressions, and even certain breathing patterns, like 2b, evoke emotions that may or may not benefit their physical and mental well-being and social interactions with others. However, actually training in and practicing the full patterns is meant for adults.

(5) The exercises shared in this book are not intended as a substitute for any therapeutic care or guidance you may currently be receiving from a mental health specialist. It is always wise to consult your therapist before practicing any emotion regulation practices. They might even be interested in reading this book and discussing the theories with you as an additional level of exploration in counseling.

The exercises and methods introduced in this book are intended for educational purposes and as a means for providing tools for somatic sensing, self-discovery, and physical self-regulation of emotions.

Throughout my years of teaching, I have seen people first drawn to learning the emotional effector patterns for professional reasons. Some want to better access and embody their emotions for acting. Others are interested in the method's potential for improving their leadership skills, business communications, or management of emotions in the workplace. Somatic educators use the method to better understand the connection between emotions and their somatic practices. Therapists and ontological coaches study the patterns so they can provide more somatic emotion regulation tools for their clients. Through learning the emotion patterns, many of these professionals gain valuable tools to apply to their stated goals. In the process, however, they often gain something unexpected, thrilling, and potentially even more valuable: an incredible amount of self-knowledge.

The Emotional Body is an exciting and highly rewarding course, which provides you with invaluable tools that forever influence how you look at emotions, react emotionally to situations, and manage your emotions in your personal and professional life. This method will provide you with a new lens for perceiving and interacting with the world around you. Enjoy the journey!

Zero & Breathing 4

Consciously Achieving Zero

Zero (0) is the label for the neutral state, or a position of disengagement from emotional expression. When in zero, you are the closest you can come to an "emotion-less" state, and it may feel like a resting point, a state of calm, or a feeling of harmonious balance. You might unconsciously reach this state after sleeping. However, consciously achieving zero requires establishing a balanced calm state, absent of conflict, emotions, excess body tension, or distracting thoughts. Attaining this while awake can be challenging and, for some, may take a lifetime to perfect. After all, it has taken us a lifetime to create our individual expressions, mixed emotions, physical patterns, deep layers of thoughts, and feelings about those thoughts. With this in mind, as we approach the study of achieving zero, it is important to recognize it requires conscious application of a gradual, step-by-step process, with the goal of becoming more and more "neutral" with each practice session.

The first step in approaching the study of zero is to recognize how much you are actually expressing. Your daily behavioral habits are complex, adopted through a lifetime of social and cultural influences. You might refer to them as your personality, temperament, character, traits, or moods. These expressive habits are projected uniquely by you and layered with emotions, movement habits, and vocal patterns. Unless someone has spent many years on somatic sensing and self-awareness practices, an individual is typically aware of only a small percentage of their conduct and its perceived meaning or impact on others.

Consider a time when someone's first impression of you was quite different from what you believed you were projecting. Your own habitual expressions can often elude you. For example, you may believe you have a friendly, open demeanor, but others perceive you as unapproachable. You may want to give off the impression of confidence, but others see subtle nervous behavior sending them the opposite message. In addition, your days are filled with reactions to events, which add more layers of emotions. This creates a varied collection of bodily expressions, some known to you, and some unknown.

Once people learn the emotion patterns, they share insightful stories of self-discovery, particularly concerning the difference between self-perceptions of behavior and how that behavior comes across to others.

One participant, who has an intensely passionate personality, shared her story. People would often say to her, "Why are you so angry?" and she thought, "I'm not angry. Why are they saying that about me?" After taking several Emotional Body courses, she finally realized she had facial muscle entanglements associated with anger around her eyes and mouth. These were not only present in her other emotional expressions, but also in her zero state. After realizing this, she said, "I guess I have been angry for years, and didn't even know it!"

Another young woman, who is a studious, dedicated academic, had a habitually worried look on her face all the time, even when "resting." Every time I saw her I wanted to gently rub my finger across her brow, as if to erase her habitual sadness. Once she was aware of this entanglement, she worked on clearing it through many workshops. When I saw her again a couple years later, I was amazed at how her face had relaxed and transformed into a glowing and radiantly calm expression.

I also learned about a masking habit I had employed throughout my lifetime. Once in a graduate school acting exercise, we were each required to stand up in front of the class and do nothing but stand "in neutral" and look at the rest of the class for five minutes. While the entire class stared at each individual, they wrote down impressions of that person's character or type. When five minutes were over, classmates passed their little slips of paper to the instructor who read off the list of impressions. When it was my turn, I was surprised the majority of the slips revealed words like nurturing, mom-like, tender, *or* caring. *I actually thought I was standing in neutral, but clearly this was not the case.*

Later, when training in Alba Emoting, I understood why this was their impression of me. I had adopted a constant masking smile of tenderness, present even when I relaxed or slept. Although this entanglement did not concern me as much as the sadness and fear emotional parasites mentioned earlier, it was enlightening information about my supposed neutral state.

Practicing the zero pattern regularly has the potential to help clear habitual entanglements while also quieting our systems, allowing us to disengage from our busy lives, if only temporarily. Some workshop participants say zero could be the new, natural face-lift secret. Indeed, I have seen so many people, including myself, transform habitual facial expressions, as well as postural attitudes and emotion-inducing breathing patterns, by practicing all the patterns, including zero.

Regular practice of zero can reveal your habitual behavior and provide you with a process for changing these habits. Imagine developing your own internal camera to film every aspect of your behavior. You could scan your entire body for movement, zooming in on particular areas that carry excess tension or patterns associated with emotions. The lessons for achieving zero help you activate this internal camera so you will become aware of the slightest introduction of tension, emotion, or new thought. It will raise your awareness about feelings and expressions you habitually carry from moment to moment. You will start to recognize excessive movements or tensions keeping you from truly disengaging from emotional expressions. Gradually, through regular practice, you will learn to release over-engagement and move closer to attaining a neutral state. Then, once you understand how to achieve zero, you will be ready to start your practice of the emotion-inducing patterns.

Did you know…?

We collect evidence directly from the vocal intonations and facial expressions of those around us, as well as from our own, and then translate the first reaction into one of two simple choices: approach or withdraw. This is called regulation of attention. It is a right brain process that enables us to acutely observe our surroundings while monitoring our own physical state and assigning appropriate social behaviors for the situation. If the clues collected indicate safety, we approach. If anything we sense signals danger or caution, we withdraw.[1] The actions of approach and withdraw are not always obvious to us or to others. They can be small, often overlooked, subtle gestures, like eye movements, held or exhaled breath, or muscle movements.

1. Stephen W. Porges, *The Polyvagal Theory: Neurophysiological Foundations of Emotions, Attachment, Communication, Self-regulation* (New York: Norton & Company, 2011), 139–143.

Zero and Active Rest

Active rest is an activity used to consciously release emotional engagement, like napping, resting, taking a long bath, lounging, or meditating. It is possible to reach a zero state, at least temporarily, during active rest activities. Some people manage to hold onto a neutral state for a while in these activities—that is, until they are met with the first cognitive or physical influence, which induces emotion. It is important to recognize that these activities don't necessarily guarantee a zero state has been achieved. You could nap fitfully, rest sadly, bathe sensually, lounge anxiously, meditate with a forced smile, or wake angrily or fearfully, particularly if startled awake by an alarm.

It is best to consider zero a conscious act of clearing, balancing, and calming your entire system. This does not mean that active rest activities cannot evoke a zero state but that it is necessary to become conscious of how and when you are actually achieving a zero state.

Consciously Scanning Active Rest Activities

Try this exercise the next time you partake in active rest activities, like waking from restful sleep, lounging around, or preparing to rise after a good massage, soothing bath, or meditation session.

1. Take a few minutes, with eyes open, to pay attention to how you feel physically and emotionally.

2. Become aware of your breathing, body alignment, facial muscles, emotions, and thoughts.

3. As you mentally attend to this raised level of awareness, ask yourself if all parts of your body are truly disengaged from emotion and in a state of active rest.

4. Consciously take a personal inventory of any physical, emotional, or thoughtful engagement.

5. Most likely you will notice at least a minor level of engagement somewhere in your body. It might be thoughts you were mulling over or a point of tension in your neck, back, legs, feet, or hands.

This is the first step in raising your awareness of over-engagement when attempting to actively rest. At first you may notice very little or even believe you have truly reached a state of neutrality. However, after moving through the exercises in this book and refining your somatic sensing skills, you may find, as you return to this exercise, many more areas of over-engagement will be discovered.

Continued Practice for Scanning Active Rest Activities

1. Conduct a physical and emotional inventory a few times a week as you come out of active rest activities.

2. Compare each new observation to previous inventories you conducted in the week.

3. Gradually raise your awareness of how your body feels when actively resting.

4. Become aware of persistent habits, tensions, and feelings keeping you from achieving a truly restful state.

▌▌ Pause & Reflect

Write down emotion words to describe how each active rest activity feels. Do the words change as you increase your somatic sensing within the activities? With each practice, do you find you get a little closer to disengaging? Are you able to fully embody rest and relaxation? If not, do you sense how much you habitually hold bodily tensions, excessive movements, or obsessive thoughts?

Practicing this somatic sensing exercise is an important first step in raising your awareness of habitual patterns, and it prepares you for lessons in the zero pattern. Attaining a zero state requires paying close attention to external and internal influences that stimulate emotion and physical tension, and then learning how to release them. The exercises in this chapter will give you tools for achieving zero. With time and practice, you will reach this state quickly and efficiently and will be ready to practice the emotion-inducing patterns.

Breathing Techniques

Breathing practices are often used as the first step in calming the body and balancing out emotional states. Breathing techniques are practiced in yoga, meditation, Tai Chi, physical therapy, breath therapy, movement training, voice training, exercise programs, and more. Many believe breathing is the only function of the autonomic nervous system (ANS) that we can willingly manipulate and change, and certain types of breathing can actually reset the ANS. This reset decreases blood pressure and pulse while it increases parasympathetic activity, making us feel more alert and reinvigorated.[2]

We have the ability to control our breathing by changing our breathing patterns. Breathing patterns consist of three areas: (1) an air path (nose or mouth), (2) a rate or duration, and (3) an area of muscle activation controlling the inhalation and exhalation. The first area, a breathing pathway, is easy to understand, but the second and third areas (rate and muscle activation) take some practice to ensure full understanding and control. Before we get into the breathing used in the zero pattern, let's first explore muscle activation areas influencing inhalation and exhalation. Then, we will practice breathing rate.

The muscle activation areas influencing inhalation and exhalation are referred to as *abdominal, thoracic,* and *clavicular breathing.*

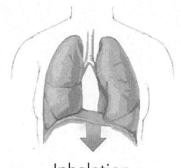 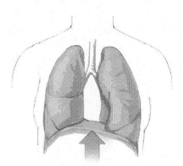

Inhalation   Exhalation

Abdominal Breathing

Abdominal breathing has been referred to as "deep breathing," "belly breathing," and "diaphragmatic breathing." The diaphragm is the large dome-shaped involuntary muscle that sits beneath the lungs. Involuntary muscles are not directly or consciously controlled. For example, when you are asleep or unconscious, your diaphragm will continue supporting respiration. We rely on the involuntary muscles to keep working for our survival. The diaphragm acts like a large bellows for the body. When the diaphragm muscle contracts downward, it pulls air into the body through the nose or mouth, down through the trachea and into the lungs. As the diaphragm muscle relaxes upward, the air is pushed back out of the lungs, through the trachea, and out through the mouth or nose.

Although the diaphragm is an involuntary muscle, we can influence it by using voluntary muscles. Abdominal muscles are voluntary muscles and can control

2. Ravinder Jerath, John W. Edry, Veron A. Barns, and Vadna Jerath, "Physiology of Long Pranayamic Breathing: Neural Respiratory Elements May Provide a Mechanism that Explains How Slow Deep Breathing Shifts the Autonomic Nervous System," *Medical Hypotheses* 67, no. 3 (2006): 566–571.

diaphragm muscle movement. During abdominal breathing, the abdominal muscles help pull the diaphragm down further toward the pelvis while inhaling. While exhaling, the abdominal muscles control the release of diaphragm contraction. Abdominal activation in breathing influences the breathing rate/duration and flow of air on inhale and exhale. In abdominal breathing, we see the abdomen area rising and expanding with the inhalation and falling and contracting with the exhalation.

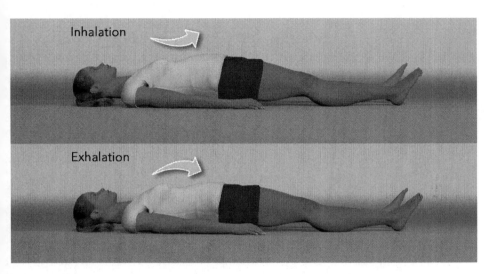

Did you know…?

The application of specific breathing practices not only helps us regulate our emotions but can also provide a host of health benefits. Conscious use of abdominal-activated breathing decreases stress and regulates cortisol (stress hormone) levels. It strengthens our immunity, and it reduces pain and the activation of pain centers in our brains. Regular deep breathing practices can make us feel happier with a more optimistic perspective while reducing symptoms associated with anxiety, depression, and trauma. Abdominal breathing can also provide us with deeper sleep cycles and help reduce impulsive behaviors and cravings.[3]

Abdominal breathing is the breathing process we naturally shift to when sleeping and relaxing. If you watch a baby breathing, you will most likely see abdominal-activated breathing. In addition to its many physical and mental health benefits, abdominal breathing allows a person to maximize breath support for speaking, singing, and physical activity.

3. Emma Seppala, *The Happiness Track: How to Apply the Science of Happiness to Accelerate Your Success* (New York: Harper Collins, 2016), 54–61.

Abdominal Breathing Practices

As you wake from a restful sleep, lie there for a moment on your back with your hand resting on your abdomen. You can find the best position for your hand by placing the thumb of your hand on your navel and stretching the rest of your hand below the navel. If you are practicing abdominal breathing, your hand will rise and fall with each inhalation and exhalation. Take a few long, deep breaths and see how much movement can be achieved in the abdominal area. Imagine your lower abdominal muscles pressing down through the pelvis as you inhale. Relax the abdominal muscles as you exhale, and the pressure through the pelvis releases. Be aware of any excess tension or movement in the chest or shoulders as you practice abdominal breathing.

Here is an exercise that can help bring even more attention to the abdominal muscle area and help strengthen these muscles to better prepare them to support abdominal breathing.

1. Lie on your back, preferably on the floor, with one or two hardcover books stacked on top of your abdominal area. To find the correct spot for the books, place your thumb on your navel and spread your hand between your navel and pelvic bone. Place the books where the palm of your hand rests on your abdomen, and then remove your hand.

2. Breathe in, with the intention of making the books rise up.

3. Breathe out, with the intention of allowing the books to sink back down.

4. Practice this for about ten breath cycles, observing how much movement is achieved in the abdominal area. Can you still feel as if you are pressing your lower abdominal muscles down through the pelvis as you inhale, even though your abdominal area is rising and falling? Can you conduct this activity without adding excessive tension to your low back?

5. Place a hand or two on your high chest and shoulders during this practice so you are aware of any excess tension or movement. If you do feel any, try to reduce engagement in this area.

6. Complete the exercise by removing the books and practicing a few more deep breathing cycles. Has the use of the books helped you better locate these muscles and activate them with inhalation and exhalation?

Clavicular Breathing

When practicing deep breathing, the lower chest area may expand and rise slightly after the abdominal area rises. This is the result of the ribs and chest area expanding as the lungs fill with air. However, if the upper chest (around the clavicle bones) and shoulders rise significantly during inhalation, with only a small amount of expansion in the thoracic or abdominal area, then a person is practicing clavicular, or upper chest, breathing.

Clavicular breathing engages muscles around the upper rib cage and shoulder muscles to achieve inhalation, resulting in a low volume inhale, sometimes called shallow breathing. This kind of breathing uses only a small amount of lung capacity. The clavicular breathing process requires muscle tension in the chest, shoulders, and neck—maximal effort for minimal results, which adds excessive tension to the neck and throat area. A person who uses clavicular breathing on a regular basis denies the body its fullest and essential life support with every breath. Regular clavicular breathing practices add excessive muscular engagement to the breathing process, causing habitual tension build-up around the neck and shoulders. Habitual clavicular breathing causes vocal strain, promotes neck and back mobility limitations, and also triggers anxiety and fear states.

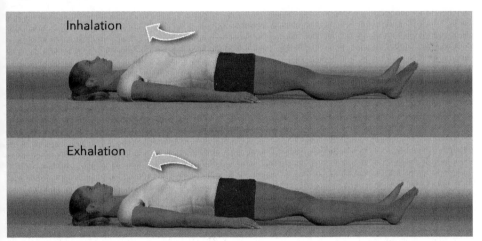

Did you know...?

The habitual clavicular breather, or chest breather, is chronically in a state of hyperventilation, which causes too much carbon dioxide discharge with every breath, making the heart work harder. This is similar to an engine straining because of a poorly adjusted carburetor. Since the respiratory system and heart fuel the rest of our body, habitual chest breathing results in a body in constant deprivation, which is effectively operating with a faulty engine. Chest breathers also tend to have high blood pressure, cardiovascular and respiratory problems, heightened pain levels, and increased tendencies for anxiety and depression.[4]

4. Gay Hendricks, *Conscious Breathing: Breathwork for Health, Stress Release, and Personal Mastery* (New York, Bantam Books, 1995), 16–18.

Comparing Abdominal with Clavicular Breathing

1. While lying on the floor, place one hand on your upper chest and one hand on your abdomen. To find the upper chest area, place your thumb at the base of your throat and stretch your hand so your smallest finger, or pinky, reaches for the sternum. This is what we will refer to as the upper, or high, chest area.

2. Take a quick breath in through your mouth, with the intention of raising your chest with the inhalation while allowing the abdominal area to sink in slightly.

3. Then, exhale out the mouth, with the chest sinking back and the abdomen rising slightly, causing an opposite action.

4. Use your hands to feel the areas that rise and fall with this type of breathing. It may feel a bit like a seesaw action between the chest and abdominal area as you inhale and exhale.

5. Do this for at least three breath cycles, exhaling out the mouth. (A breath cycle is one inhale and one exhale).

6. Then, take an inhalation through the nose, with the intention of expanding your abdominal area and keeping the upper chest area from rising. As you exhale, the abdomen sinks back, and the upper chest remains relaxed.

7. Do this for at least three breath cycles, exhaling out the mouth, and notice whether this feels different from the previous type of breathing.

 Pause & Reflect

Write two lists of words comparing how you felt (1) while breathing with the upper chest area activated and then (2) while breathing with the upper chest area disengaged. What are the differences in the lists of words? How did these two breathing areas evoke different feelings throughout your body, and in which areas of your body? How many of the words are physical, how many are emotional, and how many deal with thoughts or images?

Thoracic Breathing

Thoracic breathing practices can help connect breathing with the expansion of the ribs and the development of core muscles. Thoracic breathing can be very beneficial in strengthening the core muscles in the thorax and developing the fine muscles around the rib cage for expanding and contracting the lungs. During thoracic breathing, the rib cage expands as a way of creating a vacuum in the lungs, resulting in an inhalation. The muscles around the rib cage then relax to expel the air. The abdominal muscles may engage during thoracic breathing, helping to pull the ribs downward, creating a deeper inhalation. With a muscular focus around the upper ribs, some people have a difficult time isolating the thoracic region from the clavicular region. As you practice thoracic breathing, be aware of excessive upper chest, shoulder, and neck tension, and try to keep muscular activation to the rib area and below.

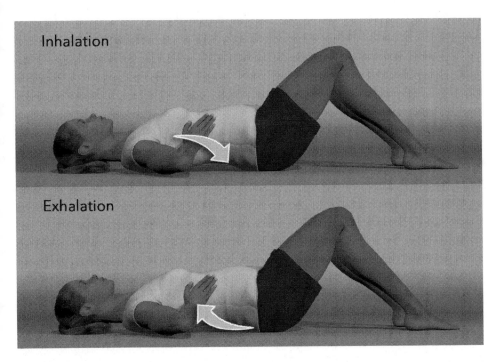

Inhalation

Exhalation

Comparing Thoracic and Abdominal Breathing

1. Lie on your back with legs bent and feet flat on the floor. Place both hands on your sides, with your palms resting on the rib cage a few inches below your armpits and your fingers pointing toward your stomach.

2. Inhale through the nose while concentrating on pushing your ribs out to the sides, pressing the ribs toward the hands.

3. Then, exhale out the mouth as the muscles around your ribs relax back.

4. Practice this movement with three slow, equal breath cycles, mentally counting

during inhalation and exhalation, attempting to exhale the same count as the inhale.

5. Then, take one hand away from your ribs and place that hand on your abdominal area. Now, inhale, still focusing on moving the ribs out, and notice any movement in the abdominal area. Practice this movement with three slow breath cycles, still noticing the breath cycle length.

6. Finally, keeping one hand on the ribs and one on the abdomen, inhale, focusing on movement only in the abdominal area.

7. Take three slow breath cycles, counting the lengths of inhalation and exhalation, while trying not to allow as much movement in the thoracic region.

8. Compare the breathing lengths for both thoracic and abdominal breathing. Are your breath cycles the same or different? If different, which type of breathing allowed you to have longer breath cycles?

Practicing all the exercises listed will raise your awareness of your own habitual breathing methods and help you achieve clarity and control of conscious breathing practices. Most of the emotion patterns use abdominal breathing. This practice will strengthen your abdominal breathing control, diminish any habitual clavicular breathing, and prepare you for the breathing patterns in the emotional effector patterns.

Teaching deep abdominal breathing practices has been a personal mission of mine for most of my teaching profession. Over the years, I have witnessed an increase in habitual clavicular breathing everywhere I turn.

In college classrooms, I see students filled with the stress of achievement as they constantly venture into new territories of learning and growing. Adopted chest-breathing practices eventually hinder their physical and mental health. Panic attack, eating disorder, and PTSD have become common terms used among peers, which speaks volumes about the amount of stress their bodies are habitually carrying. Professors, campus staff, and administrators are all affected by the strong imprint this intense microcosm makes on everyone's emotional lives.

Throughout the arts community, I continue to see chest-breathing practices associated with stressful professional environments. Breathing patterns and their use are particularly obvious as I watch artists present their creative products to the public for feedback. I see writers and visual artists practically holding their breath in their chests, waiting for a critique of their latest work.

Performing artists, who often feel as if they are placing themselves on personal public display for their art, are acutely aware of how their breathing changes before, during, and after they perform. Many struggle with pre-show jitters as their breathing creeps up into their chests, potentially causing hyperventilation or stage fright.

Corporate, business, legal, and political fields also pose stressful workplace challenges. Intense competition and a make-it-or-break-it mentality ignite a constant fight response, and with it come heightened fear levels associated with possible income and reputation loss at any turn.

Professionals serving in the healthcare, first-responder, police force and armed forces fields deal with elevated life-or-death situations daily. Without a means for releasing the stress-inducing physical patterns associated with these professions, habitual patterns emerge and create a host of problems.

In all the fields represented above, I see plenty of people holding up chests and shoulders and tightening necks as they breathe high into the clavicle area on a regular basis. Their abdomens are tucked in, held hard and strong, as if to guard against the world.

My wish for them, and for you, is to learn to consciously take moments to release this tension and breathe deeply when you can. Adopt regular time to practice deep abdominal breathing. Create a new default to support your well-being. It might even help improve your work life.

Breathing Rate

Breathing rate is the length of time it takes to inhale and exhale, measured by breathing cycles per minute. A breathing cycle begins with an inhalation and ends with an exhalation. The average resting breathing rate falls somewhere between 10 and 16 breath cycles per minute (BCPM). Breathing faster than 16 BCPM can induce hyperventilation.[5] Breathing slower than 10 BCPM has a calming effect on our bodies and lowers blood pressure.[6]

You can get a general idea of your average resting BCPM by setting a one-minute timer and counting the number of breath cycles you take until the timer goes off. Test your BCPM a few times to acquire an average reading, because the very act of observing what you are doing often makes you want to change what you do. A more accurate measure of your resting BCPM would be taken by someone else while you

---

5. Ibid.

6. MH Schein, B Gavish, M Herz, D Rosner-Kahana, P Naveh, B Knishkowy, E Zlotnikov, N Ben-Zvi, and RN Melmed, "Treating Hypertension with a Device that Slows and Regularizes Breathing: A Randomized, Double-Blind Controlled Study." *Journal of Human Hypertension* 15 (2001): 271–278.

are not aware they are counting your BCPM. Ideally, the zero breath pattern will employ less than 10 BCPM.

Try this exercise to acquire a slow breathing pattern in preparation for learning zero breath:

1. Set a timer for one minute and start it as you begin a slow, deliberate breath pattern.

2. Keep practicing until you reach an average of about 8 BCPM.

3. Once you achieve an 8 BCPM average, practice without the timer, mentally counting the lengths of your inhalation and exhalation to get a sense of this BCPM.

4. Then, test it again with the timer while you also mentally count the lengths of your inhalation and exhalation to see if they match up.

5. Keep practicing this exercise until your inhalation and exhalation match up and you consistently reach an 8 BCPM average.

The Zero Breath Pattern

Zero breath employs abdominal breathing with an inhalation through the nose and exhalation through the mouth. Follow these steps to engage the zero breath pattern:

1. Using abdominal breathing, inhale through the nose and exhale through the mouth in equal lengths of inhalation and exhalation. Try counting, in your mind, the lengths of your inhalation and exhalation. Attempt to make the breath cycle fairly slow (about 8 BCPM) and the in-breath and out-breath of equal lengths. For example, if the inhalation is a 5-count, make the exhalation a 5-count.

2. Breathing in through the nose and out through the mouth creates a circular pattern of airflow. There is no hold or pause between inhalation and exhalation, or between exhalation and inhalation. There is a gentle turnaround, taking the amount of time needed to change directions between expiration and inspiration.

3. The mouth and jaw muscles are relaxed. Allow the back of the jaw to drop down a degree with the mouth open slightly and lips parted slightly. The upper teeth should not touch the lower teeth during this breath pattern.

At first, you might feel strange applying this jaw release and circular breath pattern, which is most likely not habitual for you. However, if you practice zero on a daily basis, it could eventually become your default breath pattern when you want to relax.

Pause & Reflect

Write down words to describe how you felt while practicing the zero breath pattern. How did it feel to slow your breathing rate down to below 10 BCPM? Were you able to keep your breathing activation area in the abdomen and allow the upper chest and shoulders to remain still and relaxed? What did you sense physically, mentally, and emotionally while practicing this pattern?

Sitting in Zero

1. Sit in a straight-backed chair where your feet can easily touch the floor.

2. Slide your tailbone all the way to the back of the chair. If your feet no longer touch the floor, place a few books or a pillow under your feet until they can rest comfortably.

3. Align your feet directly under your knees, with your toes pointed forward.

4. Rest your hands on your thighs so your elbows are directly below your shoulders. Roll your shoulders up, back, and then release them down, allowing them to relax back rather than round forward.

5. Lift the back of your head toward the ceiling and let your chin tuck in slightly.

6. Begin zero breath. During the entire breath pattern, place your visual focus straight ahead, neither looking up nor down. Let the eyes soften and allow your peripheral vision to widen slightly.

7. Relax the jaw, allowing the back of the mouth to release downward. The mouth is open a small amount and the lips are relaxed and parted just enough to let the air out.

8. Breathe in through the nose and out through the relaxed, slightly open mouth, engaging abdominal breathing. The breath cycle is slow and relaxed (about 8 BCPM), with the inhalation length the same as the exhalation. Count the duration of each, in your mind, to ensure they are equal.

9. With each inhalation, remind yourself to empty your mind as the air flows in through your nose, bringing a sense of lightness to your body and mind.

10. With each exhalation through the relaxed, open mouth, remind yourself to let go of tension in the body. Release this tension as you release the breath toward your area of eye focus.

11. Practice this pattern for about ten breath cycles and then slowly release the pattern back to your own habitual way of sitting and breathing.

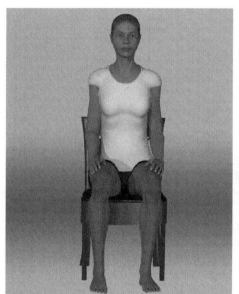 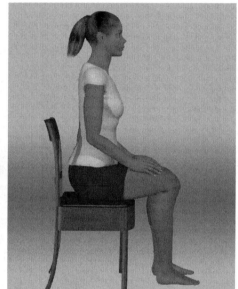

▌▌ Pause & Reflect

After practicing sitting in zero, write down a few descriptions of how you felt while in this pattern. Could you sense specific areas of your body not wanting to center, relax, or become still? Were you able to keep your eyes open and actively engaged in the give-and-take from a focal point during the entire exercise? When you shifted back to your own habitual breathing pattern and sitting pattern, what did it feel like in comparison to zero?

What if you were to sit in zero while watching TV? Try this while observing emotional scenes or commercials. Are you able to maintain zero while doing this? Can you sense when emotions come into your body, and where, as you attempt to maintain a state of zero?

Standing in Zero

1. Stand with your weight evenly distributed on your feet, with your feet lining up just underneath your hip sockets.

2. Stand up straight, finding a sense of harmony and balance in your physical alignment. Rest your arms at your sides, keep your shoulders relaxed, and allow your head to float upward as if an imaginary string were pulling the back of your head up to the ceiling.

3. Complete steps 6–10 in the "Sitting in Zero" lesson to finish.

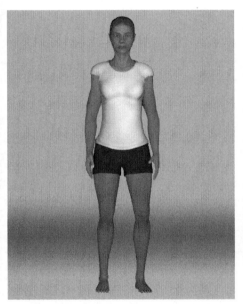 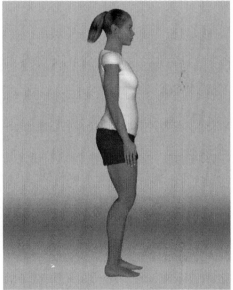

Walking in Zero

1. Once you are standing in zero, slowly step forward, rolling from heel to toe with the body relaxed and eyes focused straight ahead on the horizon. Use peripheral vision as you walk.

2. Keep breathing in zero, with your posture balanced and stacked from toe to head as you walk.

3. Let your movement flow gently, without being stiff and maintaining as much balance and harmony in your posture as possible.

4. Be aware of your surroundings, but don't interact with them, which would cause emotional experiences. Notice all aspects of your surroundings using your peripheral vision while walking.

 ## Pause & Reflect

Describe your experience with the zero pattern while standing and while walking. Write down any words to describe the differences between standing still and walking in zero. How did it feel to incorporate more of your posture and movement into the pattern? Was it challenging to keep all parts of your body committed to zero when walking?

Try to practice walking in zero in different settings, like outside in nature or in a public place. Were you able to achieve a zero state in spite of the events surrounding you? Could you sense when anything you saw, heard, felt, or thought caused a shift in your state? Could you sense any habitual movement patterns emerging, causing you to move out of zero?

Relaxing Into the Zero State

One effective way to reach greater levels of relaxation and emotional disengagement is to initiate the zero breath after a good relaxation exercise. This acts as reinforcement for the zero pattern, reminding your body of how relaxed, harmonious, and balanced it truly can be when in zero. With regular practice, you will need fewer relaxation exercises and will be able to simply utilize zero breath techniques to obtain the same results with less time and greater precision. For example, restful deep sleep can bring us to an extremely relaxed and neutral-feeling state. If you also consciously connect the zero breath to the act of waking and rising from sleep, you can eventually train your body to associate the zero breath with this calm, centered state.

Aligning Zero Breath with Waking

1. As you wake from a restful sleep, shift into zero breath.

2. While lying on your back, softly gaze at the ceiling and practice zero breath.

3. Notice how it feels to actively apply this breathing pattern to your restful state.

4. While maintaining zero, roll to your side, gently swing your legs over the edge of the bed, sit up, and come to a standing position beside your bed.

5. Try to maintain zero as you stand and walk around your room.

6. Remember how this feels when you work on the following exercises, and compare.

The following exercises will also help you associate relaxation with zero. With time and practice, you will be able to achieve a truly neutral zero state on a much more comprehensive and relaxed level. At first, you will want to practice these exercises regularly. Eventually, you will no longer need such complex exercises to help you reach zero—much like the first time you rode a bike, which took instruction, guidance, and a lot of practice to learn to balance on two narrow wheels while peddling forward, steering, and traveling at fairly high speeds. After much practice, you learned how to accomplish such a complex set of actions by simply sitting on the bike and pushing off; the rest became automatic. The same holds true for learning to achieve zero. Your body will eventually follow the simple cue of zero breath as a pathway to a relaxed, disengaged, and neutral-feeling state.

Extreme Tension to Extreme Relaxation

This exercise applies an extreme amount of tension in order to bring about a greater level of relaxation. It also helps you become more aware of where you are holding tension. It is important to associate relaxation and the release of tension with an exhalation through the mouth. This will help your body associate the act of relaxing with exhaling in the zero breath. In this exercise, you are instructed to inhale through the mouth, rather than the nose, so your body does not associate an inhalation through the nose with tension in the body.

Complete the following tension and release exercise while lying on your back:

1. Take a brief personal inventory of your body. Notice where you feel any tension, aches, or pains. Do you sense any emotions present? Are you aware of any distracting thoughts?

2. Inhale through the mouth and then hold your breath while you tense the muscles in your face as much as you can. Exhale through the mouth, and release the tension and relax the face.

3. Inhale through the mouth and then hold your breath while you tense your face, neck, shoulders, arms, and hands as much as you can. Exhale through the mouth, and release and relax.

4. Inhale through the mouth and then hold your breath while you tense your face, neck, shoulders, arms, hands, chest, and stomach as much as you can. Exhale through the mouth, and release and relax.

5.   Inhale through the mouth and then hold your breath while you tense your face, neck, shoulders, arms, hands, chest, stomach, buttocks, legs, and feet as much as you can. Exhale through the mouth, and release and relax.

6.   Change your breathing pattern to zero breath for a few breath cycles and notice any new levels of relaxation in your body.

7.   Take a second brief physical and emotional inventory of your body. Notice any physical changes from your first inventory? Did this exercise help clear your mind of distracting thoughts?

Practice the "Extreme Tension to Extreme Relaxation" exercise a few times a week until you discover that most of the previously observed tensions, emotions, and thoughts have, to the best of your knowledge, vanished.

Thoracic Stretch and Breathe

This exercise helps vertically stretch the upper part of the body around the thorax while engaging the lower abdominal muscles in deep breathing. The exercise stretches the thoracic region, providing room below the lungs for muscular breath support. It also helps to isolate the upper thoracic and clavicular muscles from the lower muscles engaged in abdominal breathing. Once again, it is important to coordinate the release of tension with an exhalation through the mouth.

1.   Stand with your feet hip-distance apart, toes pointed forward, and arms resting at your sides.

2.   Try to balance your weight equally on both feet and then balance your body with a sense of symmetry. In other words, check that your knees are over your toes and your hip sockets over your knees, and imagine your head is floating up toward the ceiling. Then, imagine "zipping up the front of your torso" with a big zipper that goes from your navel to your clavicle, which might help you lift and open your posture.

3.   Roll your shoulders up toward your ears, then back, and rest them down again, letting your arms hang with your palms right next to your thighs.

4.   Lift the back of your head up as your chin pulls in slightly, as if you were creating a straight line from your back all the way to the top of your head.

5.   Focus your eyes straight ahead and breathe in the zero breath pattern.

6.   During an inhale through the nose, sweep your straight arms up from your

sides until the backs of your hands meet above your head. When your hands meet, the inhalation should end. Then, hold your breath for steps 7 and 8.

7. Keeping your arms stretched above your head with backs of hands connected, lean to the right side from the waist, bending your entire upper body and stretched arms to the right. Still holding your breath, and without releasing your arms and hands, return to center. Then, lean the entire upper body to the left. Return to the center stretch position again.

8. Still holding your breath, bring your stretched arms down along the sides of your head to shoulder height, creating a *T* with your body.

9. Then, release your breath in an exhalation through the mouth as you slowly lower your arms down to the beginning position in step 1.

10. Repeat steps 6–9 two more times.

Rag Doll Stretch

This exercise gently stretches the lower part of your body, using gravity and slow methodical releasing movements to gradually stretch the back muscles while delivering additional oxygen to the brain. Deep breathing while bending at the waist and bringing the head below the heart provides more blood flow and oxygen to the brain, which can make you light-headed. With this in mind, you are advised to conduct this exercise while standing in front of a chair. You can also do the exercise on a mat or carpeted area. Wear loose-fitting clothing, particularly around the waist.

1. Stand up straight with your feet hip-distance apart, toes pointed forward, and arms resting at your sides. Try to balance your weight equally on both feet.

2. Roll your shoulders up toward your ears, then back, and rest them down again, letting your arms hang with your palms right next to your thighs.

3. Lift the back of your head up as your chin pulls in slightly, as if you were creating a straight line from your back all the way to the top of your head.

4. Focus your eyes forward and breathe in zero breath.

5. On the next exhale, slowly release your neck and lower the head until your chin rests on, or toward, your chest. Then, continue to release down the spine as you exhale, rolling down your back, one vertebra at a time, until you hang from your hips with your arms and head dangling toward the floor, like a limp rag doll bending at the waist. Allow your knees to bend slightly so they don't lock, and continue breathing as you hold this position. With each exhale, try to release any noticeable tension in your back, shoulders, neck, and legs.

6. Hang in "rag doll position" for two breath cycles, releasing tension and giving into gravity with each exhale. Check that your neck and shoulders are relaxed by gently swinging your arms and head from side to side.

7. With the next inhale, VERY SLOWLY roll up the spine to the chin-on-chest position and then float the head up, rolling the shoulders up, back, and then resting them down. Once fully upright, stand looking straight ahead and utilize neutral breath.

8. Take a physical and emotional inventory of your body, noticing any changes in body tension or emotion, and then repeat steps 6–7 two more times.

Practice all the exercises described so far in this chapter until you find you are able to reach a truly relaxed, centered, calm, and neutral-feeling zero whether lying down, sitting or standing. Once you reach this understanding of zero, you will be ready to learn Step Out and then move on to the emotion-inducing patterns.

During a series of workshops focused on emotions and workplace wellness, I taught the zero pattern as a primary stabilizer and "reset button" anyone can use during stressful work situations. I explained, "When emotions are heightened, so are our blood pressure and pulse. If some level of anger or fear is provoked, then we are also more likely to act impulsively, without taking time to think things through clearly. Applying the zero pattern during these times gives us the opportunity to take a moment to pause, think, and consider options without strong emotions leading our decisions."

Throughout the workshops, we explored how the emotion patterns felt in our bodies and then practiced calming them down using the zero pattern. Participants then learned how to sit, walk, and even speak using the zero pattern. It soon became an easy default pattern in which they could temporarily rest or take a moment away from their workplace stress to rethink issues. As we finished the workshop series, I encouraged coworkers to remind each other of this useful zero, or neutral, default, particularly during stressful times. I explained, "The more you practice this pattern, the more likely it is to become your new default. It could also become so subtle no one would know you are consciously applying a breathing pattern."

Months later, I stopped by an office where two women, who happened to have taken my workplace wellness workshop, worked. As soon as they saw me they said, "We use your method all the time now!" These two women handle the minute details of managing hundreds of financial accounts on a daily basis. One woman commented, "I get a lot of phone calls where people are very upset. Then I get upset. But now, my coworker over there whispers to me, 'Zero!' and I use the pattern and calm down right away." The other woman in the office added, "Yep, and if we say it to each other while someone is standing in the office, they think we are referring to something about the finances. You know, 'zero,' and no one is the wiser to our secret calming code."

Did you know…?

The Feldenkrais Method® is an excellent form of somatic education that brings attention to neuromuscular patterns and rigidities and helps a person improve range of motion, flexibility, and coordination as well as rediscover the body's innate capacity for graceful, efficient movement. Based on principles of physics, biomechanics, and human development, the lessons use gentle movement and directed attention to improve and enhance human functioning. After completing a typical Feldenkrais Awareness Through Movement (ATM) lesson, a person often expresses feeling extremely relaxed, physically harmonious, and balanced. Participating in regular ATM lessons can help you relate to and understand your potential for achieving a zero state. It can also provide you with valuable information on your own habitual movements and enhance your potential for greater physical expression.

To learn more, go to the official Feldenkrais website, www.feldenkrais.com. If you can't find a local Feldenkrais teacher, many are now offering lessons online as well as in video and audio formats.

Step Out

Step Out was first introduced by the BOS team to physically clear emotion and disengage the posture and muscles that signal emotion patterns, helping bring the body back to a more neutral or calm state.[7] Step Out starts with the zero pattern and adds a series of movements calibrated by breathing rhythms. It is informed by the practice of psycho-calisthenics, specifically the Integration Breath exercise designed to unite body movement with breathing.[8] It is essential to use Step Out regularly when practicing the emotion patterns, like a ritual to end each practice session, to help release emotional hangover.

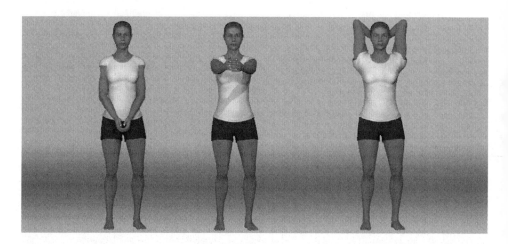

1.   Stand in zero, engaging zero breath. Keep your eyes focused straight ahead, neither looking up nor down, for the following sequence until you "shake out."

---

7. Susana Bloch, Pedro Orthous, and Guy Santibañez-H, "Effector Patterns of Basic Emotions: A Psychophysiological Method for Training Actors," *Journal of Social Biological Structure* 10 (January 1987): 1–19.

8. Oscar Ichazo, *Master Level Exercise: Psycho-Calisthenics* (New York, Sequoia Press, 1986), 50–51.

2. Bring your hands together in front of your hips by loosely interlacing your fingers.

3. Inhale through your nose as you raise your arms up over your head and bend your elbows so your clasped hands end up hanging behind your head. Use this entire movement for your inhale.

4. Gently squeeze your palms together, behind your head, as you complete the inhalation and hold your breath for a few seconds, to signify an ending point.

5. Exhale through your relaxed open mouth as you loosen your palm squeeze, raise your hands back over your head, and bring your interlaced hands back down in front of your body. Use this entire movement for your exhale.

6. Repeat steps 3–5 two more times to complete three cycles of breathing with this arm movement.

7. After the third breath cycle, bring your hands up to gently wipe your face to release any residual tension. Use a very gentle touch on the face, barely making contact with the skin, and wipe from eyes to ears, nose to ears, and mouth to ears.

8. Shake your body out by lightly jumping and then twisting and stretching limbs out at various angles, essentially throwing off the axis of your body's midline. While shaking out, make audible sound bursts like "ha!" or "ho!" or "hee-ah!" to help release any residual tensions hanging on anywhere in the body, including within vocal expression.

The arm swing movement, combined with zero breath, stretches the muscles related to the three lung segments, filling the lungs fully with air and reenergizing the body. The gentle face wiping reminds these fine muscles to release and let go of residual tension associated with emotions. The final shake-out essentially disengages postural muscle tension, keeping the body from holding onto emotion patterns or excessive muscular tension.

Practice Step Out until you have the sequence memorized and you find it brings you to a relaxed, loose, and calm state. Step Out will be used throughout this book as a method for concluding emotion pattern exercises. You can also use Step Out after a particularly stressful day or to transition into a relaxing evening, releasing the day before retiring to sleep.

Uses of the Zero Pattern

Now that you know how to achieve a zero pattern and apply it to different positions and actions, you can use zero as a practice, which will provide you with numerous benefits. The following list describes various ways in which you can use zero to support your practice of the Emotional Body as well as incorporate it into daily emotion regulation and somatic sensing practices.

1. To establish an "emotion-free" starting point from which to launch your practice of emotion patterns. Much like an artist starting with an empty canvas, zero breath helps you reach a state as close to neutral as possible before opening channels to the basic emotions.

2. As a sensor for habitual entanglements or emotional residue. When practicing the zero pattern, you will continually scan your entire body for any evidence of emotion patterns present in your breath or muscles and work to clear them to a point closer to true zero. Regular practice in this manner helps you recognize habitual blocks and entanglements and provides you with a tool for releasing the emotions you explore in patterns one through three.

3. To bridge the shifts between emotion patterns. This is similar to how a car's manual gearshift uses the clutch to briefly disengage an active level of movement in one gear before moving to another. Zero disengages the current emotion pattern and provides a brief reset before moving to another emotion pattern. Eventually, the zero bridge between emotional shifts is not consciously applied, but in initial practice sessions, zero is an important transitional step when shifting between emotion patterns. It helps provide you with control and clarity in your pattern application.

4. To release emotions, allowing you to reset and rest after exploring emotion patterns. Each lesson will conclude with returning to zero, and most will also include a Step Out to make sure all aspects of potential emotional hangover are cleared before finishing your practice of the emotion patterns. This serves as an important process for learning to clear the patterns fully. It also helps you attend to your personal well-being, making sure you reset and rest regularly, particularly when practicing the b-patterns.

5. As a regular life-practice for calming and centering. Zero and Step Out are the two exercises Emotional Body teachers enthusiastically encourage people to practice and share with others. These exercises provide valuable tools for calming our biological alarm systems and bringing us to healthier states. Many people use the zero breath as a way to prepare for sleep, to transition from work to home life, and to better manage challenging moments.

Summary
Achieving a relaxed, neutral-feeling zero state takes time, practice, and acute personal observation. Many who practice this on a regular basis recognize that the

zero state they discovered early on becomes quite different after extended attentive practice. Remind yourself to associate zero with relaxation, a full disengagement from excess tension, emotions, and distracting thoughts. As you work on this personal awareness, you will eventually achieve a more relaxed, centered, and grounded zero state.

Zero and Step Out will be used throughout this book as methods for clearing away the emotion patterns and releasing your practice sessions. Susana Bloch actually describes the Step Out exercise as a way of resetting the system back to a zero level of emotional excitement and recommends that a person use it as many times as necessary to clear away emotions.[9] Zero serves as a transitional state to shift into and out of emotion patterns. It also relaxes you and provides a calming restful state, essential for obtaining balance and supporting your well-being. Regular use of zero and Step Out can help safeguard against emotional residue and physical exhaustion. It is important to perfect your use of zero and Step Out before you proceed with practicing the emotion-inducing patterns in the following chapters.

9. Susana Bloch, *The Alba of Emotions: Managing Emotions through Breathing* (Santiago: Grafhika, 2006), 151.

The Nose-Breathing Patterns   5

Nose Breathing Preferences

When teaching Emotional Body courses, I often start with an exercise where participants explore their habitual breathing patterns. I then take a quick poll to see what people learn about themselves with this exploration. A consistent majority report they habitually breathe through the nose. When asked why they prefer breathing in this way, most state it feels comfortable, takes less effort, and reduces the dry-mouth feeling associated with mouth breathing. Let's examine why so many might habitually nose-breathe, and why others may not default to this breathing pathway.

Health Benefits of Nose Breathing
When we breathe in through the nose, air is filtered, warmed, and moisturized as it passes through the sinuses and pharynx and travels to the lungs through the trachea, or windpipe. The nose is the "air conditioner" for the entire body. It is a common practice to breathe through the nose in cold, dry, or polluted areas to gain better control of the air quality entering the lungs. Beyond these

air conditioning advantages, nose-breathing practices can also improve blood pressure, cardiac health, muscle tone, metabolism, digestion, sinus health, mental concentration, sleep patterns, and dental development.[1]

Did you know...?

The sinuses produce nitric oxide, and a nose inhalation brings this beneficial gas into our bodies with every breath. Nitric oxide's inclusion in our breathing provides two important health benefits not present when breathing in through the mouth: (1) small doses of nitric oxide, which is lethal to bacteria and viruses, help to keep the sinuses sterile, and (2) nitric oxide dilates blood vessels. When we breathe in through the nose, the nitric oxide travels down into the lungs and increases oxygenation.[2] As a result, the gas exchange between the alveoli and red blood cells becomes much more efficient, and the blood oxygen level increases.[3]

The Expressive Nose

The nose plays a leading part in our expressions. With the nose placed center stage on our faces, pointing outward and leading us through life, it is no surprise our language is filled with "nosey" expressions. The following nose-centered sayings depict vastly different expressive behaviors, depending on how the nose is acting in a given circumstance. These idioms involve nose-centered behaviors and forward motion that is led, at least externally, by the nose:

- Don't be nosey
- Stick your nose in
- Turn up your nose
- Get up someone's nose
- Look down your nose
- Nose in the air
- Win by a nose
- Keep your nose to the grindstone

What about when the nose plays a different role, as the receiver taking in our

1 Jefferson Yosh, DMD, MAGD, "Mouth Breathing: Adverse Effects on Facial Growth, Health, Academics, and Behavior," *General Dentistry* 58 (2010): 18-25.

2 John O Lundberg, "Nitric Oxide and the Paranasal Sinuses", US National Library of Medicine, *The Anatomical Record: Advances in Integrative Anatomy and Evolutionary Biology 291*, no. 11 (2008): 1479-1484.

3 J.O. Lundberg, G Settergren, S Gelinder, JM Lundberg, K Alving, and E Weitzberg, "*Inhalation of Nasally Derived Nitric Oxide Modulates Pulmonary Function in Humans*", *Acta Physiologica Scandinavica* 158 no. 4 (1996): 343-347.

surroundings? As you read through the sayings below, do you visualize someone receiving information through the nose?

- Stop and smell the roses
- To smell a rat
- The nose knows
- A nose for wine
- Wake up and smell the coffee

These expressions suggest a more centered or still posture, with a focus on inhalation. Another word for inhalation is *inspiration*, which evokes ideas of illumination and insight. The nose-sayings above suggest insight is gained by taking in information through the nose. That information is quickly sent to the olfactory bulb, located directly under the brain. Our nasal anatomy has a direct line of communication to the brain and thereby to our emotions, and it acts as an important receptacle of information for the entire body.

Before we explore the nose-breathing patterns, let's look at some basic nasal anatomy that will be referred to throughout this chapter.

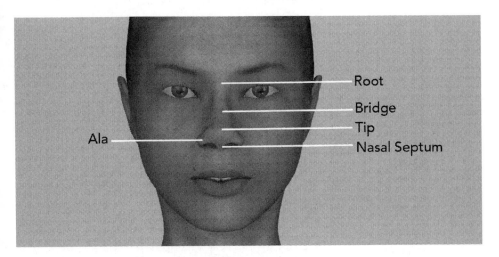

Basic Nasal Anatomy and Functions

Think of the nose's framework as a three-sided pyramid, composed of bones, cartilages, and muscles. The *nasal ridge*, or *bridge*, formed by two bones joined in the center, runs the length of the nose from its root (between the eyes) to its tip. The nasal bones are connected to the face by a fibrous membrane, creating the sides of the nose. At the base (on the upper lip), nasal cartilages connect up to the nasal bones. The vertical structure located between the two nostrils attaches the nasal tip to the upper lip and is called the *columella*, or the *nasal septum*. The structures attaching the nostrils to each side of the cheeks are called *ala*, or *nose wings*.

The nostrils and nasal cavity are lined with *mucous membrane* and *cilia* (little hairs). The mucous filters the air while the cilia prevent microorganisms from entering the body. The nasal cavity has shelves, called *nasal concha*, or *turbinates*, stacking from low to high. Inhaled air is warmed and moisturized in these turbinates before traveling to the lungs. Air can travel through any of the turbinates, and on either side of the nose, for its journey to the lungs; however, the lowest and largest turbinate is used the most.[4]

Did you know...?

Each nasal turbinate has its own function and reaction. The lowest, or inferior, turbinate responds to allergens, becoming inflamed and secreting more mucous when experiencing an allergic reaction. The middle turbinate protects the sinuses from coming into direct contact with pressurized airflow. The top, or superior, turbinate is located directly under the brain, where millions of nerves whose purpose is differentiating individual smells are housed. When we sniff, or inhale small amounts of air quickly, the air travels to the topmost turbinate in order to activate the nerves in the olfactory bulb.[5] Consider times you sniffed the air to determine a particular smell or watched an animal sniffing around, tracking smells. Both are instinctive actions for quickly acquiring information about our surroundings through the superior turbinate.

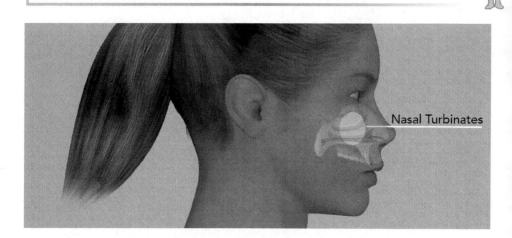

Nasal Turbinates

Muscles Affecting Nose Breathing Patterns
Distinguishing between individual nasal muscles is difficult since the muscle

4 Henry Gray, *Anatomy of the Human Body* (Philadelphia, Lea & Febiger, 1918; Bartleby.com, 2000), 991-996.

5 J.B. Watelet and P. Van Cauwenberge. "Applied Anatomy and Physiology of the Nose and Paranasal Sinuses," *US National Library of Medicine, The National Institute of Health: Allergy 54*, no. 57 (1999): 14-25.

fibers intertwine with each other. Although eight different muscles have been identified in nasal anatomy, for our purposes, we will recognize just three main muscle areas contributing to movements and expansion of the nasal membrane.[6]

1. The *procerus* muscle runs along the nasal bone and inserts into the area located near the eyebrows and forehead. You will feel this muscle move upward and downward as you raise your eyebrows and then lower them toward the root of your nose.

2. The *nasalis* muscle is like a band stretching across the nose behind the tip and attaching just behind the ala. You can feel the nasalis when you try to move the tip of your nose toward your lower lip.

3. A set of three interconnected muscles create the *nasolabial furrow*, which runs from the inside corners of the eyes down to the corners of the mouth. You can feel these muscles move as you try to pinch your nose with your muscles, or constrict your nasal passage.[7]

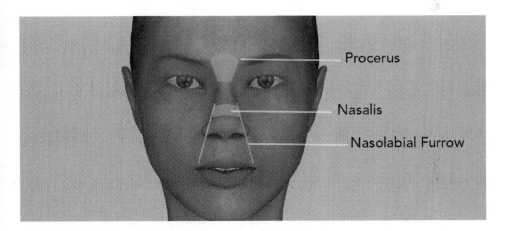

Did you know...?

Not everyone has the same number of facial muscles, and the face is the only part of the human anatomy with such massive differences in muscle structure. It is no wonder false claims abound over the number of muscles in the face as well as how many muscles it takes to smile or frown.

6 K.J. Anderson, M. Henneberg, and R.M. Norris, "Anatomy of the Nasal Profile," *Journal of Anatomy 213*, no. 2 (2008): 210-216.

7. Ibid.

However, the first systematic scientific study, published in the *American Psychological Journal*, investigated the variations in human facial muscles and found a total of 19 possible facial muscles. The study also revealed that the amount of muscles (up to 19) varies from person to person, with some individuals possessing only 60% of the available muscles. This variation from person to person can explain why the more complex emotions are expressed in so many different ways. Conversely, the study also revealed that all humans have the same five basic muscles used to express basic emotions.[8]

Dr. Bridget Waller, the study's author, states, "There is a great deal of asymmetry in the face and the left side is generally more expressive than the right." Waller continues, "As humans we are able to change the level of control we have over our facial expressions," and she stresses, "we need not worry too much about these variations because people can compensate for the lack of one muscle by using another."[9]

Exploring Nasal Muscle Movements

Let's explore moving the nasal muscles and see how they affect the airflow of your nasal passages. If at first you find you are unable to activate one of these muscle areas, don't despair. The facial muscle work we are about to explore can develop over time and with practice. Learning to control these muscles can help isolate specific activation areas to regulate an emotion in more subtle ways and to avoid unintentional emotional mixes.

Follow these steps for this investigation:

1. Gently rest your left hand over the root area of the nose, between the eyes and where the procerus muscle connects to the forehead.

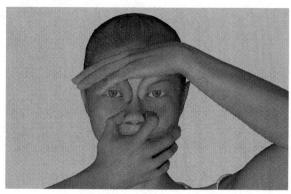

2. Then, place the fingers of your right hand around your nose, just behind the

---

8 B.M. Waller, J.J. Cray and A.M. Burrows, "Selection for Universal Facial Emotion," *Emotion* 8, no. 3 (2008): 435-439.

9 University of Portsmouth. "Learning From The Dead: What Facial Muscles Can Tell Us About Emotion." *Science-Daily.* www.sciencedaily.com/releases/2008/06/080616205044.htm (accessed July 11, 2017).

ala and where the nasalis muscle connects with the nasolabial furrow. The right hand will look as if it is trying to pinch your nose, although you will not be applying any pressure to this area.

3.   With your hands in these two positions, focus on the nasalis and nasolabial furrow areas near the right hand and try to constrict your nasal passage using only these muscles. Avoid activating the procerus muscle or any other muscle under the left hand.

4.   Once you feel you can constrict your nasal passage with these muscle areas, then work the muscles in the opposite direction, to open up, or dilate, the nasal passage. Try not to activate the procerus muscle in the forehead to complete this.

5.   Practice constricting and dilating the nasal passage using the nasalis and nasolabial furrow areas until you feel you can consciously activate these muscles without depending on the muscles in the forehead. Check that this action is not dependent on the muscles around the mouth either.

Muscles Around the Eyes and Mouth

The muscles in the nasolabial furrow reach from the eyes to the mouth, creating a clear connection between the movements of the nasal muscles to the movements of the eye and mouth muscles. For example, when you scrunch your nose, can you feel the muscles around your mouth and eyes compress as well? Let's investigate the interconnectedness of these facial muscles before we begin to apply the nose-breathing patterns.

Our eyes and our mouth are surrounded by ring-like bands of muscles, called sphincter muscles.[10] There are many voluntary movements that we can execute with these muscles, such as opening, closing, spreading, lifting, narrowing, or widening the eyes and mouth areas. Due to daily speech patterns and eating, we have much more practice voluntarily activating the mouth muscles. Also, the mouth muscles execute significant muscle actions affecting a larger opening, which makes them more obvious to us than those of the eye muscles. However, muscular movements around the eyes send powerful signals to the brain about emotions and feelings.

Let's explore a few voluntary movements possible with eye and mouth muscles. You may be surprised at how these two muscle areas relate to each other, and how they can evoke very different emotional responses when the muscles are moved in different directions.

---

10 Henry Gray, *Anatomy of the Human Body* (Philadelphia, Lea & Febiger, 1918; Bartleby.com, 2000), Section IV, 4b.

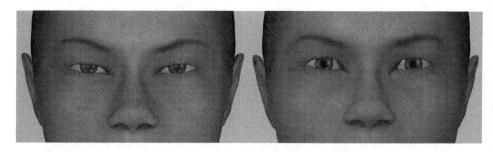

Engaging Muscles in Elevate and Depress Actions
Follow these steps for this investigation:

1. Allow your mouth to gently drop open, and then close your mouth by bringing your upper and lower lips together simultaneously. Then, relate this same movement to your eyes. Encourage your eyes to gently open, and then close them by bringing your upper and lower lids together simultaneously. Pretty easy, right?

2. Now let's isolate the movements of the upper portion of the muscle from the lower portion of the muscle. From the open mouth position, try to bring the upper lip down (depress) to meet the lower lip, without moving the lower lip or jaw. You may want to place a hand on your chin so you can detect movement. Can you achieve this? You will probably notice a great deal of activation in the lower lip and jaw, but by attempting to achieve this action you will discover the use of specific muscle areas in your upper lip. After successfully depressing the upper lip, relate this same movement to your eyes. You may want to place a finger under each eye so you can detect movement there. Bring your upper eyelid down to your lower eyelid, without raising the lower lid. You will likely find this fairly easy to achieve.

3. Let's reverse the action. Starting with an open mouth, try to bring the lower lip up (elevate) to meet the upper lip, without moving the upper lip. You may find this action easy. Then, relate this same movement to your eyes, trying to bring the lower eyelid up to the upper eyelid. You may want to very lightly place a finger on top of each upper eyelid or look in a mirror to detect any movement. This action may be quite challenging.

Adducting and Abducting Muscles
Throughout the following exercises, the terms adduct and abduct will be used to refer to muscle movements. To adduct muscles in our bodies is to move the muscles toward the midline of the body, like pulling the arms in toward your chest or bringing your feet together. To abduct muscles is to take them away from the

midline of the body, like extending your arms out to your sides or spreading your legs into a wide stance. One easy way to remember the difference is abducting is to "take away," like an abduction of a person.

Adduct and Abduct Facial Muscles

Follow these steps for this investigation:

1. With your mouth gently closed, abduct the mouth muscles by sending the corners of your mouth toward your ears, essentially widening your closed mouth and perhaps feeling a smile forming. Release the smile and then, with your eyes gently closed, try to complete the same action with your eye muscles. Send the corners of your eyes toward the ears. This will be a very subtle movement and may feel quite challenging since only a very small amount of movement is possible. See if you can complete this eye muscle movement without moving your mouth. Gently place a hand around your mouth to detect any muscle movement while you work on the eye movements.

2. Complete the actions in step 1, but with your mouth and eyes open. Can you feel the muscles moving farther now? Do you feel other muscles in the cheeks and around the temple area moving back toward the ears as well?

3. Reverse the action of the mouth muscle movement. Adduct the muscles by bringing the corners of the mouth inward. You might feel your lips pursing or making a kissing motion. Notice the muscle contracts on the upper and lower lips in order to complete this action. Then, apply the same actions to the eyes. Bring the corners of your eyes toward the root of your nose. Do you notice the upper and lower eyelid areas contracting in order to complete this action? Can you feel your vision narrowing?

4. Take a moment and yawn. Open your eyes and mouth wide to help release some of the intense muscle work in these exercises. Take a break away from this work for a while and allow your muscles to rest before moving on to more exercises.

Did you know...?

Our faces have a "two-way street" for activation of expression. Facial expressions can result from physiological changes coming from within us, and muscles formed to create facial expressions can stimulate physiological changes throughout our bodies. Our facial expressions are controlled by cranial nerves that also regulate salivation, tearing, breathing, heart rate, tongue and mouth movements, and eye and eyelid movements. When our senses detect something causing us to move our eyes, salivate, change our heart rate, or tear up, facial expressions are also activated. Likewise, when the facial muscles are consciously activated, the cranial nerves are stimulated and can result in changes in tear production, salivation, breathing, and heart rate.[11]

While learning to regulate facial muscle movements, you may be surprised at how simple movements of eyes, eyelids, mouth, and even the tongue can cause noticeable shifts in bodily sensations. You may also learn about some of your own facial muscle habits. Keep this "two-way street" of facial muscle activation in mind as you practice the Emotional Body lessons and recognize our ability to consciously evoke and control the cranial nerves through physical regulation of the facial muscles.

I worked in an environment where fellow employees engaged in workplace bullying behavior for many years. Workplace bullying is emotionally disturbing for employees, particularly when you consider we probably spend more time in the work environment than we do in our own homes and that we rely on our employment for financial stability. Many of us remain in these emotionally unhealthy environments for far too many years due to our dependence on the income or our determination to move beyond what we see as juvenile behavior in a professional adult setting. Over the years, I used all my emotion regulation abilities to remain calm and centered while staying strong and rational around the bullies. I made sure I always dealt with facts rather than opinions and worked hard not to take their comments and actions personally.

Although our employers knew of the bullying behavior, no matter how much they tried to help remedy the situation, the hostility remained, and actually increased, as if to fight against attempts to reduce the abusive stronghold.

I was finally given a great opportunity to move to a new place of employment. My new work environment was amazingly pleasant and peaceful. I could go to work each day without bracing myself for emotional warfare. No longer did I need to constantly control my facial expressions so I wouldn't show the absolute disdain I felt for the tactics and behavior I was witnessing on a daily basis.

Interestingly enough, once released from many years of constant facial

11 Stephen W. Porges, *The Polyvagal Theory: Neurophysiological Foundations of Emotions, Attachment, Communication, Self-regulation* (New York: Norton & Company, 2011),163-164.

muscle control, I suddenly developed a facial tic! It emerged within a couple months of my move. It was a subtle muscle lift on the upper left side of my mouth. At first I worried, "What is going on with my face? I am free from all that workplace stress now. Why would I develop an involuntary tic now?" Then, I noticed the tic appeared whenever I thought about my old job or one of the bullies. This was not an involuntary tic; it was completely voluntary and associated with an emotional reaction to my past work life. Considering the muscle engagement area, I realized the tic was most likely the manifestation of unresolved feelings of disgust I had suppressed for many years. In emotional effector pattern terms, disgust is a complex mix of most of the basic emotions and involves a distinct curl of the upper lip muscles. My feelings of disgust over the workplace bullying situation were finally coming to the surface because I was no longer consciously controlling and masking my facial muscles for hours a day.

I knew I needed to calm down the facial muscles and cranial nerves that were overstimulated from so many years of strong physical emotion regulation measures. I immediately engaged in a regular schedule of relaxation and centering, like zero pattern and Step Out work, Feldenkrais method exercises, massage therapy, and regular walks in nature. I also made sure I emotionally embraced my new work life and detached from my old work environment.

Within a few months, the emotional facial tic disappeared completely, and as that happened, my old job looked more like a bad dream and my new work environment felt even more peaceful and fulfilling.

Practicing the Breathing Exercises

Once you have practiced the facial muscle isolations long enough to gain some control over the muscles around the nose, eyes, and mouth, it is time to integrate the breath patterns. As you explore the breathing exercises, practicing while lying on your back is best. This allows you to relax all other areas of the body and place the majority of your focus on your breathing and on the muscles in your face. Since it could be a challenge to read while lying on your back, you may want to read the exercise first and then lie down to practice its application. Another option is to record the instructions for these initial exercises and play them back as you lie down for your practice sessions.

Comparing Zero Breath and Nose Breathing

1. While lying down on your back with your eyes gazing up at the ceiling, start the zero breath pattern (see previous chapter).

2. Once you have established a few cycles of zero breath, close your mouth and breathe in and out through the nose, maintaining all other aspects of the zero breath pattern. How does it feel to simply change the pathway of the breath?

3. After exploring nose breathing in this pattern for a while, go back to zero breath. Do you sense any changes in your body as you switch back to zero? Remain in zero breath for a few cycles to conclude this exercise.

Incorporating Facial Muscles with Nose Breathing

Practice exploring adducting and abducting muscles while you breathe through the nose.

1. As you breathe through the nose, contract, or adduct, the nasal muscles, essentially constricting nasal airflow. Encourage the muscles around the eyes and the mouth to move in the same direction. How does it feel to have these muscles moving toward the midline of your face while you breathe through the nose?

2. Now abduct the nasal muscles by opening up the nasal airway and stretching these muscles toward the ears. Encourage your eye and mouth muscles to move in the same direction. How does it feel to have these muscles moving away from the midline of your face while you breathe through the nose?

3. Gently experiment with going back and forth between adducting and abducting the nasal, eye, and mouth muscles while you breathe in and out of the nose. Do you notice any subtle changes in your feelings or emotions as you move muscle directions while breathing?

4. Find a midpoint where the muscles are not adducting or abducting. Later, this midpoint location can be identified as the zero muscle pattern, or resting state, for the eye, mouth, and nasal muscles.

5. Once you establish the midpoint while nose breathing, switch to the zero pattern to end this exercise. If you feel any residual muscle tension or emotion still present after shifting to zero, conduct a Step Out (see previous chapter) until the tension or emotion is released.

 Pause & Reflect

Take a few moments and write down any discoveries made while exercising these two degrees of nose breathing. Try to describe how the two directions of abducting and adducting felt physically. Describe sensations occurring throughout the exercises, and acknowledge areas within your body where there might have been activation, tension, and release. Were any other areas of your body triggered into responding to these small shifts in your breath and facial muscle movement? Could you sense any feelings or emotions emerging during these exercises? If so, try to describe them using emotion words. Keep this list of words as a reference for comparison with future lessons.

Take a Break
Try a few cycles of zero and Step Out or go on a walk outside, and plan some additional time away from your practice before you continue. Taking regular breaks and letting go of the pattern work is essential to your ability to absorb and retain the technique as well as to support your overall health and well-being.

Introduction to the 1a and 1b Patterns
The 1a and 1b breathing patterns may at first seem to be only very subtly different. However, this apparent subtlety may be the result of your own initial limitations in controlling your breathing while managing the movements of the small muscles around the nose and eyes. The more you learn to control and increase the degrees of abduction and adduction possible with these muscles, the more obvious and intensely different the two patterns become.

As you explore these exercises, remember to practice in a quiet private space so you can place all your attention on combining the breathing with the muscle movement and isolation. As you practice, make sure you are maintaining deep diaphragmatic breathing and actively using abdominal and thoracic muscles to support it. Also, check the high chest area regularly to make sure you are not associating exercise or practice effort with high chest, or stressful, breathing.

1a Breath Pattern

1. While lying down on your back with your eyes gazing up at the ceiling, begin zero breath. Once it is established, change only the pathway of the breath—to nose breathing. The inhale and exhale are both soft, even, and relaxed while you engage deep diaphragmatic breathing and active use of abdominal and thoracic muscles to support the breath.

2. Then, abduct the nasal muscles, moving them outward toward your ears.

Can you also move your temple muscles and the tops of your cheeks toward the ears? With your mouth closed, encourage the mouth muscles to abduct towards the ears as well.

3. Inhale through the nose, with a gentle turnaround to the exhale (as if tossing a ball up in the air and watching it transition from going up to going back down). Exhale through the nose, allowing a short pause after exhaling (as if holding the ball for a moment) before inhaling again (tossing the ball lightly up in the air). The pause is a soft moment of inaction, where you are neither inhaling nor exhaling. Avoid excess tension for this pause.

4. Establish this pattern for a few cycles. Notice if any sensations, feelings, or emotions emerge as you maintain this breathing pattern.

5. When you feel you have exercised this pattern enough, find the midpoint where you are neither adducting nor abducting the muscles in your face.

6. Once you have established a midpoint while nose breathing, switch to zero to end this exercise.

Did you know...?

The 1a pattern lowers the heart rate to below the average resting heart rate. In subjects studied during the initial research of the emotional effector patterns, the heart rate achieved when in this emotional state averaged 60 beats per minute or lower,[12] which is an excellent resting heart rate, falling just below the average resting heart rate of an athlete.

1b Breath Pattern

Although 1a has the potential to lower your heart rate, 1b evokes more muscular tension throughout the body and can raise your heart rate. Keep this in mind as you practice this pattern and be sure to apply low levels of muscle activation at first, only increasing intensity as you gain a sense of control and comfort in pursuing your exploration. You can learn a great deal about how these emotions can be present in your day-to-day life, and under your radar, by exercising subtle

12 G. Santibañez-H and S. Bloch, "A Qualitative Analysis of Emotional Effector Patterns and their Feedback," The Pavlovian Journal of Bilogical Science 21 (1986): 108-116..

low-intensity levels and becoming more sensitive and aware of their presence in your body.

At this point in your practice, try to interpret sensations felt with the patterns as enlightened moments of self-discovery. Remember, at any time during your practice, if you don't like how you are feeling and want to stop, go to zero until you clear. If you need to, stand up and complete a Step Out as an extra process for letting go of the emotional pattern.

1. While lying down on your back looking up at the ceiling, begin the zero pattern. Once it is established, change only the pathway of the breath—to nose breathing. Make sure you maintain deep diaphragmatic breathing and active use of abdominal and thoracic muscles to support the breath throughout the rest of this exercise.

2. Then adduct, or constrict, the nasal and eye muscles, moving them inward toward the bridge of your nose. Feel the tops of your cheeks pressing inward, gradually constricting the nasal passages even more and affecting the intensity of your inhale and exhale. You may feel some tension build on your upper lip as your mouth muscles constrict slightly; however, do not try to create a strong adduction of the mouth and form a pucker.

3. Inhale through your tense nasal passage with a short stop at the end, and exhale through the nose with a similar tension and stop action. Immediately inhale again, obtaining a breathing rhythm with equal lengths of inhale and exhale. (This breathing rhythm may resemble the tension of directly throwing and catching a ball, with no lob or arc. It is direct, forceful, and sharp.) Keep the inhalation and exhalation lengths fairly long, which will establish a low level of the pattern. It is best, at this point, to keep the levels low and controlled, allowing yourself to maintain the ability to observe and regulate your first experience with the pattern.

4. Maintain the 1b pattern for a few cycles. Make sure the breath movement does not sneak up into the chest or clavicle area. Use deep abdominal controlled breathing throughout the pattern.

5. Once you feel you have exercised this pattern long enough, find the midpoint where you are neither adducting nor abducting the muscles in your face. Sometimes adducted muscles in the face are more difficult to release to the midpoint. If you find this is the case, move the muscles in the opposite direction by abducting toward the ears, and then return them to the midpoint. Try this a few times if you need to establish a release of the muscle constriction in the nasal passage and across the upper cheeks.

6. Once you feel you are no longer adducting the facial muscles while nose breathing, switch to the zero pattern to end this exercise. If you feel any residual muscle tension or emotion still present after shifting to zero, conduct a Step Out until the tension or emotion is released.

Pause & Reflect

Take a few moments and write down any discoveries you made while practicing patterns 1a and 1b. Make a list of words to describe feelings, sensations, or emotions experienced during your practice. Can you sense specific areas in your body where the pattern created a domino effect, where one small muscle movement initiated the reaction of another, then another, etc.? How much of your body eventually reacted to these seemingly simple breathing and facial muscle movements?

Now, take a good long break before continuing with any other exercises or revisiting these two patterns. Before your break, you may also want to do an extra Step Out. The act of recalling and writing about the emotions derived from these exercises can bring back subtle levels of the emotional state. Regular use of the zero pattern and Step Out as practice session completion rituals is highly recommended.

Did you know...?

When engaged in the 1b pattern, the muscles around the eyes tense, narrowing eye focus, and the muscles around the jaw are tight and ready to bite. These facial muscles send strong signals to the rest of the body to tense and press forward as if ready to engage with anyone or anything in its path. 1b also raises the heart rate to a range that is far above recommended levels for a resting heart rate. In subjects studied during the initial research of the emotional effector patterns," the heart rate achieved when in this emotional state averaged over 100 beats per minute.[13]

Facial Expressions
As you experiment with the facial muscle movements, adducting and abducting, can you feel familiar facial expressions emerging? You might feel a smile forming

---

13 ibid

when abducting the muscles and moving them toward the ears in pattern 1a. The eye muscle movements of a fully integrated smile are often overlooked if we assume a smile is only formed with the mouth. However, if the eye muscles are not engaged in the smile, the expression is read as insincere or incomplete. The eye muscle movement is very subtle, and you may feel it more easily than you would see it. If you practice the 1a facial expression in the mirror and concentrate on moving the muscles around the eyes first, before engaging the mouth and cheek muscles, you may notice a slight change in your eyes. You may also notice the pupils dilate a little and the eyes become slightly glazed or glassy looking. Familiar sayings of "that glint in your eye" and "eyes that sparkle" refer to these subtle yet recognizable changes that occur when we are engaged in emotions associated with 1a.

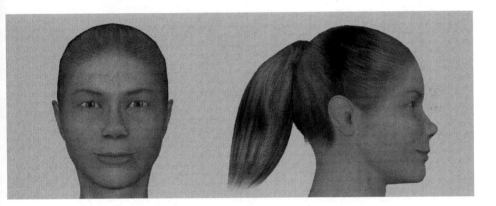

Did you know...?

The fully integrated smile, or the Duchenne smile, was identified in the late 1800s by French physician and physiologist G. B. A. Duchenne, who later shared his discoveries with Charles Darwin. Duchenne experimented with the manipulation of human facial expression of emotion and tested photographic plates of these manipulations against people's perceptions of authentic expressions of emotions. Dr. Duchenne revealed the cause of an insincere smile was a lack of involvement in the orbicular muscles of the eyes.[14]

Continued practice with controlling and expanding the range of the muscles around the eyes will help you develop a more sincere, authentic, and fully integrated smile.

14 Peter J. Snyder, Rebecca Kaufman, John Jarrison and Paul Maruff, "*Charles Darwin's Emotional Expression 'Experiment' and His Contribution to Modern Neuropharmacology,*" *Journal of the History of the Neurosciences 19* (2010): 158–170.

When you practiced the 1b pattern, could you sense an intense glare forming in your eyes? Did your eyes narrow and want to fix their focus on something or someone? You might have noticed your jaw clenching, and as the muscles in your face adducted, moving toward the middle of your face and pressing the muscles against your teeth. Did you feel your jaw move forward slightly as the muscles around the cheeks and mouth pressed forward and inward and the upper lip tightened?

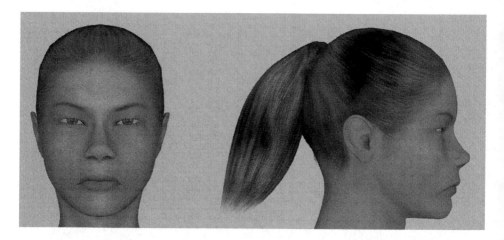

Did you know…?

Our facial muscle movements send strong signals to the autonomic nervous system (ANS), which regulates key involuntary functions of the body, including in the heart, intestines, and glands. Studies conducted where subjects were taught to move specific facial muscles associated with basic emotions resulted in dramatic changes in ANS response. The greatest degree of change occurred in the facial muscle movements associated with 1b, resulting in the subjects' skin temperature increasing significantly and heart rate rising by 25 beats per minute. The study also revealed not all negative emotions had the same effect on the ANS and that each basic emotion had its own specifically patterned effect. For example, the facial expressions evoking other emotions, like fear or sadness, decreased skin temperature, and heart rate averages were not nearly as high as the rate evoked by 1b.[15]

Incorporating Postural Attitudes

Once you have practiced the breathing patterns and facial aspects of 1a and 1b, it is time to experiment with the postural attitudes for each pattern. Postural attitude

15 Paul Ekman and K. Scherer, *Approaches to Emotion* (Hillsdale, NJ, Erlbaum, 1984): 325-327.

work requires the coordination of many large muscle groups into movement and gestures. It is wise to begin their study in a sitting position and eventually move to standing and walking since these become more complex as a person stands, walks, and then engages in activities. The following exercises will take you through gradual developments of the postural attitudes for 1a and 1b.

Sitting in 1a

Use a firm straight-backed chair that allows your feet to touch the floor when sitting toward the front of the chair seat. Sit in the zero postural attitude (see previous chapter).

Look directly across the room and identify a focal point located at eye level, so that you are neither looking up nor down at the floor. Your focal point can be anything like a spot on the wall, a doorknob, a window, or a picture. You will look at this focal point throughout the exercise.

1. From the zero sitting position, place your attention on the muscles along the left side of your neck. See if you can relax those muscles enough so you find your head slightly sinking or tilting toward the left.

2. Place your attention on the front of your neck and relax those muscles enough so your chin sinks down slightly toward your chest, but still retain eye contact with your focal point.

3. Bring your attention to the left side of your rib cage, and see if you can relax the muscles on your left side so your posture sinks slightly toward the left, essentially bringing your left shoulder closer to your left hip, creating a side bend or curve to your spine.

4. As you bend your entire torso to the left, from neck through the spine, can you sense weight shifting in your seat? Do you feel more weight on your right buttock as your body curves toward the left? If so, your body is adjusting to a contralateral posture to counterbalance the left-side lean. So that you may more clearly feel this contralateral movement, lift the heel of your left foot slightly. This heel lifting can be an extremely small movement, so subtle that someone watching you may not be able to see it. Do you have a clearer sensation of the right hip pressing into your chair seat?

5. Allow your forearms to rest on the tops of your thighs with your palms facing up toward the ceiling. This allows your arms to rotate outward slightly, opens up the thoracic region, and initiates an open posture.

6. Now explore steps 1–5 for the right side—with your head tilting to the right, with your side bending on the right, and while lifting your right heel slightly

to feel the left hip press into the chair seat. Make sure you maintain eye contact with your focal point.

7. Practice moving gradually and slowly between the two side-bending postures so you gain a sense of how this postural attitude affects your entire body from head to foot. As you practice this, encourage your muscles to relax as much as possible. Check for any excessive tension emerging in the neck. The muscles in the non-bending side will stretch slightly to accommodate the tilt. If you feel pain or tension during the tilt, decrease its intensity. A smaller tilt and side bend achieved with ease and comfort is far better than one with a greater degree of intensity. There may be habitual body tensions that will take time and repeated practice to release. Be patient and don't push for a big result here.

8. Finish the exercise by returning to the zero sitting position.

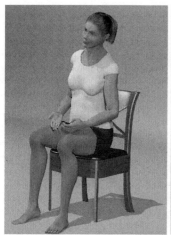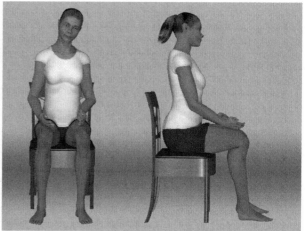

During a phone conversation with my cousin one day, she asked if there was an emotion pattern she might use to create a calm environment in her household. Married with two young children, she feels breakfast time is particularly tense as she tries to get everyone fed and out the door. Every morning, breakfast turns into a tense situation with the baby crying, her five-year-old whining, and her husband acting grumpy. I told her about the calming benefits of the 1a pattern and then instructed her on how to do the pattern. I advised her to embody the pattern in her own behavior and in interactions with her family during breakfast and see if it made a difference. I added, "At the very least, it will provide you with an inner state of calm during this hectic morning routine."

She called me a week later and reported the following: "I practiced the 1a pattern on my own for a few days until I felt I had all the elements clearly integrated. Then, I thought I would give it a try around my family. Yesterday morning, I started the pattern during my own morning routine and kept it going while I was waking up the children, making breakfast for everyone, and getting us all ready for the day. Would you believe there was absolutely no whining, crying, or grumpy behavior the entire morning? The baby was smiling, the five-year-old was singing some favorite school songs, and my husband was telling jokes. I found I was actually enjoying the entire morning as well! Incredible!"

My cousin had applied a form of emotion regulation called Situation Modification.[16] She emotionally prepared for the situation and consciously maintained it to support her own experience, meanwhile her emotions radiated out to others in the room and they were clearly influenced by her choice.

Integrating All Three Aspects of 1a

Once you have practiced the 1a postural attitude while sitting, it is time to integrate the breath and facial aspects to complete the full pattern. Complete the following steps while sitting in a firm straight-backed chair and maintaining eye contact with your focal point.

1. Begin by sitting in zero and engaging the zero pattern.

2. After a few breath cycles in zero, change your breathing to nose breathing and gradually engage the 1a breath pattern by breathing with an inhale that is slightly shorter than the exhale, allowing a small hold after the exhale and a gentle turnaround between the inhale and exhale.

3. As you solidify this breath pattern, gradually add the facial aspect of 1a by inviting the muscles on the outsides of the eyes and along the nasal ridge to abduct, or move back toward the ears. Allow the muscles in the cheeks and corners of your mouth to abduct up and back, completing the fully integrated smile.

4. Then, increase the full embodiment of this pattern by engaging the postural attitude. Start by tilting the head toward one side and softening the front of the neck so the chin tilts downward while still maintaining eye contact with your focal point. Follow through with the side-bending, recognizing how this affects your weight distribution all the way down to your feet. Remember to rotate your arms slightly so your palms open toward the ceiling.

5. Hold the side bend toward the first side for a few breath cycles and then try shifting slowly and gradually to the other side. To engage the shift to the other

---

16 James J. Gross, "Emotion Regulation," in *Handbook of Emotions*, 3rd ed., ed, Michael Lewis, Jeannette M. Haviland-Jones, and Lisa Feldman Barrett (New York: Guilford Press, 2008): 502.

side, inhale through the nose to bring your head to center and then exhale through the nose to sink into the neck tilt and side bend on the other side. Maintain that side bend for a while as you engage the full pattern. Does the second side feel different to you? Is one side preferred over the other?

6. With all three aspects of the pattern applied, take notice of how you feel as you gaze at your focal point. Can you sense any emotions or recognizable feelings emerging?

7. Finish this exercise by switching your breathing back to zero. Then, gradually adjust your posture and facial expression back to zero as well. Remain in the zero pattern for as many cycles as it takes to feel you have fully released the 1a pattern.

 Pause & Reflect

Take a few moments to write about your experience with the full 1a pattern in the sitting position. Did this pattern evoke any familiar feelings, images, or emotions? Could you feel the effects of the pattern from head to toe as you engaged the subtle weight shifts from side to side, through the hips, and down to the heel lift? Did this posture remind you of any familiar scenarios or situations where you might sit, breathe, and look at something or someone in this way?

The Nature of Side-Bending

The side-bending posture you practiced in the 1a pattern exercises can be seen all around you. Watch any parent holding a baby and you will see how they sink one side of the body in the direction of the child and tilt the head in the same direction. Take a moment to do an internet image search on "mother and child" or "famous paintings of mother and child," and you will see plenty of examples of this posture depicted throughout the ages as well. For example, both Klimpt and Picasso's "Mother and Child" paintings show classic side-bending postures. The maternal and paternal instinct to nurture is strong within our bodies, and our posture immediately curls in the direction of those for which we feel a kinship or the desire to nurture. The same holds true for our relationship with certain animals. Many people will hold their pets in the same way, even if the pet is larger than a baby. Try another internet search—this time for "people holding their dogs" or "people hugging their pets"—and you will see similar examples of people curling their posture toward one side, tilting the head in the direction of the pet, and most likely wearing a warm smile on their faces.

Did you know...?

A study conducted with 76 heart failure patients compared the health effects of patients who received hospital canine therapy with patients who had visits from friends and family. Patients who were visited by therapy dogs experienced a significant drop in anxiety and stress hormone levels whereas patients who were visited only by friends or family experienced less significant drops. Additionally, for patients who survived heart failure, the risk for cardiovascular disease or morbidity one year after the episode was lower in those who were pet owners than those who were not.[17]

Why might this happen? Consider the health benefits of the 1a pattern mentioned earlier. When a person is comfortable around a dog, they can often adopt the 1a pattern while spending time with it, thereby giving themselves the health benefits of that emotion at the same time as the social benefits of bonding with a beloved pet. A dog who is trained to provide a calm presence can form a reciprocally soothing relationship with a person, with no social constraints or demands. However, family and friends require conversation, and depending on the relationship between the patient and the visitor, these visits can come with a mixed bag of emotions causing various health effects.

Sound and the Emotion Patterns

Incorporating sound can be considered the fourth aspect of an emotion pattern. Sound vibration resonates throughout the body, helping to holistically integrate the pattern. When we add sound to a pattern, we tend to feel and connect with the emotion more fully throughout our bodies.

The type or quality of sound we make is also affected by how we feel and how much tension or relaxation is applied to the production of sound. The initial creation and then the resonation of vocalized sound are both affected by our muscles. Our vocal folds, where sound is first produced, are dramatically influenced by muscle tension or relaxation. After leaving the vocal folds, vocalized sound travels to various small and large cavities throughout the body, each of which act as resonation chambers. Within these areas, the sound waves grow and bounce, causing distinct variations in vocal quality and volume. Each resonation chamber is also affected by muscular tension and relaxation. The body becomes a full instrument of sound, directly affected by how we feel and how much muscle tension or relaxation we have in our

17 Kathie M. Cole RN, MN, CCRN, Anna Gawlinski, RN, DNSc, Neil Steers, PhD, and Jenny Kotlerman, MS, "Animal-Assisted Therapy in Patients Hospitalized with Heart Failure," *American Journal of Critical Care* 16, no. 6, (2007): 575-585.

bodies. Consider a time when you called someone on the phone and, after hearing their hello, you could sense how they felt. Our voices project our feelings quite clearly through subtle variations in sound qualities.

Sound quality depends on the following three areas affecting vocal production:

Power – Flow of air connecting with the vocal folds, causing vibration and initiating sound production

Source – Vocal fold vibration, creating and establishing pitch and tone

Filter – Resonation process, affecting voice quality, treble-bass balance, and volume[18]

Vocal production is powered by the breath coming from the lungs, which is in turn powered by the muscles in the abdomen that control the movement of the diaphragm. In the emotional effector patterns, the breathing pattern influences the power aspect of sound production. Each emotion pattern has a different breathing pattern that may have a smooth, choppy, or seeping breathing power and directly affects the quality of sound produced. Likewise if the pattern is powered by a deep, long exhale or a short,

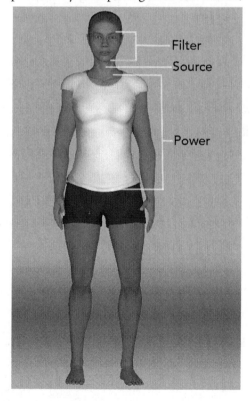

fast exhale, it also affects the quality of the sound. Throughout the chapters ahead, you will explore how the power affects your sound quality. For now, be aware of your breath power's potential to influence vocalized sound.

Once the breath comes into contact with your vocal source, vibration occurs and sound and pitch are produced. Sound is produced by air passing through vocal folds coming together while the folds stretch to various lengths to control pitch. If an emotion pattern has relaxed muscle tone the muscles around the vocal folds tend to relax as well. This results in smooth vibration patterns, with a light contact of the vocal folds, causing a gentle, flowing vocal tone. However, when the muscle tone is tense, the same muscular reaction tends to occur around the vocal folds,

18 Mary McDonald Klimek, Kerrie Obert and Kimberly Steinhauer, *Estill Voice Training System: Level One* (Estill Voice Training Systems International, 2005): 5-32.

resulting in stiff vibration patterns, with heavy contact of the vocal folds, causing a dark, harsh vocal tone. The pitch range potential depends on vocal folds stretching to various lengths while vibrating. It is also directly affected by the amount of tension accumulated in the vocal folds. Less tension allows for greater degrees of pitch variation. More tension limits pitch range and often produces more monotone sounding voices. As you keep this in mind during your practice of the patterns, you may find when you are in the a-patterns you have a softer vocal tone with greater pitch variations. Conversely, when in the b-patterns with more muscle tension there may be darker vocal tone with less pitch variation.

The sound is then *filtered* in resonation areas. In the human voice, the filter areas make up the pathway from the larynx up through the head and out the mouth or nose. This includes parts of the larynx, then the pharynx, mouth, sinuses, and nose. The neck, jaw, and facial muscles influence the shape and pliancy of each of these areas, thus changing their sound quality. The vocal instrument is highly malleable, and the sound quality varies remarkably as the muscles surrounding resonation (or filter) areas tense, release, stretch, or move in different directions. During facial muscle movements of the emotion patterns, many other muscles—like those in your larynx, pharynx, and mouth—are responding to those initial facial muscle cues. They may abduct while you practice 1a, as your facial muscles move toward your ears. Doing so will make these filter areas larger and more resonant, directly affecting the quality of sound produced. As you practice 1b and press your facial muscles toward the bridge of your nose, the filter areas may constrict and you may feel areas of your throat and larynx become tighter and smaller. When sound resonates through these tighter filter areas, it will sound quite different from when the muscles are more relaxed.

As you proceed with the application of sound to the emotion patterns, start to bring your somatic sensing deeper inside your body:

1. Pay attention to how the breath pattern affects the flow of air on and through your vocal folds.

2. See if you can sense how the surface muscle activations of facial expressions and postural attitudes affect deeper structures influencing sound production and resonation.

3. When practicing the emotion patterns with short sound bursts, try to produce them in slow motion. During sound production, try to sense all three steps of sound production (power, source, filter) and feel how the emotion pattern is affecting your vocal quality.

Adding Sound to 1a
To explore sound application of 1a, follow steps 1–4 in the "Integrating All Three Aspects of 1a" exercise, and then add the steps that follow.

1. While sitting in the full 1a pattern, during every other exhale, try a little touch of sound or small hum through the nose as you exhale. The next exhale should be simply air, with no sound. Go back and forth between sounding the exhalation through the nose and exhaling with just air but no sound.

2. Pay close attention to how the sound is produced and feels while in this pattern. Sense the power, or flow of air, connecting with your vocal folds as they close to create the source vibration of sound. Notice how the sound travels through your body to filters where it resonates and then forms a certain quality of sound as it goes out your nose.

3. Maintain the same degree of muscular effort used in the 1a pattern when adding vocalization. Compare the amount of effort used to make sound through the nose. Try to match, as much as possible, the effort used during the sounded exhale with that used during the unsounded exhale. This will help you maintain the integrity of the pattern while engaging sound.

4. Begin to extend the tone from a small vocalized burst to a sustained vocalization that lasts through the entire exhale. Can you detect a pitch change as you extend this tone? You might notice a slightly higher pitch at the onset and a gradual sliding of the pitch downward as the exhalation completes. If this is not your observation, see what happens if you try a gentle slide of pitch from high to low.

5. Continue practicing with sound through the nose on every other exhale, while engaging the full 1a pattern. Keep checking that you have not lost the breath pattern, facial aspect, or postural attitude as you explore sounding the pattern.

6. Once you are able to maintain the integrity of the full pattern while engaging sound, apply sound to all exhales and play with your sound by humming. Explore various pitch changes, scales, or familiar tunes.

7. While humming in 1a, allow yourself to bend from side to side, acknowledging the weight shifting from hip to hip. Can you feel the impulse emerging to rock from left to right? If so, follow this impulse, engaging a gentle left-to-right rocking or shifting of your weight as you hum.

8. How does the 1a pattern with sound exploration feel? Do you notice any emotions emerging more clearly due to this integration of sound and movement?

9. Finish this exercise by switching your breathing back to zero as you bring your posture and your facial expression back to zero as well, with no sound on the exhale. Remain in the zero pattern for as many cycles as it takes to feel as if you have fully released the 1a pattern.

Pause & Reflect

Take a few moments and write down any discoveries you made while practicing these aspects of the 1a pattern. How did your voice sound in 1a? When applying sound production in slow motion, could you feel the effects of the pattern on all three stages of sound production (power, source, filter)? Did the addition of sound production, humming, and pitch variation help you connect more with identifiable emotions, feelings, or images?

Write down words describing feelings, sensations, images, or emotions you felt during your practice of 1a with and without sound. After examining the word lists and journaling about your experience, take a good long break before continuing with any other exercises. Before your break, you may also want to take a Step Out.

A year after teaching an Emotional Body workshop at my church, one of the participants shared an exciting discovery she had made during her regular practice of the emotion patterns. She exclaimed, "I have learned I cannot possibly think bad or disturbing thoughts when I am in 1a!"

She continued by explaining she regularly practices the emotion patterns to keep them fresh and available to her; however, she tends to practice 1a longer than the other patterns because it relaxes her so much. During one practice session she realized she had slipped out of 1a while pondering over some disturbing thoughts. She quickly returned to the 1a pattern, and the bad thoughts went away. However, the disturbances over a recent unresolved event in her life kept occurring. Each time the thoughts came in, she noticed she was no longer in pattern 1a.

"I stopped my practice session and went to work out the unresolved issue. But, a week later, when I was practicing the emotion patterns again, I tested my theory. While in 1a, I purposely started thinking about disturbing things but also tried to maintain 1a. I found when I put my attention on the thoughts more than the pattern, the thoughts won, and I slipped out of the pattern. But, when I put more of my attention on the pattern, and made sure I maintained all aspects of the pattern, the pattern won and the disturbing thoughts disappeared!"

After hearing her story, I decided to test it myself, several times. To my delight,

I found the same conclusions. Since hearing her story, I have often used 1a as a transitional pattern to remove me from a disturbing situation, coast me into a restful night of sleep, or provide me with some distance from relentless thoughts. I have found the use of 1a in these moments allows me to disengage from tension and negativity long enough to fully release and even to process possible positive attributes to a situation that had previously looked dark and grim. This participant's delightful discovery could be a precious gift to us all!

Lexicon of Emotional States for the 1a Pattern

The following words can be thought of as a lexicon of emotional states associated with the 1a pattern. Each pattern is associated with one or two primary names, which emerged during the initial pattern research in the 1970s and 1980s. The additional words provided in the columns imply levels of intensity, or degrees, of this pure state. These degrees are represented by the terms *Low*, *Mid*, and *High* in the following columns. Applying words to emotional states is highly subjective and varies depending on individual interpretations of meaning as well as life experiences. These words are provided as guides to help you relate your experiences with the 1a pattern to familiar words used in our language.

Emotion Words for Pattern 1a
Primary Names: Tenderness or Tender Love[19]

Low Level	Mid Level	High Level
Amiable	Approving	Adoring
Appreciative	Affectionate	Benevolent
Calm	Caring	Compassionate
Considerate	Cordial	Devoted
Content	Courteous	Favoring
Dreamy	Fond	Flirtatious
Gratified	Friendly	Loving
Heartfelt	Genial	Loyal
Peaceful	Gracious	Romantic
Satisfied	Kind	
Serene	Sensitive	
Tranquil	Warm-hearted	

19. Susana Bloch, Pedro Orthous, and Guy Santibáñez-H, "Effector Patterns of Basic Emotions: A Psychophysiological Method for Training Actors," *Journal of Social Biological Structure* 10 (January 1987) 1-19.

When subtle elements of other patterns merge with pattern 1a, mixes are evident. Another emotional pattern can mix in by simply moving an extra muscle in the face, lowering the eyes to the floor, or extending an exhalation or a hold a little too long. Any chronic tensions in your posture not easily released can also contribute to another emotion mixing into this pure pattern. Always keep in mind the practice of these patterns alone, and without the aid of a qualified and experienced instructor providing you with feedback, subtle mixes may occur.

The words below are offered to help you see the kinds of mixes that can emerge in your practice of the *1a* pattern.

Mixed Emotions with 1a as a Primary Pattern

Empathetic	Patient	Sentimental
Good-hearted	Patriotic	Sincere
Hospitable	Pitying	Sympathetic
Narcissistic	Polite	Tolerant
Mellow	Proud	Concern
Melancholy	Relief	

Mixes can be identified within emotion words as well. For example, some might interpret *concern* as a subtle mix of 1a and 1b, but others might interpret *concern* as having elements of sadness mixed in. Whereas the word mellow might be pure 1a to some, others might perceive mellowness as including some sensuality. Remember, mixed emotions are based on life experiences and individual interpretations. These individual expressions of the same words are not necessarily indications of being incorrect, entangled, or even unclear about the meaning of the word. They are simply a person's expression of highly subjective secondary and tertiary words describing feelings. These are not universal basic emotions.

Did you Know...?

Our perspective on the world around us can change dramatically depending on if we are in an a-pattern state or b-pattern state. Emotion can actually alter our focus and attention. Attention is a valuable instrument that serves as a telescope through which we select, bring into focus, and magnify the stimuli we experience in our world.[20] Executive attention (also referred to as selective

20 B.A. Wallace, "The Buddhist Tradition of Samatha: Methods for Refining and Examining Consciousness," *Journal of Consciousness Studies* 6 (1991): 75-187.

or focused attention) is the ability to focus on specific details. It reflects the individual's capacity to select relevant information and to ignore irrelevant information.[21]

Certain a-pattern emotions broaden the scope of attention and widen the array of thoughts and actions that come to mind in a given situation.[22] This provides us with a "big picture" view of things. However, if we remain constantly in this broad scope of attention, it can impair our executive attention, keeping us from perceiving important details.[23]

Certain levels of b-pattern emotions provide detailed observation, concentration, introspection, and analysis and may promote aspects of emotional growth.[24] For example, low intensity levels of 1b can help us stay focused on details and analyze a situation in greater depth.

Standing in 1a

Follow these steps to see how this pattern can be incorporated into your standing posture:

1. Start by sitting in the 1a postural attitude and with your attention on your eye-level focal point.

2. Engage the side-bending practice described previously by lifting the heel of the foot on the same side you are bending toward. For example, if you bend to the left, lift your left heel slightly. Move gradually and slowly between left and right side-bending postures while you gain a sense of how this postural attitude affects your entire body from head to foot.

3. Minimize the heel lift so you now become aware of the weight shift only on your feet and hips.

4. Now, stand up and change your focal point to a place at your current eye level. While standing, practice the same movement described in step 3. Shift your weight from left to right while you side-bend slightly and tilt your head.

21 M.I. Posner and M.K. Rothbart, "Research on Attention: Networks as a Model for the Integration of Psychological Science," *Annual Review of Psychology 58* (2007): 1-23.

22 B.L. Fredrickson, "What Good Are Positive Emotions?" *Review of General Psychology 2* (2002): 300-310.

23 R.L.C. Mitchell and L.H. Phillips, "The Psychological, Neurochemical and Functional Neuroanatomical Mediators of the Effects of Positive and Negative Mood on Executive Functions," *Neuropsychologia* 45 (2007): 617–629.

24 Heather A Wadlinger and Derek M. Isaacowitz, "Fixing our Focus: Training Attention to Regulate Emotion," *Personality and Social Psychology Review* 15, no. 1 (2010): 75-102.

5. Add the 1a breath pattern and facial expression to fully engage the entire 1a pattern. Add sound, like a hum, occasionally through the nose.

6. Occasionally switch to side-bending and tilting to the other side. Allow the inhalation to bring your head up to center, and the exhalation to initiate the side bend on the other side.

7. Finish the exercise by returning to the zero standing position.

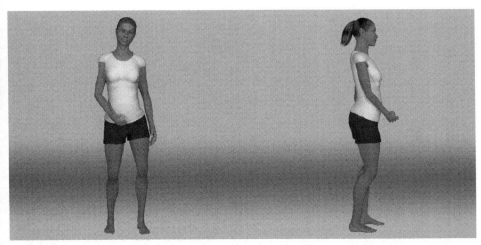

Walking in 1a
Let's explore how this pattern moves:

1. Start by standing in the 1a pattern with your attention on your eye-level focal point.

2. Engage the side-bending practice described previously by lifting the heel of the foot on the same side you are bending toward.

3. While still standing in one place, incorporate the arms by swinging the left arm forward slightly while you lift the right heel. Then swing the right arm forward while you lift the left heel.

4. See if you can incorporate a slight twisting of the torso by engaging the entire arm and shoulder into the arm swing and swinging the hand in the direction of the opposite knee. For example, as the left knee bends to lift the heel, swing the right hand forward and toward the left knee. Do you feel a slight twisting of your entire torso?

5. While still standing in one place, practice going back and forth with this heel lift and opposite arm swing. Reduce the side-bending and head-tilting angles so they are of more subtle degrees.

6. Now move forward by lifting the entire foot, instead of just the heel, and placing that foot down at a comfortable place just ahead. Repeat with the other side, and walk around for a while, practicing this postural attitude in motion. Allow your eyes to move around the space and look at things at eye level. Try not to look down while you walk. Remember to engage the arm swing and torso twist as well as a slight degree of side-bending and head-tilting. If you feel as if your head is bobbing from side to side too much, reduce the degree of the head tilt even more.

7. Add the 1a breath pattern and facial expression to fully engage the entire 1a pattern. Add sound occasionally through the nose by humming or holding onto a tone during exhales through the nose.

8. Finish the exercise by returning to the neutral standing position and completing a Step Out.

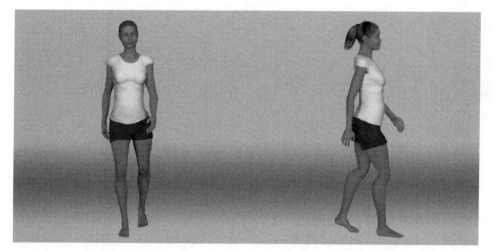

▌▌ Pause & Reflect

Take a few moments to write about your experience with standing and walking in the 1a pattern. How did it feel to stand and walk in this pattern? Did your sense of the space around you change as you engaged in walking and looking at things at eye level? How would others perceive you if you stood and walked in this way? Did you find this contralateral movement to be challenging or easy?

Incorporating the 1b Postural Attitude

Sitting in 1b
Use a firm straight-backed chair that allows your feet to touch the floor when sitting

toward the front of the chair seat. Sit in the zero postural attitude. With eyes open and looking directly across the room, identify a focal point at eye level. You will look at this focal point throughout the exercise.

1. From the zero sitting position, place your attention on the sternum area of your chest. Can you press your sternum forward, and allow your entire torso, from shoulders down to waist, to move forward as well?

2. Once you move the torso forward, lift it slightly. Can you feel your weight shift in your seat? Do you notice more weight on the tops of your legs and the fronts of your feet? Go back and forth between the zero sitting position and this forward movement of the 1b posture to practice shifting your center of gravity.

3. While you look at your focal point and press your torso forward, hold your head as if the face is also pressing directly forward, with no tilt of the head in any direction. Your jaw might also move forward slightly, aligning your lower teeth with your upper teeth.

4. Allow your hands to slide forward so your arms move in the same direction as your torso. With your palms facing the tops of your legs, you might feel that your hands want to grip your legs or knees.

5. Allow your toes to grip the floor, as if getting ready to rise quickly. Then, encourage muscle tension to increase through the legs, buttocks, and arms.

6. Finish the exercise by returning to the zero sitting position. Take your time releasing any muscle tension associated with this postural attitude. Complete a Step Out to release the pattern fully.

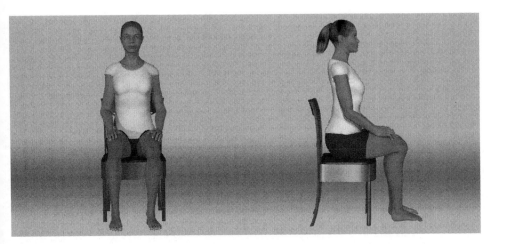

Integrating All Three Aspects of 1b

Once you have practiced the 1b postural attitude while sitting, it is time to integrate the breath and facial aspects to complete the full pattern. Practice the following steps while sitting in a firm straight-backed chair and looking at an eye-level focal point.

1. Begin by sitting in zero and engaging the zero breath pattern.

2. After a few breath cycles in zero, change your breathing to nose breathing and gradually engage the 1b breath pattern by keeping the inhalation and exhalation lengths equal to each other while incorporating a clear, strong stop after each (remember the ball-catching image).

3. Gradually add the facial expression of 1b by inviting the muscles on the outsides of the eyes and along the nasal ridge to adduct, moving in toward the midline of the face. Constrict the muscles inside the nostrils, causing tension in the breath pattern. You may feel tension increasing under the eyes, as if the lower eyelid is trying to cover your eye or your eyes are narrowing.

4. Now engage the 1b postural attitude. Start with moving the entire torso forward, and then lift it up slightly. Make sure the arms and hands move forward as well and that the face presses directly forward. The jaw may also press forward, staying true to this posture's intention to initiate forward movement.

5. Invite a gripping tension in the toes and allow it to follow all the way up the legs, through the arms, and down to the hands.

6. With all three aspects of the pattern applied, take notice of how you feel as you look at your focal point. Can you sense any emotions or recognizable feelings emerging?

7. Finish this exercise by switching your breathing back to zero breath as you bring your posture and your facial expression back to zero as well. Remain in the zero pattern for as many cycles as it takes to feel as though you have fully released the 1b pattern. Complete at least one Step Out. You may need two Step Outs to fully release the muscle tensions associated with this pattern.

Adding Sound to 1b

To explore sound application of 1b, follow the steps 1–5 in the "Integrating All Three Aspects of 1b" and then add the steps that follow.

1. While sitting in the full pattern of 1b, during every other exhale, try a little touch of sound or small hum through the nose as you exhale. The next exhale

should be simply air, with no sound. Go back and forth between sounding the exhalation through the nose and exhaling with just air but no sound. Compare the amount of effort used to make sound through the nose. Try to match, as much as possible, the effort used during the sounded exhale with that used during the unsounded exhale. This will help you maintain the integrity of the pattern while engaging sound.

2. Begin your sound exploration with a short vocalized burst. Try to slow down the pattern enough to sense the sound production in slow motion. This will allow you to feel how the emotion pattern affects the production of vocalized sound from breath power, through vocal fold source contact, and into filtered resonation of sound. Gradually elongate the sound so it sustains through the entire exhalation.

3. Continue practicing with sound through the nose on every other exhale while engaging the full 1b pattern. Keep checking that you have not lost the breath pattern, facial aspect, or postural attitude as you explore sounding the pattern.

4. How does this full integration of the pattern with sound exploration feel?

5. Do you notice any emotions emerging more clearly due to this integration of sound?

6. Finish this exercise by switching your breathing back to zero breath as you bring your posture and your facial expression back to zero as well, with no sound on the exhale. Remain in the neutral pattern for as many cycles as it takes to feel as if you have fully released the 1b pattern. Then, complete at least one Step Out.

❚❚ Pause & Reflect

Take a few moments and write down any discoveries you made while putting together all these aspects of the 1b pattern. Write down words describing feelings, sensations, visualizations, or emotions you experienced. Did the inclusion of sound help you make any new discoveries about this pattern? Did the postural attitude evoke images of events or occasions of the past that seemed familiar?

After this reflection, take a good long break from any practice of emotion patterns. Since the act of recalling emotional experiences can bring up the emotions again, you might need to take an extra Step Out before you go on a break.

Did you know...?

Our vocal folds are made up of two pairs of folds, called the true vocal folds and the false vocal folds. The true folds are responsible for vibrating and creating sound. The false folds (located just over the true folds) are responsible for creating a seal over the true folds and closing the larynx. The act of closing the larynx is very important in keeping unwanted food, water, or particles from entering the windpipe and lungs. False fold closure also helps build up air pressure behind the vocal folds to create a cough or throat clearing. [25]

During vocalized sound, the false folds are meant to remain open so the true folds can vibrate and operate fully in sound and pitch production. However, when experiencing pain or strenuous physical, emotional, or mental activity, our bodies trigger false fold closure signals.[26] False fold closure, even in small amounts or degrees, puts pressure on the true folds, keeping them from vibrating fully and causing strain. The short-term result is a voice that sounds tense, harsh, and brassy. This is why our voice might sound different when we are under stressful emotions or in pain.

Long-term false fold closure over vibrating true folds could result in permanent limitations of vocalized range, temporary loss of voice, and development of vocal nodes or polyps on the true folds.[27] But vocal lesson training can provide tools for overriding the false fold closure triggers and for retracting the false folds so they do not constrict true vocal fold vibration.

Lexicon of Emotional States for the 1b Pattern

The following words name emotions you might have felt while practicing the 1b pattern. Since each pattern has levels of intensity, the words are categorized within low to high levels. Keep in mind the subjectivity of words, and simply use these words as an aid for assigning meanings to your experiences with this pattern.

---

25 Mary McDonald Klimek, Kerrie Obert and Kimberly Steinhauer, *Estill Voice Training System: Level One* (Estill Voice Training Systems International, 2005): 33-39.

26 ibid.

27 Rachael L. Gates, Arick Forrest and Kerrie Obert, *The Owner's Manual to the Voice: A Guide for Singers and Other Professional Voice Users* (New York, Oxford University Press, 2013): 45-47.

Emotion Words for Pattern 1b
Primary Names: Anger or Aggression[28]

Low	Mid	High
Aggravated	Acerbic	Aggressive
Ambitious	Daring	Brazen
Annoyed	Demanding	Cantankerous
Bitter	Fervent	Cruel
Concentrating	Fuming	Ferocious
Examining	Insistent	Fierce
Focused	Malicious	Furious
Frustrated	Relentless	Hateful
Grumpy	Ruthless	Heartless
Impatient	Seething	Hostile
Irritated	Sour	Predatory
Rigid	Spiteful	Raging
Willful	Vehement	Savage
	Vexed	Vengeful
	Vicious	Wrathful

The following words are offered to help you see how mixes can emerge in your practice of the 1b pattern. The slightest shift in muscle tension, breath pattern, or angle of the postural attitude can easily engage a subtle mix of basic emotions. The following words suggest some of these possible mixes.

Mixed Emotions with 1b as a Primary Pattern

Adamant	Curious	Jealous
Arrogant	Disdainful	Livid
Assured	Disgusted	Outraged
Belligerent	Envious	Pompous
Bold	Exasperated	Pretentious
Brave	Fanatical	Proud
Chivalrous	Greedy	Sarcastic
Conceited	Haughty	Stubborn
Confident	Indignant	Vain
Contemptuous	Inquisitive	
Courageous	Irate	

---

28. Susana Bloch, Pedro Orthous, and Guy Santibáñez-H, "Effector Patterns of Basic Emotions: A Psychophysiological Method for Training Actors," *Journal of Social Biological Structure* 10 (January 1987) 1-19.

Standing in 1b

Now you can incorporate what you have learned about 1b into the standing posture.

1. Start by sitting in the 1b postural attitude with your attention on an eye-level focal point.

2. While pressing the torso forward and lifting it up slightly, face directly forward with no head tilt in any direction. Is the jaw also pressing forward slightly?

3. Engage the 1b breath pattern, breathing in and out through the nose with sharp equal inhales and exhales, pushing air through constricted nasal passages.

4. Invite the adducting muscle movements, allowing the muscles around the outsides of the eyes to press inward toward the nose. Build tension under the eyes, causing your vision to narrow.

5. Slide one foot forward slightly, as if ready to advance, and engage a gripping action with your toes. Spread the gripping muscle tension up through your legs and down through your arms to your hands.

6. With your chest leading your movement, press the torso further forward while pushing your feet into the floor and then push off from the chair, bringing yourself up into a standing position. Change your focal point to eye level while standing.

7. Stand with your muscles still gripping and pressing forward. You may find that your buttocks muscles and your leg muscles can more fully tighten and

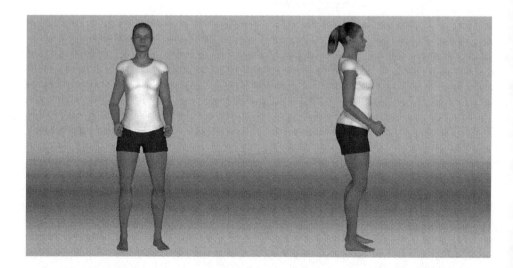

help complete this postural attitude of pressing forward.

8.   Incorporate sound into some of the exhalations and practice this full 1b pattern engagement for a few cycles. Check that all elements of the pattern are still present while standing.

9.   Finish the exercise by returning to the zero standing position and engaging the zero breath pattern. Complete at least one Step Out to fully release the tensions associated with this pattern.

Did you know...?

Children become increasingly sensitive to being accepted by their peers throughout their school years, and they learn from their peers about acceptable behavior and emotions. Studies have shown less tolerance among peers for overt expressions of anger, and many school-age children feel anger is difficult to control. As a result, the peer norm during middle childhood is to try to avoid negative emotions altogether and mask, or attempt to cover what they are really feeling by superimposing displays of other more acceptable emotions. They will try to give the impression of being cool, calm, and unruffled so as to be more accepted by their peers.[29] When expressing negative emotions, particularly anger, they will express the emotion in ways they have seen displayed by others, which is a form of emotional masking. Masking emotion helps them feel a distance from the true emotion and a sense of control over its expression, with the added bonus of feeling accepted by their peers.[30]

As a result, school-age children eventually repress their negative emotions and so don't learn how to manage all the basic emotions or express them in authentic ways. When events occur where negative emotions emerge, they feel incapable of handling them. Instead of managing the situation emotionally, they resort to uncontrolled emotional outbursts or self-isolation. Eventually, these practices could result in various social disorders. Unless new methods for emotion regulation are learned, these children will grow into adulthood with the same limiting and potentially isolating expressive patterns and practices.[31]

29 J.G. Parker and J.M. Gottman, "Social and Emotional Development in Children: A Step Toward a Theory of Aggression," *Monographs of the Society for Research in Child Development* 32, no. 5 (1989): 113.

30 M.K. Underwood, "Peer Social Status and Children's Understanding of the Expression and Control of Positive and Negative Emotions," *Merrill-Palmer Quarterly* 43 (1997): 610-634.

31 N. Eisenberg, R.A. Fabes, S.A. Shepard, B.C. Murphy, I.K. Buthreie, S. Jones, et al., "Contemporaneous and Longitudinal Prediction of Children's Social Functioning from Regulation and Emotionality," *Child Development* 68 (1997): 642-664.

Walking in 1b

Let's explore how this pattern moves. Since all the muscles are primed and ready for advancement, the 1b postural attitude tends to push us into action quickly and forcefully. As you prepare for this exercise, give yourself plenty of unobstructed space to walk around, so you can fully explore the pattern's inherent movements and gestures.

1. Start by standing in the 1b pattern with your attention on an eye-level focal point.

2. Engage your muscles in the pressing forward posture while gripping the floor with your toes, and then step forward. Can you feel the weight primarily on the fronts of your feet as you walk?

3. With your arms and hands actively gripping, you will not feel as much ease of movement in your arms as you walk. The muscle rigidity of this pattern does not support as much arm swing or torso twist as you felt in 1a.

4. Walk around your space, maintaining the full 1b pattern and looking at things found at your eye level. Check that all the elements of the breath pattern, facial aspect, and postural attitude are retained as you explore moving with this pattern.

5. Engage sound on occasional exhales through the nose to explore sounding in the 1b pattern.

6. Notice how you feel as you walk through your space, looking around while in this full 1b pattern.

7. Finish the exercise by returning to the neutral standing position. Engage the zero breath pattern and complete at least one Step Out to fully release the tensions of the 1b pattern.

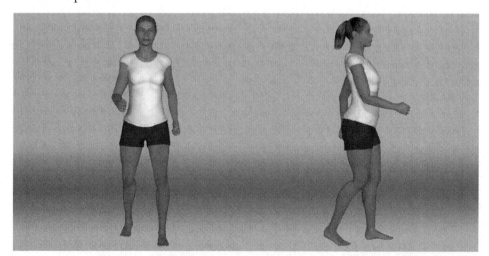

Pause & Reflect

Take a few moments to write about your experience with standing and walking in the 1b pattern. How did it feel to stand and walk in the pattern? Did your feelings for the space around you change as you walked and looked at things at eye level? How would you be perceived if you stood and walked in this way in a public setting?

Did you know...?

Aspects of the 1b posture can make you feel more powerful and confident while also increasing testosterone levels and decreasing cortisol (stress hormone) levels. Hormone levels respond to internal and external cues, rising and falling regularly for short terms in response to certain situations. Testosterone naturally rises when we anticipate competition or achieve something that makes us feel proud. Cortisol levels rise in our bodies when we experience stress, as when facing a threatening situation, experiencing loss, or feeling helpless or defeated.

People who feel powerful most of the time often exhibit aspects of open and lifted posture, and typically maintain higher testosterone levels coupled with lower cortisol levels, resulting in disease resistance, adaptive behaviors, and strong leadership abilities.[32]

A person who consistently feels as if they are in a state of "low power" not only exhibits closed and folding postural habits, but often has chronically elevated cortisol levels, which can cause various health problems such as impaired immune functioning, hyper-tension, and memory loss.[33]

To reap the benefits of power poses, you do not need to take up more space in every room you enter or grandstand among your peers to demonstrate your power. Aspects of powerful postural attitudes can be practiced in private spaces and can directly affect your public life. You can also adopt subtle adjustments in your everyday posture to increase overall feelings of openness, empowerment, and confidence.

32 P.H. Mehta and R.A. Josephs, "Testosterone Change After Losing Predicts the Decision to Compete Again," *Hormones and Behavior* 50 (2006): 684–692.

33 S. Segerstrom and G. Miller, "Psychological Stress and the Human Immune System: A Meta-Analytic Study of 30 Years of Inquiry," *Psychological Bulletin* 130 (2004): 601–630.

Empowering and opening postural aspects are present in patterns 1a, 1b, 2a, and 3a. Learning the postural attitudes of basic emotions and how they affect your health, attitude, perception, and behavior can have substantial implications for your everyday life and professional career.

Polarities Between the 1a and 1b Patterns

You can shift between one nose-breathing pattern to the next by making gradual changes in muscular tension, direction of muscle movement, and breathing pattern. Slow, subtle changes like this can bring you from one emotional state to another and allow you to experience the mixed emotional states in between. We will call this an emotion pattern polarity exercise, with the a-emotion as one pole, the b-emotion as another pole, and the mixed emotions experienced on the line between the two poles. You can practice a polarity exercise by starting with either pattern (a or b) and explore the mixed states by moving from one pure emotional state to the other.

a: The a-state represents an emotion that has the least amount of muscle tension and a postural attitude that is open and approachable.

b: The b-state represents an emotion that either has the greatest degree of muscle tension or uses muscle movements to close the body off to others, making it unapproachable.

Minor changes of tension and directional movements can easily shift a person from an a-state to a b-state of expression, or vice versa.

Shifting Between Polarities of 1a and 1b

This exercise will help you explore the mixed emotions felt when elements of the 1a and 1b pattern are combined in your expression. As you experiment with this exercise, proceed slowly so you can sense subtle shifts in the mixed emotion states and recognize how they differ from each other. Most likely you will experience a long list of mixed emotions as you move from one pure emotion to the other and back again.

1. Select an object or a picture of someone and place it a few paces from your

chair. It should be at eye level when you are sitting in the chair.

2. While sitting, look at your chosen object and breathe in and out of your nose with your mouth closed. Consider the muscles inside your nasal passage constricting and tensing as you breathe. Gradually allow the full 1b pattern to build, including postural attitude and facial expression. Build it very slowly so you can feel the various levels of the pattern's intensity growing. Take the intensity level as high as you feel comfortable with while remaining in the chair.

3. Do you feel degrees of anger as you build this pattern? Varying levels of anger can feel like concentration, directness, assertiveness, seriousness, frustration, aggression, furiousness, or rage. Can you sense your feelings about the object, or picture, changing as you slowly build this pattern?

4. Then, while continuing your nose breathing, move your facial muscles in the opposite direction by gradually relaxing the muscle tonicity throughout your body and abducting the muscles inside your nasal passage, moving them toward your ears. Encourage the muscles located on the outside of your nose, in your upper cheeks, and even on the outsides of your eyes to abduct and elevate, moving outward and upward toward your ears.

5. Slowly invite all aspects of the 1a pattern to shift you away from the 1b pattern, bringing you step by step toward 1a. Can you sense your feelings about the object you are looking at changing as you slowly move from 1b to 1a?

6. Check that you are releasing muscle tension in the feet, legs, arms, and hands as you slowly engage the full 1a pattern in the postural attitude, facial expression, and breathing pattern. Can you feel degrees of tender love forming as you explore this opposite direction of movement, relaxing your breathing and muscle tonicity? Varying levels of tender love can express as peacefulness, ease, tranquility, or adoration. How do you feel about the object now?

7. Explore going back and forth between 1a and 1b while you look at your object or picture. Can you also sense the mixed emotions present in the transition between the two extremes? The mixed emotions occur when you are moving from one pole to the other. The elements of both patterns are still present, creating mixes, until you fully release one pattern and settle into the pure state on the other side.

8. Finish this exercise by going into the zero pattern, and then complete at least one Step Out.

While teaching an Emotional Body workshop, I gave the assignment, "Take the next hour before our break and apply some of the patterns to a common activity in your life. Take a walk, go for a swim, shop for groceries, etc. Do the same activity a few times, but apply different patterns to the same action or event and see what happens." One participant came back after the break and shared this story about his 1a/1b experiment:

I went home to have lunch. As I approached my house I engaged in the 1b pattern and walked up to the house. I have two dogs who normally greet me with great excitement when I come home. However, as I stormed up to the house and practically attacked the door handle as I opened the door, the dogs took one look at me and scattered. I didn't say anything to them or do anything else, but they seemed to read my anger instantly and didn't want any part of me. I left the house and went back to my car, where I did a Step Out and then started the 1a pattern. I approached the house again while engaging the 1a pattern and gently opened the door this time. The dogs came running and, upon seeing me in the changed state, they were back to their usual hearty greeting.

Polarity Degrees and Our Behavior

Emotions in action create behavior, which affect our interactions with others. The postural attitudes of *1a* and *1b* are focused forward with eye contact placed on someone or something, creating a postural attitude of advancing. However, the muscular intensity variations between the two emotion patterns specify the type of advancing being conducted with the emotion. Someone expressing 1a is softly and gently advancing, sharing degrees of love and tenderness, whereas a person expressing 1b is advancing forcefully and with excessive tension, expressing degrees of anger and aggression.

Practicing exercises like Shifting Between Polarities not only helps you understand the many emotional mixes possible between *1a* and *1b*, but also provides you with practice for conscious self regulation of emotion. For example, if you are a habitual nose breather, and you want to physically adapt to a challenging situation for better emotional outcome, you can shift your emotional state from one pole to the next by gradually adjusting your breathing, posture, and facial expression. The words that follow represent some of these possible shifts. The direction of each emotional shift can move from right to left or left to right on the list depending on your desire for the situation. For example, you could be in a situation where you start off soothing someone, and then conditions change where you need to protect or even control the person or situation, and perhaps shift right back to soothing again. Likewise, if you were in a habit of undermining or belittling someone, the ability to compliment them is not far away when you consider the simple physical adjustments it takes to obtain an a-pattern emotional state. When you realize these emotional shifts can occur with slight muscular adjustments, they may seem less daunting and much more attainable in the moment.

The words under 1a and *1b* are fairly high intensity levels of the pattern; therefore, one can assume there are even more words possible between the two polarities. This list of words simply suggests general degrees and how mixes occur in the middle.

1a	Mixed State	1b
Soothe	Protect	Control
Compliment	Belittle	Undermine
Assure	Reinforce	Demand
Support	Counsel	Accuse
Entice	Needle	Badger
Flatter	Interview	Investigate
Nurture	Lead	Fight
Cling	Harbor	Confront
Contain	Manage	Pursue
Please	Tolerate	Argue
Spoil	Preserve	Enforce
Advise	Remind	Scrutinize
Recommend	Guarantee	Declare

Summary

Most people have habitual breathing patterns that have been adopted and developed throughout their lives. These breathing habits could be influenced by any number of experiences, including, but not limited to, environmental conditions, social influences, health issues, and internal psychological messages. Regardless of how we learned to default to certain breathing patterns, these breathing habits still influence our emotional range and expressive capabilities. This does not mean that the other basic emotions are not felt or expressed, but it does suggest such habits might influence what could become dominant states of expression.

Learning and practicing the emotion patterns will help you become much more sensitive to subtle shifts in your emotions and expressive behavior. Practicing emotion patterns that feel less familiar to your habitual expressions also provides you with pathways into new emotion choices and increases your expressive capabilities.

Practice the 1a and 1b exercises in this chapter regularly, until you no longer need to read about how to replicate all aspects of each pattern when breathing, sounding, sitting, standing, and walking. Once you have achieved this level, you will be ready to explore the exercises provided in the final chapter of this book, "Applications and Practice."

The Mouth-Breathing Patterns $\qquad$ 6

Mouth-Breathing Practices

We naturally revert to mouth breathing when our instincts tell us we require a large of amount of air in a short period of time. It is a logical shift from using the narrow inhalation passageway of the nose to using the large, open, and more unobstructed passageway of the mouth. An inhalation through the mouth provides a path of least resistance, and studies show the mouth provides three times the maximal oxygen consumption of nose breathing.[1] When we exert ourselves and become out of breath, our mouths instinctively open to allow for the greatest amount of oxygen input at the fastest rate. If the nose or sinuses are blocked, making nose breathing even more difficult, our bodies sense the potential for oxygen deficit and communicate the need to shift to mouth breathing.

Health Effects of Mouth Breathing

Biologically, mouth breathing is intended as a short-term remedy to intense situations, like oxygen deficit, or as a tool for short-term activities. Swimming, for example, requires mouth breathing in order to pull in as much air as possible when briefly bringing the head above water. Similarly, when a person is at risk of drowning, they instinctively use every effort to bring their mouth above water to quickly exhale and inhale air before their head drops below the surface again. A baby who is given early floating and swimming lessons instinctively closes the mouth as the face drops below the water's surface. As the instructor rolls the baby

---

1. A.R. Morton, K. King, S. Papalia, C. Goodman, K.R. Turley, and J.H. Wilmore, "Comparison of Maximal Oxygen Consumption with Oral and Nasal Breathing," *Australian Journal of Science and Medicine in Sport* 27, no. 3 (Perth, University of Western Australia, 1995): 51-5.

onto the back, bringing the mouth above water, the baby mouth-breathes quickly and fully and then produces a cry to express distress.

Not all mouth breathing is associated with oxygen deficit and distress. Mouth breathing also allows for expressions of feelings and emotions. It is central to a yawn, an exhilarating moment, or a passionate love scene. Mouth breathing provides us with a vast array of expressive states that you will explore later in this chapter.

However, long-term or chronic use of mouth breathing can have negative effects on our health and well-being. Studies show children who are dominant mouth breathers develop sleep disorders, allergies, and dental problems. Even facial and skeletal development are affected by chronic mouth breathing. Ongoing use of mouth breathing can also affect mental and emotional states as well as physical growth.[2]

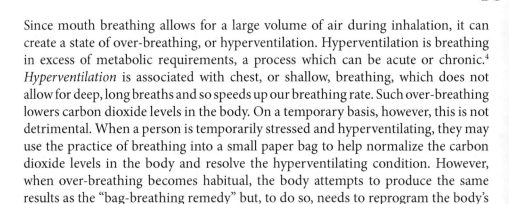

Did you know...?

Historical documentation reveals that many American Indian tribes recognized the importance of limiting mouth-breathing practices for health and well-being. After babies finished breastfeeding and were lying back, asleep in their mothers' arms, with their mouths still open from feeding, the mothers gently pressed the babies' lips together so they would close their mouths while sleeping. The practice of swaddling or bundling while sleeping, and placing a small pillow under the head, also encouraged a position that would keep mouths closed while sleeping.[3]

Since mouth breathing allows for a large volume of air during inhalation, it can create a state of over-breathing, or hyperventilation. Hyperventilation is breathing in excess of metabolic requirements, a process which can be acute or chronic.[4] *Hyperventilation* is associated with chest, or shallow, breathing, which does not allow for deep, long breaths and so speeds up our breathing rate. Such over-breathing lowers carbon dioxide levels in the body. On a temporary basis, however, this is not detrimental. When a person is temporarily stressed and hyperventilating, they may use the practice of breathing into a small paper bag to help normalize the carbon dioxide levels in the body and resolve the hyperventilating condition. However, when over-breathing becomes habitual, the body attempts to produce the same results as the "bag-breathing remedy" but, to do so, needs to reprogram the body's entire respiratory system to a lowered carbon dioxide level. In this case, the body

2. Jefferson Yosh, DMD, MAGD, "Mouth Breathing: Adverse Effects on Facial Growth, Health, Academics, and Behavior," *General Dentistry* 58 (2010): 18-25

3. George Catlin, (1870) *Shut Your Mouth: Notes of Travels Amongst the North-American Indian*, (London, Truebner & Co., 1870), 60.

4. W. Gardner, "Hyperventilation Disorders," *Journal of the Royal Society of Medicine* 83, no. 12 (1990): 755–757.

will strive to maintain this new level, causing hyperventilation to become chronic.[5]

Carbon dioxide controls the diameter of blood vessels, and low levels of carbon dioxide cause constriction and reduce cerebral blood flow, decreasing oxygenation of body tissues. As a result, many health problems are directly associated with chronic hyperventilation, including cardiovascular, neurological, gastrointestinal, and respiratory issues as well as general complaints of fatigue and sleep disturbance. Research indicates over-breathing can contribute to 40% of symptoms presented to general practitioners.[6]

This chapter will help you recognize how certain breathing practices can trigger hyperventilation and produce negative health effects. You will occasionally be cautioned to limit the practice of one particular pattern that may significantly raise stress. As with any physical and emotional exploration, it is important to practice the emotion patterns in low levels and take regular breaks so you don't over-stress your system. This chapter will also provide regular check-ins to remind you to return to deep, slow breathing in the zero breath pattern, which will rebalance your respiratory system and help clear away any emotions evoked.

A Caution Before Practicing 2b

If you have experienced respiratory problems in the past, suffer from panic attacks, or have regular symptoms of hyperventilation, it is recommended that you seek the advice of your physician before practicing the emotion patterns in this chapter. Learning the deep breathing patterns in this book can help you overcome over-breathing and hyperventilation issues; however, one pattern in this chapter, pattern 2b, may exacerbate respiratory problems and panic attacks. Additionally, if you are under the care of a therapist, particularly for any trauma therapy, it is advisable to discuss your work on these exercises with your therapist. Exploring the 2b pattern at low intensity levels can help you learn how these conditions may be linked to holding onto chronic hyperventilation in your everyday life, which could be a very valuable self-discovery. However, it is important to keep the health warnings in mind as you proceed and not to force or push the 2b pattern too hard or into high levels of intensity too quickly. In my classes and workshops, I introduce pattern 2b slowly and gradually and give plenty of breaks away from the pattern, always returning to zero in between explorations.

> In a university course I taught on Conscious Breathing for Health and Wellness, a number of the students had a history of panic attacks. One student could not lie on his back or engage in any kind of breathing work without evoking a sense of panic and the need to leave the room.

---

5. Ibid.

6. Anne Pitman, "Hyperventilation: An Under-Recognized Condition," *Pulse* 64 no. 43 (2004): 52-58.

We gradually worked through his challenges by having him practice the breathing patterns sitting in a chair near the door so he felt the safety of both being near an exit and working in a seated position. We also agreed he would not practice pattern 2b if the class lesson included instruction on it. He was to just listen to the lesson while in the zero breath pattern, which still allowed him to learn about the physical manifestations of the emotion and how it contributed to panic attacks.

Gradually, he found the zero pattern was very helpful for him to use when listening to lessons on stressful emotions, like 2b. He also discovered when any feelings of panic emerged, the 1a pattern was very effective in quelling his anxiety. By the end of course, he was able to engage in all class activities, including lying on the floor practicing deep breathing lessons. In his final journal entry for the course, he reported that by learning these breathing techniques and regularly practicing deep breathing, zero, and the a-patterns, his panic attacks had reduced significantly.

The Benefits of Mouth Breathing with Deep Breathing

Although chronic shallow mouth breathing can cause many health issues, short-term mouth breathing, when using deep-breathing practices, is absolutely necessary for moments of physical exertion and catching our breath after strenuous activities. In these cases, mouth breathing is essential for rebalancing oxygen and carbon dioxide levels. In addition, we need to breathe through the mouth when compensating for nasal obstructions. Anyone who suffers from allergy and sinus issues will often need to mouth-breathe.

Breathing in and out of the mouth is necessary to support various activities, such as playing certain musical instruments, swimming, or scuba diving. Consider the breathing pattern needed to support public speaking, singing in a musical, or serving as an auctioneer. During these activities, it is common practice to inhale quickly through the mouth to acquire enough air to support sustained speaking or singing. As long as these mouth-breathing practices utilize deep diaphragmatic breathing, one can easily sustain them for long periods of time without causing any health problems. Throughout your exploration of this chapter, you will also find that mouth-breathing patterns allow us to express a vast array of emotions that are essential to our emotional well-being.

Our Sensitive Mouths

The mouth plays an active role in our lives as the sole entry point for food and water, and as the primary exit point for vocalized expressions of our feelings and needs. As the taste center of our bodies, our mouths react instantly with taste sensors even when we are not actually eating or drinking anything. Just the thought of certain foods, drinks, and even emotional feelings can cause our saliva to respond and ether build up or dry up in our mouths.

Mouth idioms fill our language, suggesting how central the mouth is to our lives. We can be mealy-mouthed, down-in-the-mouth, foul-mouthed, or end up putting a foot in our mouths. Someone could be accused of running at the mouth, speaking from both sides of the mouth, or being so cold that butter wouldn't melt in their mouth. A situation could make your mouth water, leave a bad taste in your mouth, cause you to foam at the mouth, or make you feel like your heart's in your mouth. Someone might even take the words right out of your mouth. Some sayings—like "Go wash your mouth out with soap!" or "Would you kiss your mother with that mouth?"—imply that our mouths will continue to carry any offenses we may utter, as if our oral expressions were absorbed into the lips and walls of the mouth.

We may be sensitive about our mouths, given how central they are to our survival and to our personal expression. Some feel very uncomfortable opening their mouths wide, which can cause feelings of vulnerability. On the other hand, others may feel uncomfortable having their mouths covered, an action that evokes fear of suffocation.

Thousands of taste buds reside on the tongue, lips, roof, sides and back of the mouth as well as on the pharynx, larynx, and epiglottis.[7] This fact could contribute to our mouth sensitivity. We indulge in good food and drink, or resist them, depending on how our taste buds react. We also savor deep passionate kisses with our mouths and express feelings of love and tenderness by softly kissing our children, pets, and even objects for which we hold a special fondness. If we don't feel such fond feelings for someone, we move our mouths away from them as they get closer. This can happen when we ignore someone or show indifference, disdain, or disgust.

Recognizing both our sensitivity to the mouth and how mouth breathing can introduce hyperventilation is important as we approach the mouth-breathing patterns. Out of all the emotional effector patterns, the two mouth-breathing patterns have the potential to evoke feelings of vulnerability and heightened sensitivity to one's surroundings. However, in a comfortable and trusted setting, allowing oneself to become vulnerable can be an exhilarating and provocative experience, like riding an amusement-park ride or giving in to a passionate moment. As you progress through this chapter, try to explore the exercises in a quiet, comfortable, and trusted environment to support an optimal learning experience with these patterns.

Complexity of the Mouth-Breathing Patterns

Mouth-breathing patterns have more complexity to their expressive qualities than the other patterns. Each of these patterns also has two modes of expression: (1) active and (2) receptive, or passive. Therefore, these basic emotions not only have degrees of expression or intensity levels, but also have variations in their expressive modes. In order to keep these forms clear, the 2-patterns are referred to as 2a (Receptive), 2a (Active), 2b (Passive), and 2b (Active).

---

7. B. Nilsson, "The Occurrence of Taste Buds in the Palate of Human Adults as Evidenced by Light Microscopy," *Acta Odontologica Scandinavica* 37 (1979): 253-8.

Because of the complexity of these patterns, whenever possible, practice them with an experienced Emotional Body teacher for clear guidance and support. Explore the exercises in quiet private places and during times of the day where you can comfortably examine how they make you feel. Always make sure you return to zero after each exercise and use Step Out to finish all your practice sessions.

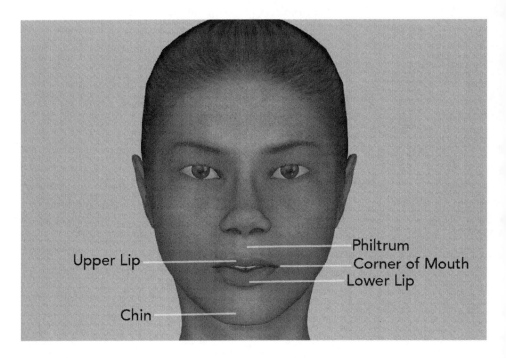

Basic Mouth Anatomy and Terms
The terms that follow will be used throughout the chapter to describe general areas of the mouth activated in these patterns.

1. The *upper lip* is the upper part of your mouth opening, which acts as a band across the top of your mouth.

2. The *philtrum* is the vertical groove between the tip of the nose and the middle of the upper lip.

3. The *lower lip* is the bottom part of your mouth opening, which acts as a band across the lower part of your mouth.

4. The *mouth corners* are where your upper lip and your lower lip meet and form a crease.

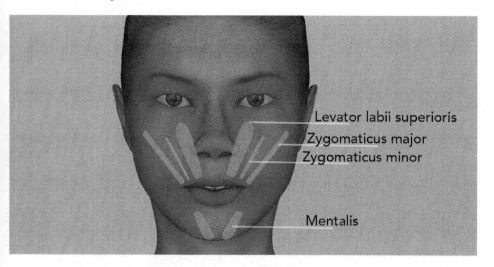

Levator labii superioris
Zygomaticus major
Zygomaticus minor

Mentalis

Basic Mouth Muscles

The *obicularis oris* muscle is the large sphincter muscle that surrounds the mouth and is the muscle most associated with the mouth. This muscle allows the mouth to open, close, pucker, and pinch. There are fifteen other muscles that affect mouth movement and expressions; however, for the mouth-breathing patterns and their accompanied facial aspects, we will focus on these four muscles:

1. The *levator labii superioris* elevates the upper lip.

2. The *mentalis* muscles are located on either side of the lower end of the chin and activate the lower lip.

3. The *zygomaticus major* draws the mouth's angle back and up.

4. The *zygomaticus minor* elevates and retracts the lip and mouth.[8]

Did you know...?

The upper lip area has a long history of references to love, passion, and lust. The line of the upper lip is known as Cupid's bow for its resemblance to the shape of a bow. The philtrum, or vertical groove between the upper lip and the tip of the nose, has Greek and Latin roots that suggest this area of the mouth is like a love potion. The levator labii superioris muscle created the snarl commonly seen on the face of 1960s hip-gyrating music idol, Elvis Presley, earning this upper lip muscle the nickname "The Elvis Muscle."

8. Body Maps," Healthline, accessed February 12, 2014 http://www.healthline.com/human-body-maps/ accessed February 12, 2014

Mouth Muscle Movements

Let's investigate what it feels like to move these muscles around the mouth and see if you can isolate their use. As you form these mouth expressions, notice if you experience any emotions.

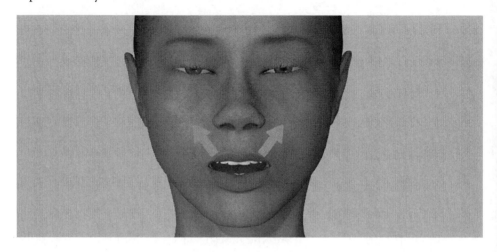

Upper Lip Muscle Movement Exploration

1. Open your mouth wide enough to place a finger between your teeth. Then, remove the finger and allow your mouth to remain open to that degree while you explore the muscle movement in steps 2–4.

2. Lift the upper lip around the area of the levator labii superioris, located on either side of the philtrum. It will feel as if you are raising the middle of the upper lip toward the eyes. Try to keep your lower lip relaxed, and isolate muscle movement to the middle of the upper lip. Then release. Repeat a couple times to get a sense of that particular muscle movement. This muscle activation area is not part of the 2a pattern, but it is important to distinguish this area from the desired movements described in step 3. End this step by releasing the muscle elevation and checking that your mouth has maintained the same degree of openness.

3. Move your attention farther out on the upper lip to the zygotmaticus minor, located approximately halfway between the philtrum and the corners of the mouth. With the mouth remaining open, try to elevate this area of the upper lip while also pulling it back at an angle toward the ears. Then release. This is the muscle engagement area for pattern 2a (Receptive). Practice this again and see if you can identify its specific location.

4. To help you feel the dual action of elevating while also angling back toward the ears, investigate these two different movements separately. Only elevate

the zygotmaticus minor, and then release. Then, angle it back toward the ears, without elevating, and release. Finish this exploratory step by bringing the two actions together, lifting and angling back.

5. For contrast, place your attention on the corners of your mouth and, with your mouth still open, see what it feels like to pull the corners of the mouth toward your ears, which will activate the zygotmaticus major muscles. As you do this, gently place your fingers on your lower lip and see if you can feel the lower lip stretching and expanding. Activating this area of the mouth forms more of a full-mouth smile, which is not the correct muscle activation for these mouth-breathing patterns.

6. End this muscle exploration by opening your mouth as big as you can, and stretching your lips before gently closing your mouth. Then, blow a large amount of air quickly out of your mouth, allowing your relaxed lips to flap with the air release, making a sound similar to that of a horse when it does the same action.

▌▌ Pause & Reflect

How did this muscle activation in the upper lip make you feel? Take a moment and write down any discoveries you made. Could you get a sense of the "Elvis lip curl" in step 2? Did you feel a slightly different sensation when moving the muscles as directed in step 3? Were you able to distinguish between the different mouth expressions in steps 2, 3, and 5?

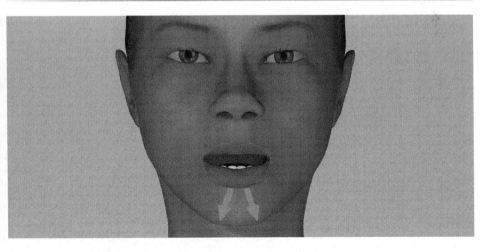

Lower Lip Muscle Movement

1. Open your mouth slightly, not quite as much as you did in the previous exercise.

This time, you are not able to put a finger between your teeth, but the teeth are parted slightly. The upper lip remains relaxed throughout this exercise.

2. With your attention on your lower lip, try to move the middle of the lower lip down very slightly, as if to expose your lower teeth. This muscle movement can be done in varying degrees, but in this effector pattern it is a very subtle movement. You might benefit from looking in a mirror while you exercise this muscle to see how subtle a movement you can achieve with the intention of barely exposing the lower teeth.

3. Let's examine the muscle that achieved the movement described in step 2. Gently place your fingers on the middle of your chin, over the mentalis muscles. The mentalis muscles are the same muscles that form a pout when elevated. Take a moment and form a pout with your lower lip, elevating the mentalis muscles—which can move a great amount in this direction—and pushing your lower lip out. Now, with your mouth still open, depress these muscles, moving them in the opposite direction. Can you feel the subtle movement of the mentalis muscles used to achieve this action? Make sure the muscle movement is in the mentalis area, and not further out to the sides of the chin in the depressor labii inferioris muscle area, or you will be forming a grimace.

4. With your fingers gently sensing the mentalis muscles of your chin, complete the muscle movement described in step 2 again, with the mouth open while you try to expose the lower teeth. The upper lip remains relaxed and the mouth remains slightly open. This mouth expression is the one used in pattern 2a (Active).

5. Release this lower-lip exploration exercise by puckering up and blowing air out through your lips, allowing them to flap and make a "raspberries" sound.

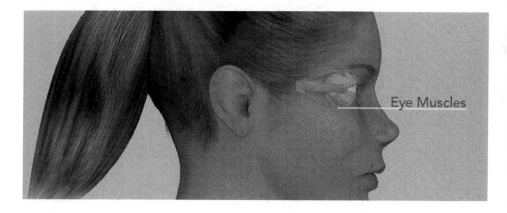

Muscles Behind the Eyes

Let's give the mouth muscles a break and investigate eye muscle movements. There are specific expressions of the eyes that we make all the time, but we are most likely unaware of how they are formed and what effect these movements have on our emotional state. In the nose-breathing patterns, we examined the muscles around the eyes and how they influence certain expressions, but now let's get a sense of how the muscles behind the eyes work.

Did you know that you have muscles behind your eyes that can move your eyes out and then back into the eye sockets? The outward motion results in a stare or bulging of the eyes, and the inward motion allows the eyes to almost close, resulting in a soft gaze. The muscles responsible for this movement are the rectus muscles. Let's investigate this eye muscle movement with a few exercises:

1. While lying on your back or sitting in a chair, focus your eyes on a point on the ceiling or across the room.

2. Without moving any other muscles in your face, try to press your eyeballs forward, toward that focal point. Allow your eyelids to retract, or get out of the way, as your eyes move forward. Hold this stare at the focal point for a while and see how that feels. Then release, allowing the eyes to rest for a moment.

3. Place a hand gently on your forehead and again send your eyes toward a focal point across the room, as described in step 2. Notice if there is any muscle engagement in the forehead. Can you complete this eye movement without engaging the muscles in the forehead?

4. Then, move your eyes in the opposite direction, going backward and deep into your eye sockets, allowing your eyelids to almost close around your eyes. While you still maintain a focus on your point on the ceiling or across the room, how does it feel to have this kind of soft, focused gaze?

Pause & Reflect

Release all this muscle work. Close your eyes. Relax your mouth. Breathe deeply. With each exhale of breath, release any tension that might have accumulated during these muscle exploration exercises. Take a physical rest away from this work.

Before moving on in this chapter to incorporating the breathing patterns, reflect on any feelings that emerged during the mouth and eye muscle explorations. Write down any words or descriptions that came to mind during these exercises and note associations made between certain muscle movements and the feelings or images evoked.

Comparing Zero Breath and Mouth Breathing

Let's look at how mouth breathing feels in comparison to the zero breath pattern.

1. While lying down on your back with your eyes gazing up at the ceiling, start the zero pattern (*see chapter 4*).

2. Once you have established a few cycles of zero, let your mouth drop open a little more and place your focus on mouth breathing by breathing in and out through the mouth while maintaining all other aspects of the zero pattern. Make sure that you continue to utilize deep diaphragmatic breathing and that you do not activate high-chest breathing. How does it feel to simply change the pathway of the breath to the mouth?

3. After exploring mouth breathing in this pattern for a while, go back to the zero pattern. Do you notice any changes as you switch back to zero? Remain in zero for a few cycles to conclude this exercise.

2a Breath Pattern

1. While lying down on your back with your eyes focused on the ceiling, begin the zero pattern. Once it is established, change only the pathway of the breath to mouth breathing. Both the inhale and exhale are soft, even, and relaxed while you engage in deep diaphragmatic breathing and actively use abdominal and thoracic muscles to support the breath.

2. Keep the 2a inhale and exhale equal in length, but shorten them slightly. For example, if your zero pattern had a six-count inhale and exhale, shorten each to four or five counts so they easily flow from one to the other.

3. Inhale through the mouth, with a turnaround similar to the "ball image" in the zero pattern, but imagine this turnaround to be softer and slower, as if it were in slow motion. The same slow turnaround is felt after the exhalation as well. There are no holds or pauses in this breath pattern. All remains as an easy, languid flow of air in and out.

4. Allow your tongue to rest on the bottom of your mouth at the place where it tends to go right after swallowing. Place your attention on how the breath flows in and out, cascading air across your tongue, down your throat, and into your system. Feel how the air is moving through your body, and imagine it is the air that is breathing you. Notice its gentle rise and fall in your body as you breathe this pattern, and consider how this feels.

5. When you feel you have exercised this pattern enough, switch to the zero pattern to end it.

2a (Receptive) Pattern with Facial Expression

We will practice the 2a breath pattern again while also incorporating the facial aspect of the receptive pattern. See if you can feel a difference in the pattern when the facial muscles are included.

1. While lying down on your back looking at the ceiling, start the 2a pattern by following steps 1–4 in the "2a Breath Pattern" exercise. As you continue with the pattern, feel how the air is moving through your body and allow the breath to become movement inside of you and throughout you.

2. While maintaining the 2a breath pattern and letting your mouth remain open, bring your attention to your upper lip. Focus on the area of the zygotmaticus minor, located approximately halfway between the philtrum and the corners of the mouth. Try to elevate this area of the upper lip while also pulling it back at an angle toward the ears. You might feel as if you are forming a very subtle upper lip smile.

3. Continuing with the breath pattern and keeping a slight upper lip smile on your gently opened mouth, bring your attention to your eyes. Allow your eyes to move back, deep into your eye sockets, and your eyelids to gently close or almost close.

4. This completes the 2a (Receptive) pattern with facial expression. Remain in this pattern as long as you would like, and then gradually shift into the zero breath pattern to end this exercise.

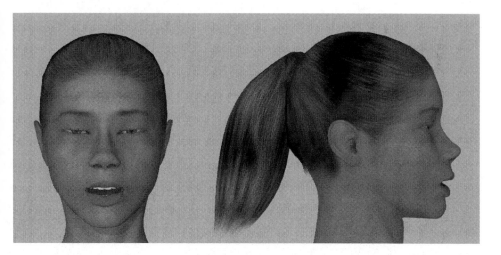

2a (Active) Pattern with Facial Expression

The active mode of the 2a pattern has a couple subtle muscular changes that provide a different experience with the same breath pattern. See if you can feel that difference as your facial muscles shift slightly in this mode.

1. While lying on your back with your eyes gazing up at the ceiling, engage the 2a pattern with the inhale and exhale through the mouth and of equal length. The inhalation and exhalation have a soft, slow-motion turnaround with no holds or pauses.

2. Your mouth will remain open, but not as open as in the receptive mode. The teeth are just barely parted, and the tongue is pressed slightly forward so that the tip of the tongue touches the back of the lower teeth. Place your attention on how the breath flows across your tongue.

3. While maintaining this breath pattern, relax your upper lip completely, and place your focus on the middle of your chin. Depress the mentalis muscles slightly, with the intention of exposing the lower teeth. This is an extremely subtle movement, right in the middle of your chin, that lowers your lower lip ever so slightly.

4. Continuing with the breath pattern and this lower lip tension, bring your attention to your eyes. Allow your eyes to move back slightly, not quite as deep into the eye sockets as you did in the receptive mode. Make the eyes a little more active and focused, but still with the intention of retracting slightly.

5. This completes the 2a (Active) pattern with facial expression. Remain in this pattern as long as you would like, and then gradually shift into the zero pattern to end this exercise.

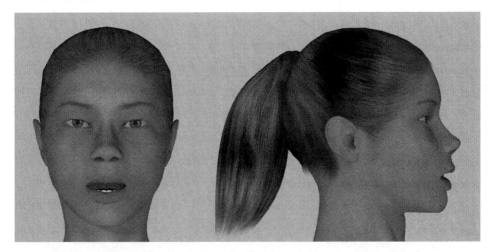

 Pause & Reflect

Take a few moments and write down any discoveries you made while practicing patterns 2a (Receptive) and 2a (Active). Can you identify words to describe sensations or emotions that emerged during your practice of these two different modes of the same breath pattern? How are they different? How are they similar? What situations in your life might evoke these different feelings? Can you imagine how different levels of these patterns could be present in daily activities? These patterns might also be present during special occasions, vacations, or moments within loving relationships.

Now, take a long break before continuing with any other exercises or revisiting these patterns. You may also want to do an extra Step Out before taking your break.

Incorporating the 2a Postural Attitude

Once you have practiced the breathing patterns and facial aspects of 2a (Receptive) and 2a (Active), we can incorporate the postural attitudes. We will begin by sitting in a chair and then move to standing and walking. The following exercises will take you through gradual developments of the postural attitude of 2a.

Sitting in 2a

1. Use a firm straight-backed chair that allows your feet to touch the floor when sitting toward the front of the chair seat. Sit in the zero postural attitude (as described in chapter 4). With eyes open and looking directly across the room, identify a focal point that is at eye level so that you are looking neither up nor down. Your focal point can be anything like a spot on the wall, a doorknob, a window, or a picture. You will look at this focal point throughout this exercise.

2. From the zero sitting position, consider adjusting your posture so it reflects a body that is "openly receiving." To accomplish this, rotate the arms slightly so the palms face up toward the ceiling, and rest the backs of your hands on your thighs. Allow your toes to point out slightly away from the midline of your body rather than pointing straight ahead. Slide your feet a couple inches away from center, to the left and right, causing your legs to open up a bit. Encourage the leg muscles to relax into this open V-shape.

3. Bring your attention to your navel area and press your navel forward, causing your lower back to arch as your pelvis tilts forward. Then bring your navel back to center so that your lower back is no longer arching. Repeat this movement a few times to get a sense of how this movement forward and backward creates a gentle rocking in your seat.

4. Now, bring your attention to the middle of your throat, where your larynx, or voice box, is located. In the same openly receiving postural attitude, see what it is like to achieve a similar forward movement, but this time leading with the middle of the throat. In order to press this part of your neck forward, allow the head to tilt back slightly, creating an arch in the back of your neck. Then, return to the starting position, with your neck straight and your face forward. Repeat this movement a few times to sense how it creates an arching forward and back in the upper part of your spine. Depending on how far back you arch your neck, you may lose eye contact with your focal point occasionally.

5. Now, combine the rocking of the spine in these two areas in the following way. Starting from the openly receiving upright posture, begin by pressing the navel forward. Soon after, let the middle of the throat press forward as well. Once the neck has reached a full arch, start to bring the navel area back to center. Have the neck follow the movement of the navel to return to center as well. Repeat this combined movement a few times, and see if you can coordinate the two movements so that you feel a gentle undulation of the entire spine. It should feel like a slow ripple, with the pelvis initiating the movement and the neck following the lead of the rocking pelvis.

6. You may find that this movement needs to be exercised in large, or even choppy, movements at first as you find the flow and rhythm of this full spinal undulation. Once you achieve the coordination of these two areas and start to feel the sense of a wave of movement through your spine, reduce the intensity to a slow and very subtle rocking forward and backward.

7. Finish the exercise by returning to the neutral sitting position.

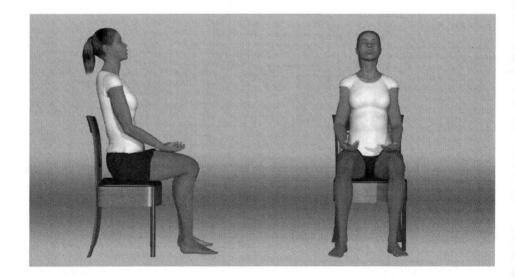

Integrating All Three Aspects of 2a (Receptive)

Once you have practiced the 2a postural attitude while sitting, it is time to integrate the breath and facial aspects to complete the full pattern. Complete the following steps while sitting in a firm straight-backed chair and looking at your focal point.

1. Begin by sitting in zero and engaging the zero breath pattern.

2. After a few breath cycles in zero, change your breathing to mouth breathing and gradually engage the 2a breath pattern by making the inhale and exhale of equal length. The inhalation and exhalation have a soft, slow-motion turnaround with no holds or pauses.

3. As you solidify this breath pattern, gradually add the facial aspect of 2a (Receptive) by first bringing your attention to your upper lip and forming a very subtle upper lip smile. Then, allow your eyes to move back, deep into your eye sockets. Your eyelids may gently close or almost close.

4. Then, increase the full embodiment of this pattern by engaging the postural attitude. Bring your body into an openly receiving upright posture. Begin the gentle and subtle spinal undulation by leading with the navel pressing forward. Soon after, let the middle of the throat press forward as well. Once the neck has reached a full arch, start to bring the navel area back to center, and have the neck follow the movement of the navel to return to center as well.

5. You now have integrated the breath, facial aspect, and postural attitude of pattern 2a (Receptive). Practice this pattern for a couple minutes and check that all aspects of the pattern are retained as you incorporate the gentle spinal undulation. Can you reach a place where the movement of the inhalation and exhalation are the cause of this spinal undulation? Can you feel as if the air is breathing and moving you?

6. Explore what it is like to go between eyes closed and eyes slightly open. Make sure the eyes are still sinking deep into the eye sockets yet softly looking at a focal point. Does the sensation of the pattern change with this subtle opening of the eyes?

7. Take notice of how you feel as you engage this full pattern. Can you sense any emotions or recognizable feelings emerging?

8. Finish this exercise by switching your breathing back to neutral breath as you bring your posture and your facial expression back to zero. Remain in the zero pattern for as many cycles as it takes to feel as if you have fully released the 2a pattern.

Integrating All Three Aspects of 2a (Active)

1. Begin by sitting in zero and engaging the zero breath pattern.

2. After a few breath cycles in zero, change your breathing to mouth breathing and gradually engage the 2a breath pattern.

3. Add the facial aspect of 2a (Active) by first placing your focus in the middle of your chin. Depress the mentalis muscles slightly with the intention of a very subtle exposure of the lower teeth. Then, bring your attention to your eyes and allow them to move back slightly, not quite as deep into their sockets as you did with the receptive mode. Allow the eyes to remain open and focused but retracting slightly.

4. Sit in an openly receiving upright posture. Begin the gentle and subtle spinal undulation by leading with the navel pressing forward. Soon after, let the middle of the throat press forward as well. However, don't bring the neck to a full arch but keep your focus on your focal point. You will find that a slight upper body undulation still occurs, but the head does not tilt back so much that you lose eye contact with your focal point. Then, start to bring the navel area back to center. The subtle neck movement will follow the retraction of the navel area to return to center as well.

5. You have now integrated the breath, facial aspect, and postural attitude of pattern 2A (Active). Practice this pattern for a couple minutes and check that all aspects of the pattern are retained as you incorporate the spinal undulation while maintaining a focal point.

6. Although your eyes are fixed on a focal point, remember they are set back slightly in their sockets and the muscles around and under the eyes remain soft and relaxed.

7. Take notice of how you feel as you engage this full pattern. Can you sense any emotions or recognizable feelings emerging? How is this pattern different from the receptive mode? To fully explore the differences, try going back and forth between the active and the receptive modes.

8. Finish this exercise by switching your breathing back to zero as you bring your posture and facial expression back to zero as well. Remain in zero for as many cycles as it takes to feel as if you have fully released the 2a pattern.

Pause & Reflect

Take a moment to reflect on these two modes of the 2a pattern. What emotions or feelings emerged with each? Where and when might you experience these two modes of expression? There is an inherent open and sensual quality to these patterns, particularly once the full postural attitude is applied. When these patterns are practiced at high levels, it may be clear how they can be associated with sexual sensations. Keep in mind that at very low levels the 2a pattern can be experienced in common interactions throughout the day. If this is difficult to imagine, bring your pattern practice down to the most subtle level, where the spinal undulations are barely perceptible. See if you can identify other words for your experiences with the pattern as you examine it in this way.

Adding Sound to 2a

Adding sound, and specifically speaking in 2a, is much easier than in the 1a and 1b patterns, because in 2a you are exhaling out the mouth. Go through the steps in "Integrating All Three Aspects of 2a (Receptive)" and "Integrating All Three Aspects of 2a (Active)" and simply add the following step before you complete the exercise.

Step for Adding Sound

Once all three aspects of the pattern are integrated, produce a gentle touch of sound on every other exhale. Allow this vocalized sound to sustain throughout the exhalation and retain the integrity of the exhale's volume, flow, and intensity. When you exhale with no sound, make a mental note of exactly how this exhalation feels in its flow of air and muscular effort. Then, when you exhale again with sound, see if you can match the same effort used when you did not emit sound. Make sure the only new element of action occurs in the larynx, where the sound is formed. Continue practicing the addition of sound by going back and forth, applying sound on every other exhale. Practice this until you have a sense that the exhalation has the same qualities with or without sound. Then, finish this exercise by switching your breathing back to zero breath and bringing your posture and facial expression back to zero.

While teaching the 2a pattern in one of my university classes, the students were working on acquiring an understanding of the difference between the receptive and the active modes as well as relating their applications to daily life activities.

During a post-exercise discussion, the students offered interpretations of their experiences with the 2a pattern. "It's so relaxing and open!" "It made me feel like I was floating in the gentle waves of the ocean." "I was on the dance floor approaching someone I liked."

When I asked if they could identify how the two modes of the pattern were different, one student provided a clear example of the differences that I still use to this day: "Both patterns are focused on receiving, but the receptive pattern is expectant while the active pattern is insistent. Sort of like the difference between 'I am willing' (receptive) and 'I want' (active)."

Lexicon of Emotional States for the 2a Pattern

The words that follow are emotional states associated with the 2a pattern. Each pattern has primary names associated with it that emerged during the initial research of these patterns. The additional words provided in the columns imply levels of intensity, or degrees, of this pure state. These degrees are represented by the terms Low, Mid, and High in the columns that follow. Keep in mind that the act of applying words to emotional states is highly subjective and varies depending on life experiences and individual interpretations of meaning. Therefore, these words are provided only as guides to help you relate your experiences with the 2a pattern to familiar words in our language.

Emotion Words for Pattern 2a
Primary Names: Sensuality, Lust, Eroticism, or Sex[9]

Low Level	Mid Level	High Level
Desirous	Amorous	Breathless
Enticed	Aroused	Enraptured
Expectant	Flirtatious	Erotic
Peaceful	Passionate	Lustful
Receptive	Seductive	Voracious
Sensual	Sexual	Wanton
Surrendered		

Try embodying some of these words and see if you can feel the elements of 2a naturally emerging as you "act out" the words. Can you sense if one emotion word connects more with 2a (Receptive) or 2a (Active)?

9. Susana Bloch, Pedro Orthous, and Guy Santibañez-H, "Effector Patterns of Basic Emotions: A Psychophysiological Method for Training Actors," *Journal of Social Biological Structure*, 10 (January 1987) 1-19. (Note: In this article, the original research team differentiated between the basic emotion's phasic [transient or stimulus bound] state, and its tonic [maintained-in-time] state and used these words to label the various states of this emotion. Many would be hard pressed to believe that babies would have this particular basic emotion developed within the first year of life if it were only labeled *eroticism*. The consideration of *sensuality* as a viable basic emotion that also transforms into eroticism, allows us to consider this possibility in early life development, and not just emerging in puberty.)

When other patterns combine with 2a, mixes occur. Another emotion pattern can mix in easily through a slight posture adjustment, like the addition of a tilted head or the inclusion of tension in the posture. A mix can come in when different muscles are engaged in the face, such as when the eyes move forward, when tension exists under the eyes, or when muscles in different areas of the mouth are activated.

If the breath pattern changes in any way, then there is a clear mix coming in as well. Be aware that in a pattern like 2a, where the posture is very open, fluid, and relaxed, any chronic tensions you may be holding onto will also mix in another emotion. Remember that when practicing these patterns alone without the aid of an experienced and qualified instructor's feedback, subtle mixes are most likely occurring.

There are plenty of mixed emotions for which the 2a pattern is a primary base of the expression. The following words offer the opportunity to see how this pattern can emerge in various modes of expression.

Mixed Emotions with 2a as a Primary Pattern

Admiring	Enamored	Invigorated	Nostalgic
Bewitched	Enthralled	Jealous	Obsessive
Captivated	Entranced	Lascivious	Passive
Casual	Fascinated	Lewd	Resentful
Coquettish	Infatuated	Mesmerized	Wicked
Coy	Inspired	Nonchalant	

Try displaying some of these words. Can you feel emotion-pattern elements emerging that are not part of the 2a pattern? For example, when you display being *wicked*, does extra tension come in around your eyes? That would be an aspect of 1b mixing in. If you embody the word *coy* or *coquettish*, can you feel where a head tilt and a little side bending may come in? This would be a mix-in of some 1a. Continue taking on other words in this list and see if you can identify where the mixes might be. Remember that mixed emotions are highly subjective, so your own interpretation of each of these words will most likely vary in some degree from someone else's. Embodying them and then deconstructing their elements will help you see how the 2a pattern is present and other elements are mixing into your expression of these states.

Standing in 2a
It is time to see how this pattern can be incorporated into your standing posture.

1. Start by sitting in the 2a openly receiving postural attitude with your attention on your focal point.

2. Engage the gentle spinal undulation of the receptive pattern, and allow the last part of the undulation (where the neck moves forward) to lead you up and into a standing position.

3. Select a new focal point that is at your standing eye level. See if you can maintain the gentle spinal undulation, and make it as slow as possible so it looks like your standing posture just has a very soft, slow sway to it.

4. Add the 2a breath pattern and the receptive facial expression to fully engage the entire 2a (Receptive) pattern. The eyes can be closed or slightly open as if looking through veils of eye lashes at your focal point. Add sound occasionally through the exhalation out the mouth.

5. Gently switch to the active mode, by adjusting your facial expression: drop the upper lip smile and place attention in the middle of the chin, depressing very slightly. Then, bring the head upright, with no neck arch on the undulation, and look at your focal point. Add sound occasionally through the exhalation out the mouth.

6. Finish the exercise by returning to the zero standing position and zero breath.

Walking in 2a
Let's explore how this pattern moves.

1. Start by standing in the 2a (Receptive) pattern with eyes open and softly focused on a point across the room. Make sure you have plenty of space in front of you to allow for walking at least a few paces in a straight line before needing to turn.

2. Using the spinal undulation as the impetus for moving forward, allow the navel to lead you, encouraging a foot to swing forward and make the first step. Then, with the next spinal undulation, the other foot swings forward, making the second step. Continue walking with the pelvic tilt (or navel-forward movement) initiating each step.

3. Both arms will swing forward, together, following the movement of this pelvic-centered, swinging walk. Remember to allow the arms and legs to rotate slightly so the palms open forward and the feet turn out. You will probably need to practice this walk with very large movements at first, to coordinate all the elements. Eventually you will want to reduce it down to a subtle spinal undulation, allowing just enough movement to keep a gentle forward swing in the walk.

4. Now, walk around your space and try to maintain this gentle spinal undulation as the core of your walk, with arms swinging forward together and legs easily swinging forward with each step. Watch that you are not swaying side to side, which would mix in the 1a pattern.

5. Switch to the active mode of 2a by reducing the neck arch and making the eyes a little more alert but still set back slightly. Drop the upper lip smile and depress the middle of the chin very slightly. Place your focus on things in your space and walk to them. You will find that there is a little less spinal undulation in the 2a (Active) walk since the neck is not arching. How does this mode of expressing the 2a pattern feel? Can you sense that the walk might have quickened slightly in comparison to the receptive mode?

6. Finish the exercise by returning to the zero standing position and zero breath pattern. Then, complete a Step Out.

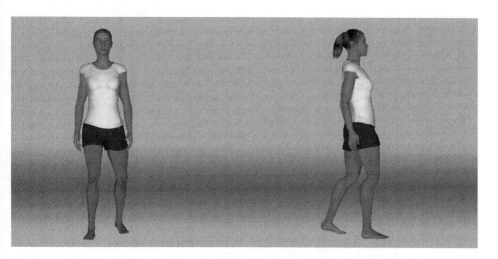

▌▌ Pause & Reflect

Take some time to reflect on and write about your experience with this pattern in motion. When we incorporate all the elements of the pattern and then include movement, our tendency is to relate this to our experiences and our observations of others. You might be thinking, "This feels so different and strange to walk this way," "This reminds me of so and so," or "This makes me feel like when I was..." A person's posture and walk can be so specific to that individual that we can recognize someone we know, even if they are a football field's length away from us, just by their walk. Were there any elements of your own walk recognizable in this 2a walking exploration? What feelings did this walk evoke in you as you moved around the room?

*I was teaching a workshop at my church with a group of women in their 30s to 70s. When I introduced the 2a pattern, the women were delighted and called it delicious and sensual. Once we applied the posture and walk, the women couldn't help but laugh and giggle as they walked around our church sanctuary in 2a. They exclaimed, "This is **not** the walk I use here, but I know it well!" and "This is my sexy walk!" I asked them where they might feel they could use this walk. Here were their responses:*

- *"When I'm wearing a dress and feeling sensual."*
- *"When I'm walking on the beach and taking in the breezes."*
- *"When I'm feeling sexy and want someone to notice."*

Then, months later, I was teaching a group of college students how to walk in 2a. The young men in the group described their walk in a different, yet no-less-delighted way:

- *"This is how I walk when I'm listening to music on my ipod."*
- *"I do this when I'm walking with my friends into a party."*
- *"I feel like I'm strolling with no care in the world."*

As you exercise the 2a pattern, you will most likely start to experience a vast array of feelings associated with this pattern by exploring levels of intensity within its two modes of expression. Perhaps you will begin to recognize even more words to describe the sensations evoked than are listed in this chapter. The more you practice the pure form of the patterns, the clearer sense you will have of when mixes might be coming in and what they might signify.

For example, an exercise I do when a group is first learning the patterns is to have everyone write down on a white board or easel tablet the word(s) that came to mind when they first experienced the pattern. This is a silent exercise completed directly after reaching zero so that no one is influenced by the words or experiences of others in the room. Below is a list of words that participants from one workshop listed as their first experience with the 2a patterns. Can you see, just from their use of a word to describe their experiences, how some were likely close to producing the pure state right away, and how others were likely experiencing mixes?

2A (Receptive)

Aroused	Love	Releasing
Bliss	Luxurious	Sad
Calm	Needy	Sensual
Dreamy	Peaceful	Surrendered
Empathetic	Relaxed	

2A (Active)

Alert	Excitement	Surprised
Ambitious	Horny	Suspicious
Curious	Pensive	Wolf-like
Erotic	Relaxed	Wonder

As the workshop progressed, participants found where those mixes were coming into the patterns and learned how to clear them and attain pure states. As you practice these patterns, see if you can do the same.

A Shift In Breathing: Preparing for the 2b Pattern

Out of the six patterns introduced in this book, only one incorporates chest-centered breathing. This is the 2b pattern. Although chest-breathing practices were covered in an earlier chapter, we will review them here as we prepare to explore the 2b pattern. High-chest breathing practices can cause anxiety and stress levels to rise up quickly. If you have been diagnosed with a stress-related condition like panic attacks or post traumatic stress disorder (PTSD), it is recommended that you practice these patterns with an experienced and qualified instructor or therapist. If you are practicing these exercises without the aid of an instructor, it is important to keep your practice at low levels, for short amounts of time, and take plenty of breaks in between. During these breaks, remember to bring your breathing back down to abdominally supported breathing and check that you have fully released the upper chest breathing.

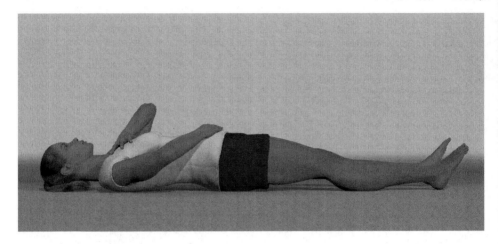

Review of Chest Breathing

1. While lying down on your back, place one hand on your high-chest area so that your thumb rests on the base of your throat and your pinky finger stretches toward your sternum. Place the other hand on your abdomen so that your thumb rests on your navel. To establish the muscle movements involved in chest breathing, hold your breath for a moment and, using the muscles in your chest, try to push the hand resting on your high chest up toward your chin, and then release. You might feel your entire chest rise, along with your shoulders, in the direction of your head. Try this a few times, and then rest and breathe deeply, making sure to engage your abdominal muscles to support the breath during these breaks.

2. Now, let's connect breathing with this high-chest movement. Engage the high-chest muscle movement as described in step 1. But, this time, as the chest rises toward the chin, inhale through the mouth, and as the chest falls, exhale through the mouth. Try this a few times, and then rest and breathe deeply, using the hand on the abdomen to check that you are engaging deep breathing and using the hand on the high chest to check that no upper chest movement is still engaged during the resting break.

3. Once you feel you have a sense of how the chest moves with the inhale and exhale, try to establish a more subtle movement of the chest, so you can get a sense of low intensity chest-centered breathing, or shallow breathing. To return to high-chest breathing, follow the instructions in step 2, focusing on a little less activation of the upper chest, and sustain for about six breath cycles. Then, rest and breathe deeply. Finish with zero breath to help clear anything that may have emerged with this exploration.

> ## ▐▌ Pause & Reflect
>
> Take a moment to reflect on anything that came up for you while practicing high-chest breathing. Did it provoke extra tension in the chest, neck, and shoulders? Could you feel any emotional sensations? Was it difficult to let go of the high-chest activation when you reverted back to deep breathing again? Was any part of this breathing practice familiar to you as part of your own habitual breathing practices?

If you feel any residual tension remaining in the chest, neck, and shoulders after exploring this initial exercise, take a break and do a Step Out or engage in an activity like stretching or exercising that could help release this area of tension. The lessons to come can wait until you know you have fully released the previous lesson. This is a good practice to keep in mind for the rest of this chapter.

Introduction of the 2b Breath Pattern

1. While lying down on your back, place one hand on your high-chest area and the other hand on your abdomen. With eyes open, looking at the ceiling, begin zero breath to start this exercise, and check that there is not any high-chest breathing sneaking into your zero breath.

2. Once you have established a few cycles of zero breath, switch your breathing pathway to the mouth only, breathing in and out through the mouth.

3. Gradually, and at a low level of muscle activation, incorporate the high-chest breathing as you continue to breathe in and out of the mouth.

4. Allow the inhalation and exhalation lengths to shorten considerably from your zero breath cycle. If your zero breath pattern length tends to be around 6 counts, try now to make the inhalation and exhalation 2 or 3 counts. The result is a shallow, fairly fast breath pattern.

5. Once you have achieved this shorter breath pattern, add a fairly long hold after the inhalation, perhaps at least as long as a breath cycle, so a 3 to 4 count hold. This hold will happen most of the time after an inhalation; it does not need to occur every time. When it does, it is of a fairly significant length.

6. Then, if you want to explore this pattern going to a slightly higher intensity,

let the breath pattern release from any regular pattern of length, as long as the lengths do not become too elongated. For example, one breath cycle is a 2 count, the next is a 3 count, followed by a couple 1 counts in a row, etc. Remember to apply the long breath holds regularly.

7. After exploring this irregular breath pattern for a short while, shift into zero breath. Start with a nice, long inhale through the nose, engaging deep breathing and letting go of the high-chest breathing. Then, exhale out the mouth in a long smooth exhale. Continue in this manner to commit to zero breath. Keep a hand on your high chest and make sure that you are not using any high-chest breathing.

8. Finally, gradually move up to a standing position and complete a Step Out. You may need to complete two Step Outs in a row in order to fully release the 2b pattern.

Did you know...?

The word stress is commonly used to describe how we feel when experiencing aspects of the 2b emotion. Stress can result from believing that the outcome of a situation may be dire and doubting our ability to cope. The situations posing the potential threat are called stressors. Stressors can range from experiences in daily life to major life events. They can be positive or negative, such as a promotion that requires significantly increased effort or a job loss that results in financial crisis.[10]

Stressors can be acute (lasting minutes to hours), subacute (lasting less than one month) or chronic (occurring over months or years). The intensity of the stress, even when acute, may have longer-lasting effects.

We may not even be aware of how long isolated episodes of acute stress have an effect on the body. For example, students taking final exams release stress hormones and experience significant neurohormonal changes during the exam. These changes may last for several weeks after the initial event.[11] Although acute stress can be detrimental, chronic stress is highly problematic. It can lead to full-body dysregulation and exacerbate problems with existing inflammatory diseases like asthma and allergies. Studies have shown a relationship between individuals experiencing chronic stress and increased

10. B.S. McEwen, "Central Effects of Stress Hormones in Health and Disease: Understanding the Protective and Damaging Effects of Stress and Stress Mediators," *European Journal of Pharmacology* 583 (2008):174–185.

11. L.Y. Al-Ayadhi, "Neurohormonal Changes in Medical Students During Academic Stress," *Annals of Saudi Medicine* 25, (Jan-Feb 2005): 36-40.

incidence of allergic disease,[12] hospitalization for asthma,[13] or even fatal cases of asthma.[14]

Stressful situations are a natural and expected part of living. Our bodies are equipped with various tools to use as strategies for adapting to stress. Emotion regulation is also a tool for stress adaption. The more we learn about emotion regulation, and how to reduce high or chronic levels of potentially destructive stress, the better we are at equipping our bodies with healthy regulation tools rather than forcing our bodies to resort to unhealthy, dysregulated levels.

Adding the 2b Facial Expression to the Breath Pattern

1. Follow steps 1–5 in "Introduction to the 2b Breath Pattern."

2. Then, with eyes open and fixed on a focal point, try to press your eyeballs forward, toward that focal point. Allow your eyelids to retract, or get out of the way, as your eyes move forward. Then, with the eyeballs pressing outward, occasionally let your eyes look around the room without moving your head. Then, allow them to come back to the focal point occasionally. Place a hand gently on your forehead so you notice if there is any muscle engagement in the forehead. Can you complete this eye movement without elevating or lifting the muscles in the forehead?

3. Allow the mouth to stay open, as if the jaw released and the chin suddenly dropped down to create a large opening for air to come in and out of the body. This will create an oval or circular opening of the mouth. This action stretches the skin around the mouth, creating facial tension. However, watch that the corners of the mouth do not try to pull downward along with the chin movement, or a mix will occur.

4. After exploring this facial expression with the 2b breath pattern for a short while, shift into zero breath. Use a hand placed on your high chest to make sure that you have truly let go of the high-chest breathing. Make sure the eyes have relaxed back to the middle of their sockets.

12. R.J. Wright, P. Finn, J.P. Contreras, et al., "Chronic Caregiver Stress and IgE Expression, Allergen-Induced Proliferation, and Cytokine Profiles in a Birth Cohort Predisposed to Atopy," *Journal of Allergy and Clinical Immunology* 113, no. 6 (2004):1051–1057.

13. N.W. Wainwright, P.G. Surtees, N.J. Wareham, B.D. Harrison, "Psychosocial Factors and Incident Asthma Hospital Admissions in the EPIC-Norfolk Cohort Study," *Allergy* 62 no. 5 (2007):554–560.

14. R. J. Wright, "Alternative Modalities for Asthma that Reduce Stress and Modify Mood States: Evidence for Underlying Psychobiologic Mechanisms," *Annals of Allergy, Asthma, and Immunology* 93, no. 2 (2004): 18–23.

5. Finally, slowly move up to a standing position and complete a Step Out. You may need to complete two Step Outs in a row in order to fully release the pattern.

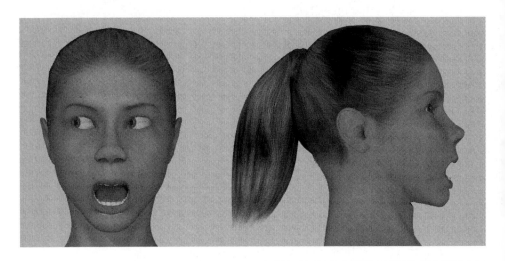

▌▌ Pause & Reflect

Take a few moments and write down any discoveries you made while practicing pattern 2b. Can you identify words to describe sensations or emotions that emerged with this pattern? Did the shallow, high-chest breathing affect other areas of the body and, if so, how? Since this is an irregular breath pattern, could you feel a difference in what was being provoked by this pattern when you held your breath or applied very short breathing cycles as opposed to slightly longer ones? How did it feel to press your eyes forward and then look around the room without moving your head? Were any fearful or anxious feelings evoked with the incorporation of this eye movement?

As you first explored this pattern, you might have found that in order to access voluntary control of the involved muscles, you needed to engage large movements, which quickly brought you to a fairly high level of the emotion. However, once you gain control of the eye muscle movement and the high-chest breathing pattern, you can bring their application down to a lower intensity and examine how the basic emotion evoked could be present in day-to-day activities. Consider any times throughout the day when you are holding your breath, breathing faster or more shallow breaths, or looking around a room with your eyes while the rest of your body remains still. These are all low-level behaviors of the 2b pattern, but both high and low intensity levels alert the same basic emotion to the brain.

Now, take a good long break from any pattern work, and make the break a physical activity, even if it is as simple as cleaning up an area of your house, taking the dog for a walk, performing another Step Out, or doing just 10 minutes of some yoga stretches. It will help you further release any pattern residue that might still be present in your muscles.

Incorporating the 2b Postural Attitude

Once you have practiced the breathing pattern and facial aspects of 2b, it is time to incorporate the postural attitude. We will begin by sitting in a chair and then move to standing and walking. The following exercises will take you through gradual developments of the postural attitude 2b.

Sitting in 2b

Use a firm straight-backed chair and sit toward the front of the chair seat so you have plenty of room between your back and the chair back. Sit in the zero postural attitude.

With eyes open and looking directly across the room, identify a focal point that is at eye level. You will look at this focal point throughout this exercise, until you receive instructions to move the eyes and look around the room without moving the head.

1. From the zero sitting position, imagine the area of your upper back between your shoulder blades is moving back and up. Now, without adjusting your seated contact with the chair, lean this area of your back toward the back of the chair and then pull upward. Do you feel your upper chest rise toward your chin?

2. Repeat this movement a few times to get a sense of how pulling the upper torso back and up creates a postural attitude of retreat.

3. While keeping your eyes focused on your focal point, imagine all the muscles in your body want to move in this way. Can you repeat the upper torso movement, going back and up, and simultaneously invite as many other muscles as you can to instinctively pull back and up? You may discover that your legs and arms pull back and your buttocks muscles contract to pull the legs back. Repeat this movement a few times to sense how this movement creates the feeling of a body in full retreat.

4. Once you have a sense of this postural attitude in full pull-back with a slight lift, let's add the eye movements. The next time you engage this retreating posture, take a moment and allow the eyes to quickly dart around the room without moving your head. Then, end the exploration with the eyes returning to your focal point.

5. Repeat this combined movement a few times. Once you have a clear sense of

how to fully embody this postural attitude, try reducing the intensity so you can see how you might experience this posture in more subtle ways. Considering a scale of 1 to 5, perhaps identifying your first big attempts in terms of a 5, then try a 4, then scale back to a 3, and then a 2, all while pulling back and up slightly to maintain the internal muscle motivation of retreating.

6.   Finish the exercise by returning to the zero sitting position.

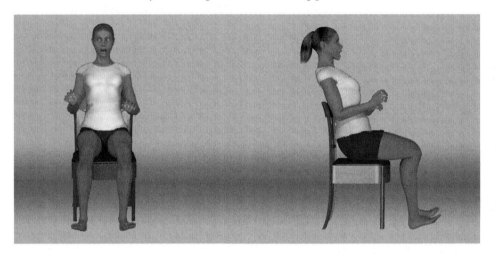

Did you know...?

Actors who use personal-life substitutions to portray fearful acting scenes not only run the risk of developing anxiety disorders and panic attacks, but can also decrease their immune responsiveness and become vulnerable to infection.[15]

Repeated or chronic episodes of fear and anxiety can manifest into anxiety disorders and may play a role in the development of panic attacks and post-traumatic stress disorder.[16] High levels of anxiety, anger, and depression have also been linked to the development of many diseases including cardiovascular disease, cancer, arthritis, diabetes, compromised immune function, and the common cold.[17]

15. John Medina, *Brain Rules: 12 Principles for Surviving and Thriving at Work, Home, and School* (Seattle, Pear Press, 2008), 177-179.

16. Margaret E. Kemeny and Avgusta Schestyuk, "Emotions, the Neuroendocrine and Immune Systems, and Health," *Handbook of Emotions* 3rd ed., eds. Michael Lewis, Jeannette M. Haviland-Jones, and Lisa Feldman Barrett. (New York: Guilford Press, 2008): 663-664.

17. Nathan S. Consedine, "Health-Promoting and Health-Damaging Effects of Emotions: The View from Developmental Functionalism," *Handbook of Emotions* 3rd ed., eds. Michael Lewis, Jeannette M. Haviland-Jones, and Lisa Feldman Barrett (New York: Guilford Press, 2008): 677.

> Conversely, actors who used happy and uplifting life memories to portray character situations in a scene revealed healthy immune systems.[18]

Integrating All Three Aspects of 2b

Once you have practiced the 2b postural attitude while sitting, it is time to integrate the breath to complete the full pattern. Complete the following steps while sitting in a firm straight-backed chair and gazing at your focal point.

1.   Begin by sitting in zero and engaging the zero breath pattern.

2.   After a few breath cycles in zero, change your breathing to mouth breathing and gradually engage the 2b breath pattern by switching your breathing activation area to the high chest. Shorten the length of the inhalation and exhalation, creating a shallow breathing effect, and add an occasional, fairly long hold after the inhale.

3.   Encourage your eyes to move forward, as if pushing out of their sockets, increasing peripheral vision. Let the eyelids get out of the way, causing the eyes to look as if they are bulging outward.

4.   Allow the mouth to drop open, and stay open, creating an oval or circle.

5.   Then, apply the full embodiment of this pattern by engaging the postural attitude. Allow the upper back to move backward and lift up, and then encourage most other muscles in the body to reflect this retreat posture while keeping your eyes and face aligned with your focal point.

6.   During the occasional breath holds after the inhale, activate the eye movement. The eyes could dart around the room while the head stays still and the body faces the focal point.

7.   You now have integrated the breath, facial aspect, and postural attitude of pattern 2b. Practice this pattern for a very short amount of time, perhaps one minute, and preferably at a low level of intensity. Using a scale of 1 to 5, try not to go beyond what you consider a level 3.

8.   Take notice of how you feel as you engage this full pattern. Can you sense any emotions or recognizable feelings emerging?

9.   Finish this exercise by switching your breathing back to zero as you bring your

---

18. John Medina, *Brain Rules: 12 Principles for Surviving and Thriving at Work, Home, and School* (Seattle, Pear Press, 2008), 177-179.

posture and your facial expression back to zero as well. Make sure you are using deep breathing in zero and that you have released upper-chest breathing tension and eye tension.

10. Take one or two Step Outs until you have fully released the 2b pattern.

 ## Pause & Reflect

Take a moment and write down any discoveries you made by incorporating the full embodiment of the 2b pattern. Are there words to describe the difference between your level 3 of the pattern and your lower levels of the pattern? What feelings or images were evoked when engaging this pattern? Could you feel the need to retreat, to freeze, or to run and hide?

Now, take a good long break from the emotion pattern work. The 2b pattern can be particularly difficult to release, and long periods of work on this pattern are not advised. If you prefer to continue with your emotion pattern work, go practice an a-pattern. Any one of the a-patterns will help you shift to a more beneficial, relaxing, and healthy state.

Did you know...?

The emotions of fear and anger immediately engage our body's alerting network. The alerting network is concerned with increasing and maintaining response readiness in preparation for any threat to self.[19] Our bodies have a double-wired alert system. One path goes directly to the amygdala, which quickly triggers a physiological response. The other pathway is slower because it is first processed through the cortex, or thinking part of the brain. Both pathways are necessary for our survival and well-being. The short path prepares the body for immediate reaction, like a startle reflex or the initial stages of fear. When we are fearful or angry, our reflexive attention is immediately focused on all movements, sounds, and expressions of others. Our alerting networks view these actions as a potential threat and are poised for attack, withdrawal, or escape. An anger response is ready to attack and defend. An anxiety reaction expects harm in the future. A fear response anticipates harm in the present.[20]

---

19. M. Bradley, M. Codispoti, B. Cuthbert and P. Lang, "Emotion and Motivation I: Defensive and Appetitive Reactions in Picture Processing," Emotion 1 (2001): 276-298.

20. Jack George Thompson, The Psychobiology of Emotions (New York, Plenum Press,1988), 245-248.

The second circuit, or thinking reaction, can then take a moment to analyze the situation to determine if the threat is real or perceived. This is where subjective feelings are established. If the threat is real, then because the reflexive action has already occurred, the body is already engaged in the act of protecting itself. If the threat is perceived, nothing has been lost. However, once an emotion has been turned on, it is difficult for the cortex to turn it off.[21]

Adding Sound to 2b

To explore how sound might occur in the 2b pattern, go through the steps in "Integrating All Three Aspects of 2b" and add this step before you complete the exercise.

Steps for Adding Sound

1. Once all three aspects of the pattern are integrated, produce a touch of sound during exhalation. Allow this vocalized sound to sustain throughout the exhale while retaining the integrity of the exhale's volume, flow, and intensity. You will notice the sound is different after each occasional hold of breath in the pattern. This is because air has built up behind the vocal folds during the hold and its release produces a louder, shorter burst of sound. During intense levels of the pattern, this will sound like a scream, but in lower levels, more like a whimper. During the exhalations that don't have a hold, you will hear a smoother, more airy flow of sound.

2. Now, try a touch of sound on the inhalation. It works best if the inhales are fairly fast. The tense and constricted postural attitude of 2b can cause the vocal folds to come together during the inhalation, thereby producing vocalized sound on the inhale. Try a few inhaled vocalizations while practicing the 2b breath pattern. Notice how it sounds different from the exhaled sound.

3. Practice this for a short while until you feel you have a sense of these three different ways to make sound within the 2b pattern (during inhalation, during exhalation with no holds, and during exhalation after holds). Finish this exercise by switching your breathing back to zero as you bring your posture and facial expression back to zero as well.

4. Complete the entire exercise by doing one or two Step Outs.

 ## Pause & Reflect

Take a moment to reflect on the feelings and images evoked by adding

---

21. *Ibid.*

sound to this pattern. Many find that the vibration of sound incorporated into the patterns triggers deeper sensations and connections with the emotions associated with those patterns. Was this the case for you? Still, others find it difficult to apply sound. The very act of vocalizing emotion makes it feel more public and pronounced, which can be intimidating to do and difficult to commit to, even in a private exercise. Was this more your experience? Take a moment to write down any words or images that came up for you during the application of vocalized sound. Then, take a good break from the work before you continue.

Lexicon of Emotional States for the 2b Pattern

The words that follow are emotional states associated with the 2b pattern. Each pattern has primary names associated with it that emerged during the initial research. The additional words provided in the columns imply levels of intensity, or degrees, of this pure state. These degrees are represented by the terms Low, Mid, and High in the columns that follow. These words are provided as guides to help you relate your experiences with the 2b pattern to familiar words used in our language.

Emotion Words for Pattern 2b
Primary Name: Fear, Anxiety, Panic[22]

Low Level	Mid Level	High Level
Apprehensive	Anxious	Alarmed
Distrusting	Bewildered	Dreading
Doubtful	Cowardly	Frantic
Flustered	Disbelieving	Horrified
Hesitant	Dumbfounded	Hysterical
Intimidated	Flabbergasted	Panicked
Nervous	Frazzled	Shocked
Reluctant	Frenetic	Stunned
Timid	Frigid	Terrified
Uncertain	Jumpy	
Uneasy	Spooked	
Wary	Surprised	

Try embodying some of these words and see if you can feel the elements of 2b emerging as you "act out" the words. Check that you are staying true to all

22. Susana Bloch, Pedro Orthous, and Guy Santibáñez-H, "Effector Patterns of Basic Emotions: A Psychophysiological Method for Training Actors," *Journal of Social Biological Structure* 10 (January 1987) 1-19.

elements of the pattern by monitoring the breath, posture, and facial aspects and making sure they are in line with the parts of the pattern described so far in this chapter. Try filming yourself while embodying these words and see if you identify when mixes come in and where. Remember, emotion words are highly subjective, so if mixes are coming in, it is most likely due to your own life experience and how you interpret and express these words.

Other emotion patterns can mix into the 2b pattern easily by adjusting the posture. For example, a sinking posture that involves pulling back can indicate insecurity, bashfulness, sheepishness, or modesty. You can easily move from expressing a pure 2b state to a mixed state when different muscles become engaged in the face, as in the addition of a grimace, where the corners of the mouth pull down, perhaps indicating repulsion or disgust. If the forehead furrows, with eyebrows pinching together and up, this can express the mixed states of worry and suspicion. If a person's jaw pushes forward slightly and tension builds under their eyes, they may be feeling insulted or offended. Remember when practicing these patterns alone without the aid of an instructor's feedback, such subtle mixes will most likely occur from time to time.

The following words offer the opportunity to see how the 2b pattern is present in many modes of expression. Try embodying these words and see if you can tell which additional patterns are mixing in and where they are expressed: in the breath, posture, or face.

Mixed Emotions with 2b as a Primary Pattern

Aghast	Disgusted	Restless
Aloof	Edgy	Revolted
Amazed	Fidgety	Sheepish
Appalled	Insecure	Shy
Astonished	Insulted	Skeptical
Astounded	Jealous	Squeamish
Baffled	Meek	Stressed
Bashful	Modest	Submissive
Confounded	Nauseated	Suspicious
Confused	Numb	Tense
Crazed	Offended	Wild
Dazzled	Overwrought	Worried
Demure	Repulsed	
Deranged	Reserved	

As you practice embodying these words, you may notice posture or expression changes that signal an emotional mix. When you are being bashful or demure, do you feel a small head tilt and smile forming? If so, this would be a mix-in of 1a. If you display being submissive or meek, see if you notice your body sinking downward, which is a mix-in of 3b. When being dazzled or amazed, can you feel a more fluid flow of breath in and out, similar to that of the 2a breath pattern? Continue taking on other words in this list and see if you can identify where the mixes might be.

Did you know...?

Flirting and seduction are not just romantic acts, but essential actions of foreplay before intercourse. Safe, healthy seduction allows intimacy to occur and, at the same time, naturally adjusts aspects of our biology to reduce any potential physical trauma during intercourse. If we are touched unexpectedly, particularly in places we consider as private, a startle reflex can result. A startle reflex is a defensive reflex elicited by an abrupt, unexpected and sometimes intense stimulus that makes us jump, pull back, or just blink.[23] A startle reflex signals the alerting networks, and instantaneously the amygdala kicks into flight mode (2b). This may express itself very subtly as pulling away, denying intimacy, or just feeling basic stiffness and discomfort. However, when touch is expected, often preceded by flirting and seduction, we perceive security and the body anticipates intercourse by automatically lubricating genital tissue, maintaining blood pressure, and raising our pain threshold, allowing us to achieve high levels of sexual arousal safely and comfortably.[24]

I was instructing a private client on the 2a and 2b patterns and telling her about how the startle reflex is an instinctive alert system that can transform into levels of fear. We then discussed how pure 2a, particularly higher and more sensual or sexual levels of 2a, is difficult to achieve if there is any 2b tension mixing in or if a person does not feel safe enough to allow the body to adapt an openly receiving posture.

My client had a wonderful aha moment in the midst of this discussion. She told me when she and her husband were courting, they enjoyed long, slow seductive sessions of lovemaking, preceded by plenty of flirting and caressing. During that time, she was always willing to engage in sex with her husband any day of the week. Later on, after they were married for

23. Andrea L. Glenn and Adrian Raine, *Psycholophysiology: An Introduction to Biological Findings and their Implications* (New York, NYU Press, 2014), 71-73.

24. Stephen W. Porges, *The Polyvagal Theory: Neurophysiological Foundations of Emotions, Attachment, Communication, Self-regulation* (New York: Norton & Company, 2011), 179-180.

some time, she found she was less willing and not enjoying their intimacy as much as she had in the earlier days. She adored her husband, was very attracted to him, and confessed she had worried a great deal that perhaps as she was getting older she had lost her own sexual drive or interest. When I asked her if she could identify anything that had changed in their way of approaching each other in intimacy, her eyes lit up:

You know, since you mention it, our foreplay has transformed from a slow, seductive style to a practice where my husband now playfully grabs and gropes at me as his way of prompting lovemaking. I think I instinctively pull back into what I guess I would now identify as a startle reflex. This makes so much sense to me now, since we are taught throughout our lives to instinctively protect those areas. So, now I am with someone who no longer feels we need a "warm-up" or to use a gradual seduction before lovemaking, but my body is saying, "Oh yes I do!"

I assured her she was not alone in this need, that this was a common need for many. I encouraged her to share this insight with her husband. We then laughed at the line she planned to use as her opener, "It's not me, it's my amygdala." She later reported back that she and her husband had changed their philosophy to that of Aesop's tortoise: "Slow and steady wins the race."

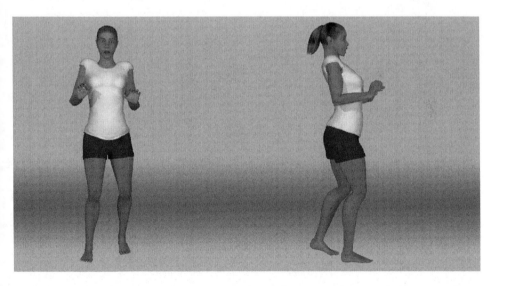

Standing in 2b
Let's see how this pattern can be incorporated into your standing posture.

1.   Use a firm straight-back chair. Stand behind it, and then turn around so your

back is against the back of the chair. Reach your hands behind you and grip the back of the chair. This will help you explore the balance center of the postural attitude while using the chair back as a support.

2. Now press your upper back, just between the shoulder blades, back and up. Allow as many muscles in your body to follow with this intention to retreat, and let your posture lean back so that your weight distributes to your heels.

3. Then, in preparation to let go of the chair, adjust the backward lean just enough that you feel you could stand without the support of the chair. When you are sure you can, let go of the chair and bring your hands in front of you. Bend your elbows and allow the palms to face outward.

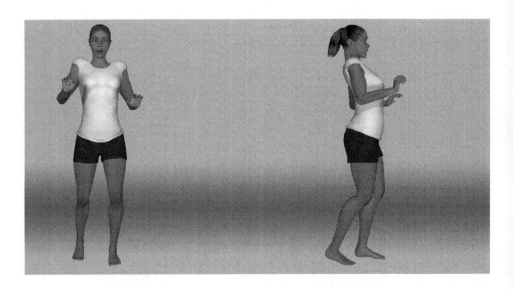

Walking in 2b

Let's explore what happens when we try to walk with this posture.

1. From the position acquired in step 3 of "Standing in 2b," try to take a few steps forward. If you remain true to the postural attitude of 2b, the only part of your body that wants to move forward is your eyes. So walking forward, in a sense, goes against the pattern's desires. Moving forward in this pattern requires doing so with as many muscles in your body contracting and pulling back. You will find your walk is slow, stiff, and tentative.

2. As you explore this posture in motion, try stepping backwards a few times or avoiding obstacles by stepping back and around them. A person moving through the world in 2b will often step back, regularly giving way to others. They may also prefer to hold objects like books or pillows between

themselves and others or stand behind objects like tables and podiums when addressing people. This is a way of coping with the posture's intention to retreat. Instinctively, the person in 2b retreats behind things or other people.

3. Once you have a sense of the posture when standing and walking, combine this exploration with the 2b breath pattern and facial expression.

4. Finish this work with at least one Step Out.

 ## Pause & Reflect

Take a few moments to reflect on what it was like to put the 2b pattern into action. Once we start moving around and doing activities in a pattern, we may temporarily be unable to control all elements of the pattern, and so mixes typically come into this initial stage of practice. In time, and with plenty of practice, feedback, and refining, you will be able to maintain a pure state of any pattern in motion and within activities. Always ask yourself if you are being true to all parts of the pattern, and run a mental checklist as you practice. Ask yourself, "Am I still doing the pure breath pattern, facial expression, and posture?"

Resist the temptation to "act" the emotion you believe you are displaying. Most often, this practice will lead to mixes, because our instinct in "acting out a word" is highly subjective and based on our own life experiences or what we have seen others do. Keeping in mind that you are practicing specific patterns of breathing and behavior will help you remain true to the pure patterns and eventually master them. Take a moment of self-reflection and ask yourself if some aspect of subjective play-acting or performing has come into your practice of the patterns. If so, consider ways you can refrain from this manner of practicing in the future. During Emotional Body workshops, you might hear an instructor call out, "No acting please. Just do the patterns and allow the emotions to emerge from the pattern work." This is our way of reminding people not to act the emotion, just to reproduce the patterns. The emotion will emerge in its pure state eventually.

Did you know...?

Severe or prolonged feelings of stress can decrease our learning abilities and contribute to poor memory, language processing, concentration, and problem-solving skills. One study showed that adults with high stress levels performed 50 percent worse on certain cognitive tests than adults with low stress. There are different kinds of stress, and some kinds of stress are beneficial, like challenging ourselves to accomplish new things or engaging in thrilling sports or amusement rides. The stress that is physically debilitating and destructive of our ability to learn and think clearly is the kind where three conditions exist: (1) the stressor is causing an aroused physiological state, like one of increased blood pressure and raised cortisol levels; (2) the stressor is an aversive stimulus, like something causing pain or bad feelings; (3) the individual on the receiving end of the stressor either is not aware of the stressor's affects or is not in control of it. For example, a person could be in a highly stressful job situation and either not be aware of how the situation was affecting them or not feel as if they can change the situation. In this case all three conditions for a physically debilitating and destructive stress level exist. In such situations, a person acquires a state of learned helplessness and loses the ability to change the situation without the intervention of others.[25]

Polarities Between the 2a and 2b Patterns

Let's explore what it is like to shift between one mouth-breathing pattern to the next and to experience shifts between polarities. To review from chapter 5, a represents one extreme and b represents the opposite.

a   b

a: The a-state represents an emotion that has the least amount of tension and a postural attitude that is open and approachable.

b: The b-state represents an emotion that either has the greatest degree of muscle tension or uses muscle movements to close the body off to others, making it unapproachable.

Minor changes of tension and directional movements can easily shift a person from an a-state to a b-state of expression, or vice versa.

25. John Medina, Brain Rules: 12 Principles for Surviving and Thriving at Work, Home, and School (Seattle, Pear Press, 2008), 173-176.

Shifting Between Polarities of 2a and 2b

Shifting between polarities of 2a and 2b is a bit more challenging than shifting between 1a and 1b. Since 2a utilizes deep abdominal breathing and 2b uses high chest breathing, this exercise requires the additional step of changing the type of breathing support. However, practicing this exercise can provide many personal benefits by helping you become much more aware of when and how your breathing shifts up into the high chest during certain expressive states. It can also bring attention to potential entanglements that are common between these two basic emotions. As you approach this exercise, take your time with these steps, as if practicing in slow motion, so you can sense throughout your body how the breath changes affect how you feel.

1. Select an object or a picture of someone and place it a few paces away from your chair. It should be at eye level when sitting in the chair.

2. While sitting, look at your chosen object and breathe in and out of your mouth using high-chest breathing. Add an occasional hold to your breath and exhale small amounts of air and then quickly inhale through the mouth again. Continue to build all elements of the 2b pattern, including postural attitude and facial expression. Allow it to grow slowly so that you can feel the intensity of the pattern increase as body tension builds. Take the intensity level as high as you feel comfortable doing while remaining in the chair.

3. Do you feel degrees of fear as you build this pattern? Varying levels of fear from low to high intensity can feel like moving through states of uneasiness, apprehension, anxiousness, disbelief, alarm, hysteria, and terror. Can you sense your feelings about the object or picture changing as you gradually build the intensity of this pattern?

4. Then, while continuing your mouth breathing, slow your breathing down gradually and remove the holds after the inhale. As you do this, reduce the muscle tension in the postural attitude and allow your eyes to become still, and then start to settle the eyes back into their sockets. With each breath, concentrate on bringing the breathing activation area down into the abdominal region and releasing upper chest activation.

5. Slowly invite all aspects of the 2a pattern to shift you away from the 2b pattern, bringing you step by step toward 2a. Can you sense your feelings about the object you are looking at changing as you move from 2b to 2a?

6. Check that you are releasing muscle tension in the feet, legs, arms, and hands as you gradually engage the full 2a pattern in the postural attitude, facial aspect, and breath. Can you feel degrees of sensuality forming as you explore this opposite direction of movement while relaxing your breathing

and muscle tonicity? As you move in this direction you might start to feel infatuation, captivation, obsession, coyness, inspiration, or admiration. How do you feel about the object now?

7. Explore going back and forth between 2a and 2b while you look at your object or picture. Can you also sense the mixed emotions present in the transition between the two extremes? The mixed emotions occur when you are moving from one polarity to the other. The elements of both patterns are still present, creating mixes, until you fully release one pattern and settle into the pure state on the other side.

8. Finish this exercise by going into the zero pattern and then completing a Step Out.

Did you know...?

We have an instant survival response to perceived danger. When we are fearful the brain sends a powerful hormone out to different areas of the body, depending on our immediate perception of potential survival for the situation. There are two modes of the fear response. We are either mobilized (active) or immobilized (passive). When we believe we have the opportunity to escape the situation, our body goes into mobilized fear and vasopressin (a hormone that increases our blood pressure) is immediately released centrally in our bodies, which stimulates mobility so we can easily shift between fight and flight. However, if we perceive that fight or flight is not an option, vasopressin is instead released systemically and the result is that we are immobilized (passive) with fear. This causes a massive vagal surge, resulting in a physiological shutdown and a severe decrease in blood pressure. The result is freezing, shutting down, feigning death, or losing consciousness.[26]

Shifting Between Polarities of 2a and 2b

Practicing exercises like Shifting Between Polarities not only helps you understand the many emotional mixes possible between 2a and 2b, but also provides you with practice for conscious self regulation of emotion. For example, if you are a habitual mouth breather and you want to physically adapt to a challenging situation for better emotional outcome, you can shift your emotional state from one pole to the next by gradually adjusting your breathing, posture, and facial

---

26. Stephen W. Porges, The Polyvagal Theory: Neurophysiological Foundations of Emotions, Attachment, Communication, Self-regulation (New York: Norton & Company, 2011), 181.

expression. The postural attitudes of 2a and 2b include reclining, which creates a state of receiving from others. The 2a attitude involves receiving pleasurable sensations, and 2b involves receiving unpleasant or alarming sensations. The words in this polarity exercise may help you see how shifting your receptive behavior between 2a and 2b can affect your reactions and relationships to others.

The words that follow represent some of these possible shifts. The direction of each emotional shift can move from right to left, or left to right on the list depending on your desire for the situation. For example, you could be in a situation where you start off feeling desirous of someone, and then this could develop into feelings of infatuation, but conditions could transform the situation to where you feel reluctance, and possibly even frigid. Likewise, if you were in a habit of being intimidated by someone, you could find that you might have the ability to then transform your feelings about them into being surprised or even mesmerized, and possibly even surrender to their personality rather than fear it. Explore this exercise as a potential new skill for shifting emotional states with slight muscular and breathing adjustments, and then consider how this might serve you in your real life.

The words under 2a and 2b are fairly high intensity levels of the pattern; therefore, one can assume there are even more words possible between the two polarities. This list of words simply suggests general degrees and how mixes occur in the middle.

2a	Mixed State	Mixed State	2b
Desirous	Infatuated	Reluctant	Frigid
Surrendered	Mesmerized	Surprised	Intimidated
Flirtatious	Enamored	Apprehensive	Shocked
Peaceful	Captivated	Dumbfounded	Spooked
Tranquil	Nonchalant	Disbelieving	Panicked
Sensual	Obsessive	Jealous	Stunned
Amorous	Coy	Distrusting	Jumpy
Receptive	Inspired	Frenetic	Alarmed

Summary
Learning and practicing the 2a and 2b patterns will help you become much more sensitive to subtle shifts in your emotions and expressive behavior. Exploring the 2b pattern in controlled, low intensity exercises can also raise your awareness to any habits you may have for high chest breathing, or maintaining chronic subtle levels of this stress inducing emotion.

Practice the exercises in this chapter until you no longer need to read about how to replicate all aspects of each pattern when sounding, sitting, standing, and walking. Once you have achieved this level, you will be ready to explore the exercises provided in the final chapter of this book.

The Nose-Mouth Breathing Patterns   7

Shortening Inhale & Elongating Exhale

The nose-mouth breathing patterns, labeled 3a and 3b, both have a relatively short inhale through the nose and a long exhale through the mouth. They may sound quite similar by this description; however, the two patterns vary greatly in their flow of air. The nose-mouth breathing patterns are also different from the others introduced so far in this book. All of the previous patterns—zero, 1a, 1b, 2a, and 2b—involve a smooth flow of air during the inhalation and exhalation. That is, although slight pauses or holds are applied between the in and out breaths, the actual flow of air during inspiration and expiration is uninterrupted. In contrast, the 3a and 3b patterns have various types of breaks in the airflow, distinguishing them substantially from other patterns introduced in this book.

Before these airflow distinctions are introduced, let's first establish ways to apply a long exhale and short inhale.

Utilizing a Long Exhale

Both the 3a and 3b patterns utilize a long exhale, exceeding the habitual exhale lengths in our resting breathing pattern. These longer exhales are often used in such daily activities as speaking, singing, sighing, and laughing. We may be unaware of our regular use of these longer exhales if they are occurring when our focus is on something else, like the source of our laughter or the content of our speech or song. During conscious application of this longer exhale, you may be more aware of the effort required to extend the exhalation. Since the extended exhale takes you beyond your habitual breathing cycle length, you may feel as if you are going to a below-empty state. To achieve the extended exhale, you will need to contract more of your abdominal muscles to push against the diaphragm in order to expel more air out of the lungs. Consider the effort it takes to blow up a balloon. To fill a balloon with air from your lungs, you utilize your abdominal muscles in the same way, by extending the exhalation and pushing out more air.

During your initial practice sessions on extending the exhalation, you may feel as though you are exerting a great deal of effort to elongate the expiration. You also may associate this excess effort with including more muscles in your body than necessary to achieve a longer exhale. Try to isolate muscle effort to the lower part of your thoracic region, and be aware of attempts to include muscular effort (like shoulder lifts or clavicle muscle activation) in your upper chest and shoulders. Pay attention to any muscle tension in the neck, jaw, shoulders, or upper back that may inhibit the loose muscle tone associated with these two patterns.

Extending the Exhalation
Let's practice extending the exhalation, without using excessive effort in other parts of the body.

1. While lying down on your back, begin the zero breath pattern, with the inhalation length equal to the exhalation length, being sure to utilize deep breathing with abdominal muscle engagement.

2. Gradually elongate the exhalation by adding one count to each exhalation. For example, if your zero breath pattern typically uses a 5-count for inhale and exhale, make your next exhale a 6-count, and then the next exhale after that a 7-count, and so on until you reach at least a 10-count, all while keeping your inhale at a 5-count.

3. While your exhale gradually elongates, try to draw the majority of your effort from the lower part of your thoracic region, keeping the focus on contractions in abdominal muscles. Check for any tension emerging in your neck, throat, jaw, shoulders, upper chest, or back. Watch for any throat clenching, an attempt to squeeze the air out using muscle efforts in the throat. To avoid this tension buildup, think about the inside of your throat widening and opening, like an open, relaxed channel for the air to escape through. Try to keep all these areas above the sternum relaxed and open as you gradually build the exhalation to its longest possible length without engaging excess tension.

4. Once you have achieved a long exhale length, practice this pattern, which consists of a shorter inhale and very long exhale, for a few breath cycles.

5. Then, return to your zero breath pattern to end the exercise. Take a Step Out if you feel as if any emotions emerged, and make sure that you have cleared back to zero before continuing your practice.

Did you know…?

An extended exhale can provide indirect natural stimulation of the vagus nerve, resulting in a calming effect as well as health benefits that include reduction of inflammation, a boost to your immune system, reduction of anxiety, heightening of your senses, and improvement of mental health.[1]

The vagus nerve is a long, wandering nerve that extends from your brain stem through your facial muscles, throat, and heart and then down into your stomach and intestines. The vagus nerve plays a major role in the mind-body connection by communicating your gut instincts back to the brain, and guiding you in many of your actions and feelings. Vagus nerve activity, known as your vagal tone, varies from person to person and can be measured by an electrocardiogram. A high vagal tone provides you with the ability to relax faster after a stressful situation and makes your body better at regulating blood glucose levels.

When you breathe in, your heart beats faster to increase oxygen flow throughout your body; meanwhile, your vagus nerve activation is suppressed. When you breathe out, your heart slows and your vagus nerve is activated. An elongated exhale provides your body with a longer period of vagus nerve activation and can raise your vagal tone, providing you with more health benefits.[2]

Medical practices use direct vagal nerve stimulation (using an electrical pulse) and recommend various indirect and natural methods for vagus nerve stimulation, including slow deep breathing, an extended exhale, and vocalizing the exhalation using an *h* before a vowel sound, like "Ha."[3] If you sing or play a wind instrument you are also naturally stimulating the vagus nerve, increasing vagal influence and creating a calming healthy practice for your body.[4]

As you progress with your practice of the 3a pattern, notice that these vagus nerve stimuli methods are inherent in that pattern.

Shortening the Inhalation
Shortening the inhalation may feel more challenging than extending the exhalation.

1. Stephen W. Porges, *The Polyvagal Theory: Neurophysiological Foundations of Emotions, Attachment, Communication, Self-regulation* (New York: Norton & Company, 2011), 253-254.

2. Ibid

3. "Natural Vagus Nerve Stimulation," Resilience Informed Therapy, accessed July 10, 2015, www.drarielleschwartz.com.

4. Stephen W. Porges, *The Polyvagal Theory: Neurophysiological Foundations of Emotions, Attachment, Communication, Self-regulation* (New York: Norton & Company, 2011), 253-254.

Throughout our day, we regularly utilize a short inhale when we speak, quickly inhaling air to sustain continued speech. We do this subconsciously and quickly, unaware of how often we inhale and how much of that inhale serves an extended period of speech. When practicing conscious breathing, we often place more stress on the act than we would when doing it subconsciously. This may be because people often associate a quick inhale through the nose with tension, as if tensing the muscles in the nose and throat would assist this quick inspiration (it actually achieves the opposite by decreasing the volume of intake). Let's practice quick inhales with the goal of acquiring as much tension-free application as possible.

1. While lying down on your back, begin the zero pattern, with the inhalation length equal to the exhalation length, being sure to utilize deep breathing with abdominal muscle engagement.

2. Gradually elongate the exhalation by adding one count to each exhalation until you have achieved the longest exhale possible without engaging excess tension in the areas above the sternum.

3. Now, gradually shorten your inhale, by decreasing the inhalation length by one count with each inhale, until you have achieved an inhale length as close to a 1-count as you can without engaging excess tension in the nose, throat, neck, shoulders, chest, or upper back.

4. In order to keep your nasal passage and throat open and relaxed, try abducting the muscles in your nasal passage and throat. Consider sending the nasolabial muscles, the ones on either side of your nose, back toward your ears. Imagine your entire throat widening, as if all the muscles inside your throat are extending out away from the midline of your body. Abducting these muscles may make you feel as if your ears are actually moving outward.

5. Practice this breathing pattern, with a short, quick inhale and a long exhale, for a few breath cycles. Watch for any excess tension emerging and try to keep the majority of your body—inside and out—relaxed and open, focusing your effort on the abdominal area.

6. Then, return to your zero pattern to end this exercise. Take a Step Out if you feel as if any emotions emerged with this practice session, and make sure that you have cleared back to zero before continuing.

Once you have spent some time practicing relaxed and open short inhales and elongated exhales, you will be ready to apply the various breaks in the airflow that distinguish the differences between patterns 3a and 3b. The 3a pattern breaks the exhalation into short choppy steps. This is called a step exhale.

Step Exhales

A *step exhale* is broken by little stops, or brief moments where no air is being exhaled, that are followed by bursts of air. This is often called a *step breath pattern*, because it looks like a stairway on a breath pattern diagram. It is also referred to as a *breathing saccade* or described as "breathing jerky" because of the rapid jumpy feeling the breath pattern evokes.

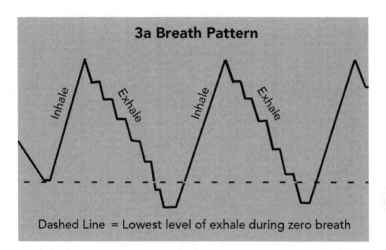

3a Breath Pattern

Dashed Line = Lowest level of exhale during zero breath

To get a sense of how this step pattern is achieved on an exhale, take a quick inhale through the nose, and then pinch your nose while you blow air out of your mouth with short bursts until you have exhaled all the air. This will help you see how your exhale efforts, including use of the abdominal and diaphragm muscles, accomplish these bursts of air on their own without inhalation through the nose or mouth during the breaks. Practice this a few times with your nose pinched on the exhalation, and then try it without pinching your nose, making sure no nose breathing is attempted during the exhalation out the mouth.

Now, let's apply the step exhales to the 3a breath pattern.

3a Breath Pattern

1. While lying down on your back with eyes open and gazing at the ceiling, begin the zero breath pattern, with the inhalation length equal to the exhalation length. Be sure to utilize deep breathing with abdominal muscle engagement.

2. Elongate the exhalation to its longest possible length without including excess tension in the areas above the sternum.

3. Shorten your inhale until you have achieved an inhale length as close to a 1-count as you can without involving excess tension in the nose, throat, neck, shoulders, chest, or upper back.

4. Now, try chopping up your exhale by adding very short stops, where the length of the stop is less than half a count. Your abdominal muscles will clench and push the air out in a little burst of air after each stop. The exhalation pattern might be described as "exhale-stop-burst, stop-burst, stop-burst, stop-burst, etc." until you have achieved an empty or below-empty feeling.

5. When you inhale, make it a short, quick, and open inhale through the nose. Then, go directly to the stepped exhale to empty or below empty. Make sure your nasal passage and throat are open and relaxed during the exhalation, and watch for any tension sneaking into the upper body and throat during the step exhales.

6. Practice this breathing pattern, with a short quick inhale and a long stepped exhale, for a few breath cycles. Make sure that you are not adding little inhales through the nose or mouth during the stepped exhale. The quick inhale through the nose happens only after a long stepped exhale.

7. Then, return to your zero breath pattern to end this exercise. Take a Step Out if you feel as if any emotions emerged with this practice session, and make sure that you have cleared back to zero before continuing your practice.

3a Facial Expression and Sound

Once you feel you have a sense of the stepped exhale out the mouth and the quick, light inhale, add the facial expression. The facial expression is quite similar to that of pattern 1a, except the mouth is open, allowing a bigger movement of the muscles of the face as they abduct back and up toward the ears.

1. While lying down on your back with eyes open, begin the zero pattern. Then, elongate the exhalation out the mouth with quick stops followed by bursts of air until you complete a long stepped exhalation.

2. When you inhale, make it a short, quick, and open inhale through the nose. Then, go directly to the exhalation with steps until you have fully expired all your air and need to inhale.

3. Now, encourage the muscles around the eyes and upper cheeks to abduct back toward the ears, and allow the muscles in the corners of the mouth to follow until you have a big open-mouth smile. Keep this facial expression throughout use of the pattern, making sure to maintain the facial expression when you inhale through the nose.

4. Then, apply sound to the exhaled bursts of air. Because of the stop-burst pattern of the exhalation, it will sound like "Ha, ha, ha, ha, ha" or "he, he, he, he, he," depending on the shape of your open mouth.

5.   Practice this breathing pattern with its facial expression and exhaled sound for a few breath cycles. Make sure that you are not adding little inhales through the nose or mouth during the stepped exhale. The quick inhale through the nose happens only after a long stepped exhale.

6.   Return to the zero pattern to end this exercise. Take a Step Out if you feel as if any emotions emerged with this practice session, and make sure that you have cleared back to zero before continuing your practice.

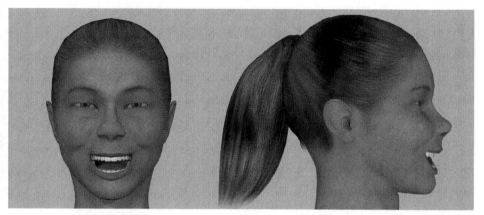

▌▌ Pause & Reflect

Write down any words or phrases that might describe what you felt as you practiced the 3a pattern. Did the stepped exhales give you a light bouncy feeling with this pattern? Did your application of facial expression and sound produce something that started sounding like laughter, even if it was not your habitual way of laughing? There are so many ways in which people laugh. Some have the open mouthed gaffaw, the roaring ho-ho-ho, or the throaty heh-heh-heh. Then there are those that laugh through the nose, snicker, or even have the silent laugh. Many times our habitual laughter patterns are learned behaviors from our family or friends, or they reflect the cultural norms for laughing in public.

If you did feel as if you were laughing, can you identify any emotions that this laughter evoked? Laughter is an action, not an emotion, and laughter can evoke many different feelings, depending on how we laugh. Some may laugh with sadness, sarcasm, seduction, fear, hysteria, tenderness, or joy. See if you can write down emotion words for how you felt during your practice of this pattern so you can become more clear about the feelings it can evoke. Remember, 3a is a pure pattern, with no mixes of other emotions or learned behaviors. Watch a very young baby's spontaneous laugh, and you will see this pattern in its purest form.

I was teaching the emotional effector patterns to a group of life coaches who took to the patterns like ducks to water. They jumped into the emotion pattern exploration without reservation and, since so much of their work is about using words to identifying the situations their clients are experiencing, the coaches quite easily found words to describe their own experiences with the patterns. After their first exploration of the 3a pattern, the group had these words to share about the emotions evoked by it. Can you see a common theme in the feelings evoked by the 3a pattern?

Words Shared by Life Coaches After Initial Exploration of 3a

Delightful	*Goofy*	*Laughter*
Friendly	*Happy*	*Mirth*
Funny	*Joyous*	*Ridiculous*
Giddy	*Jubilant*	*Silly*

Did you know...?

Our brains are hardwired for laughter, and when we experience a joyous hearty laugh we increase the "feel good" organic chemical levels in our bodies that not only make us feel better but attract others to us as well. Neural circuits for laughter exist in ancient regions of the brain, and during early stages of evolution, our brains developed the capacity for laughter even before the ability to support speech. When we laugh, dopamine reward circuits in our brains light up,[5] making us feel good about ourselves and motivating us to plan, achieve, learn, and resist destructive impulses.[6]

Recent studies of emotions also confirm that laughter is indeed infectious, promoting attraction and the desire to play. Such scientific observations will help us better understand why laughing makes us feel good, is infectious, and attracts others to us.[7]

The importance of promoting healthy humor and hearty laughter has become a mission for many organizations. The Association for Applied and Therapeutic Humor (AATH) is an international nonprofit organization that provides education, evidence-based resources, and a supportive community .

5. Jaak Panksepp, "Beyond a Joke: From Animal Laughter to Human Joy?" *Science*, New Series 308 (April, 2005): 5718.

6. Emily Deans M.D., "Dopamine Primer: How Dopamine Makes Us Human." *Psychology Today* (May 13, 2011).

7. Jaak Panksepp, "Beyond a Joke: From Animal Laughter to Human Joy?" Science, New Series 308 (April, 2005): 5718.

to promote the practice of healthy humor.[8] The International Society for Humor Studies (ISHS) is a scholarly and professional organization dedicated to the advancement of humor research. Many of their members are university and college professors who produce an annual scholarly journal and conference where the role of humor is examined in business, entertainment, and health care practices.[9] In 1976, the United States National Humor Month was founded. It is devoted to educating the public on how good-hearted humor and laughter can improve well-being, boost morale, increase communication skills, and enrich quality of life. The month was well chosen, with April 1st, April Fools' Day, kicking off 30 days of humor.[10]

Consider looking into some of these organizations to enhance your study of emotions and learn more about recommended applications of healthy humor.

Mixes Occurring on High Levels of 3a

On higher levels of this pattern, a mouth inhale might start to mix in. This is particularly likely once the stepped exhale has elongated enough that a person might automatically open the mouth on the inhalation to quickly gain as much air as possible before going on to the exhalation. Mouth inhalation is a natural occurrence for most people when they are expressing high levels of 3a. Just be aware of when this occurs and see how high you can bring the pattern before a mouth inhalation begins to sneak in.

Another common mix might creep into this pattern when the muscles in the forehead start to elevate, pulling the eyebrows up. Soon, other facial muscles might elevate along with the eyebrows, causing the pattern to mix with qualities of sadness or surprise. The sadness can mix in because of the abdominal efforts required to continue supporting this long stepped exhale; it can feel either fatiguing or painful to continue the laughter. How often have you seen someone doubled over with laughter, holding their belly, looking as if they are in pain? As long as you see them smiling, you know that they are still in a state of joy, but you might instinctively recognize their expression is something not purely joyful. When practicing the 3a pattern, to keep the facial expression pure, remember to abduct the facial muscles, with everything pulling back toward the ears. Watch for any impulse to elevate the muscles, which could cause a mix.

I was offering an emotional effector pattern workshop for YMCA LiveStrong participants who were cancer survivors learning strategies for releasing

8. www.aath.org, The Association for Applied and Therapeutic Humor (AATH) is a non-profit, member driven, international community of humor and laughter professionals and enthusiasts.

9. www.humorstudies.org, The International Society for Humor Studies (ISHS) publishes the quarterly journal, Humor: International Journal of Humor Research, the ISHS newsletter, and holds an annual international conference.

10. www.humormonth.com, National Humor Month was founded by comedian and best-selling author Larry Wilde, Director of The Carmel Institute of Humor. Steve Wilson, founder of the World Laughter Tour, is the Director of National Humor Month.

stress and cancer-related fatigue as well as reclaiming vibrant, active lives. I introduced the group to patterns 1a, 2a, and lastly 3a. Once they experienced the 3a pattern they acknowledged feeling an incredible purging effect with this pattern, as if the long stepped exhale was helping them shake out and then release their stress. As we discussed the pattern further, they also noted that during the long exhalation, it felt as if they were squeezing out the old air in their lungs, like the way we wring out a wet towel, and making room for new, rich, oxygenated air. They found the pattern to be delightfully exhausting, rejuvenating, and uplifting, whereas 1a and 2a felt more calming.

In another situation, I was teaching college students the basic emotion patterns, and when they had the opportunity to explore pattern 3b, they found that although the long seeping exhale was exhausting to maintain, it provided them with the opportunity to release a remarkable amount of stress they were carrying around from day to day in college. They also mentioned feeling briefly tired and emotionally numb after practicing 3b, but the numbness was actually a welcome change from the anxiety and the constant driving intensity to perform at their best. They were quite surprised by the releasing and clearing effect that 3b had on them.

The purging and releasing quality inherent in the extended exhale is certainly something to consider when practicing 3a and 3b.

Achieving a Seeping Exhale

The 3b exhale is also very long, but it is more like a seeping or slowly deflating exhale, with a lower volume of air being expelled at one time than in the 3a exhale. This means that the 3b exhale can go even longer than the 3a exhale. Let's try a few exercises to help you see the variation in expelled air volume for these different types of exhales.

Use a stopwatch, like those found on a cell phone or computer, to time the lengths of the exhale types listed below. Start the stopwatch as soon as you start the exhalation, and stop the timer when you have reached a point where you no longer have enough air to support vocalization.

Before each exhale, take a short, quick inhale through the nose, and then go directly to a voiced exhale out the mouth, but with these variations for each new exhale:

1. Exhale the sound "ha" on stepped exhales.

2. Exhale a sustained "ssss," like a snake or hole-in-the-tire sound, on a smooth exhale.

3. Exhale a sustained "ah," as if softly singing one note, on a smooth exhale.

How did the times vary on these exhales? Which one was longer, and which was shorter for you? You may have found that the "ssss" exhale was the longest. That is because you have the front of the mouth working as a tight valve, only allowing a small amount of air to flow out of the mouth in a controlled exhale. You may have found that the stepped "ha" exhale was the shortest, because there is the possibility of exhaling big bursts of air in a "ha" sound, expelling more volume than the "ssss" with each step. The sustained "ah" exhale might have landed right in the middle in the exhalation times, depending on how much air volume you were giving your "ah" sound.

As you approach the next exercise for building the 3b breath pattern, try to find an elongated exhale that is closer in expiration volume to the amount expelled in the "ssss" exhale, but without closing your mouth to form an *s* and instead forming an "ah" or "uh" sound as you exhale. This will help you more closely acquire a seeping or deflating exhale.

3b Breath Pattern

The 3a and 3b patterns are mirror opposites of each other. Both use a combination of nose inhale and mouth exhale; however, the opposition occurs in the steps that break up the airflow in part of the breath pattern. In the 3a pattern, the steps occur on the exhalation, but in the 3b pattern, the steps occur on the inhalation. Let's explore this pattern and see how it feels.

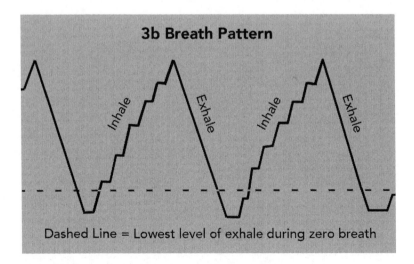

1. While lying down on your back with eyes open, begin a the zero breath pattern, with the inhalation length equal to the exhalation length. Be sure to utilize deep breathing with abdominal muscle engagement.

2. Elongate the exhalation to the longest possible length without engaging excess tension in the areas above the sternum. Keep the exhalation long and smooth until you feel as if you have expired all that you can.

3. Shorten your inhale until you have achieved an inhale length of about a 3-count.

4. Now try breaking up the airflow of your inhale by adding very short, fast sniffs that are controlled by the abdomen muscles. Try not to constrict your nasal passage as a means to accomplish the sniffs. Although some constriction will eventually occur when the facial expression is added, recognize that the majority of the effort in creating the sniffs is coming from the abdominal muscles clenching and pulling down the diaphragm muscle. It might be helpful to think of the sniffs as little tremors going into the nose or to visualize how a dog quickly sniffs around the floor, trying to catch the scent of something. This quick sniffing action is similar to that of the 3b inhalation.

5. Once you have accomplished a few quick sniffs in through the nose, go immediately to the long, smooth, seeping exhale out of the mouth. Although there are multiple sniffs on the inhalation, they are quite short and quick, so the exhalation is still much longer than the inhalation. Make sure your nasal passage and throat are open and relaxed during the exhalation; watch for any tension creeping into the upper body and throat during the step inhales.

6. Add sound to the exhalation by holding onto a vowel sound like "uh" or "ah," depending on the shape of your mouth. Try to vocalize this vowel sound, in a low volume, all the way through the exhalation until you don't have enough air to support vocalization. This will help you hear the smooth flow of air in your exhale and how it's different from the short, choppy inhalation as well as to recognize when your air support starts to weaken.

7. Practice this breathing pattern, with its few sniffed inhales, and one long, vocalized, smooth, seeping exhale, for a few breath cycles. Consider the exhalation to be like a full body deflation, where the air, along with its associated sound, is seeping out of the body, rather than being blown out forcefully. Imagine the sniffed inhales are quick grabs of air through the nose to refill before starting the long, deflating exhale.

8. Then, return to the zero pattern to end this exercise. Take a Step Out if you feel as if any emotions emerged with this practice session, and make sure that you have cleared back to zero before continuing your practice.

 ## Pause & Reflect

Did any feelings or emotions emerge with your practice of the 3b breath pattern? Did the application of a voiced deflating exhale sound anything like a sigh, moan, or groan? Take a few moments to write down any emotion words that might have emerged during your practice of the 3b breath pattern and compare them to the words you identified with the 3a pattern. Can you now see how adding these airflow distinctions between the two nose-mouth breathing patterns can elicit completely different feelings or expressions?

When I teach the 3b pattern I often encourage people to voice the exhalation quite early in the learning process because the seeping exhale can go quite long, and many people don't take it to its fullest length. Once they start to voice the exhalation, I can get a sense of how long they are really taking the exhalation, and I encourage them to go further while also expelling less air at a time. At the same time, workshop participants recognize how the vibrations caused by vocalizing help them connect more clearly to recognizable emotions. At first, I can sense that a room full of people learning the pattern for the first time are reluctant to vocalize this pattern, but as I encourage them to let it out through a voiced exhale, the vocal volume increases, the exhalations get longer, and soon I see and hear emotional inductions in the pattern throughout the space. Moans, sighs, wails, and groans fill the room like an old church organ warming up, clearing its pipes, and purging old air.

Exploring Facial Muscle Movements for the 3b Pattern

The 3b pattern engages muscles in the forehead that elevate while also adducting, forming a pinch in the forehead. Let's practice controlling these muscles. There are a couple different methods that help people find this area of muscle activation. One approach may work better for you than another.

Method One

1. Place a finger on the bridge of your nose, right where your eyes meet your nose. Then, with the tip of the finger pointing toward your forehead, slide that finger up your forehead so it is about an inch above the bridge of your nose.

2. Keeping your finger there, and using the muscles in your forehead, try to pinch that finger by adducting the muscles in your forehead, moving them inward toward the midline of your body. You will feel a pulling all around the upper part of your eyes and forehead as you accomplish this.

3. While maintaining the finger pinch with the adducting muscles, try to use those muscles to elevate the pinched finger a little bit so that you feel your finger rise up the forehead. If you can't achieve this lift using the adducting muscles, simply slide your finger up and down your forehead while working to keep the forehead muscles pinching the finger.

4. Once you have found a way to pinch the finger while also elevating it, remove the finger from your forehead while maintaining the elevated muscle pinch. See if you can duplicate this without using the finger as a guide.

5. Then, release the forehead pinch and complete the exercise by gently massaging your forehead muscles to release. Perhaps also try the 1a eye muscle abduction here, by moving the muscles on the outsides of your eyes back toward your ears. This works as an opposite muscle action to release the extreme tensions required of the forehead pinch.

Method Two

1. Look in the mirror, so you can see if what you believe you are doing is actually occurring with your facial muscles.

2. While looking in the mirror, raise your eyebrows. While keeping them raised, press them together so that they look like they are trying to meet in the upper part of your forehead. This will cause a strong pinching feeling in your forehead and around your eyes and nose.

3. Then, release the forehead pinch and complete the exercise by gently massaging your forehead muscles to release and/or abducting your eye muscles back toward your ears.

Method Three

1. While looking in the mirror, bring your eyebrows together around the bridge of your nose. It will look like you are furrowing your brow. While keeping them together, lift them up so that they look like they are trying to meet in the upper part of your forehead. This will cause a strong pinching feeling in your forehead and around your eyes and nose.

2. Then, release the pinch and complete the exercise by gently massaging your forehead muscles to release and/or abducting your eye muscles back toward your ears.

Any of these three methods will produce the same result, a facial expression in which your eyebrows are knitted, or coming toward each other in the upper area of your forehead, creating what some might call a worried look. The goal here is to figure out the pathway, or muscle movement order, that works best for you to achieve this resulting expression. The forehead pinch will feel as if many of the muscles in your forehead, eyes, and nasal passages are all pinching up and together. Prolonged use of this forehead pinch could cause a headache, and might be difficult to release. So, as you continue practicing the 3b pattern, be sure to fully release all aspects of the pattern regularly, including this particular area of the forehead. Engage a muscle movement that takes you in the opposite direction, like the 1a eye muscle abduction, to help you fully release the 3b pattern. A good face massage and stretching of your facial muscles will help as well.

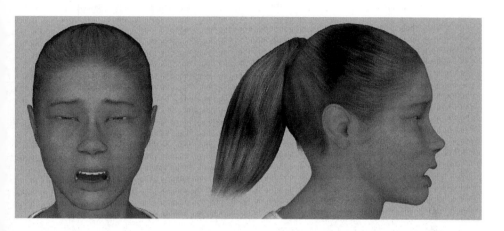

The 3b Breath Pattern with Facial Expression

1. While lying down on your back with eyes open, begin the zero breath.

2. Elongate the exhalation to its longest possible length without engaging excess tension in the areas above the sternum. Keep the exhalation long and smooth until you feel as if you expired all that you can.

3. Shorten your inhale until you have achieved an inhale length of about a 3-count, and inhale using very short, fast sniffs that are controlled by the abdomen muscles.

4. Once you have accomplished a few quick sniffs in through the nose, go immediately to the long, smooth exhale out the mouth, feeling as if you are deflating your body and letting go of any possible tension.

5. Now, let's add the facial expression. Create an upper forehead pinch with your muscles, and once accomplished, keep it there for the remainder of the pattern practice.

6. Allow the eyes to look down toward your feet.

7. As you exhale out the mouth, pull the corners of your mouth down, as if there were little hooks pulling down on the corners of your mouth. While the corners pull down, the lower lip might push up a bit, forming a frown.

8. When the exhalation elongates to the point of feeling as if you have expelled all the air you can with a seeping, sigh-like exhale, try using your abdominal muscles to push out more air to elongate the exhalation further. This may sound like a "hu, hu, hu" at the very end of the exhalation. Eventually you may feel as if the abdominal muscles start to do this on their own, like an abdominal spasm causing saccadic, "jerky" exhalations. This is a natural evolution of the pattern as it reaches a level of induction.

9. Once the open-mouth frown is engaged, you will feel as if your face is being pulled in two different directions. The forehead is pinching together and up, and the mouth corners are pulling down.

10. Add a vocalized exhale by holding onto a vowel sound like "uh" or "ah." A pouting mouth may eventually appear, as the mouth muscles attempt to adduct, similar to the forehead muscle action, creating a puckering pout when you attempt to vocalize.

11. Practice this facial expression with the 3b breathing pattern, which is a few sniffed inhales and one long smooth exhale.

12. Then, return to the zero breath pattern to end this exercise. Take at least one Step Out and make sure that you have cleared back to zero before continuing your practice.

▌▌ Pause & Reflect

Take a few moments to reflect on how this pattern made you feel. The facial expression involved can evoke some very strong emotions that are difficult to clear. If this was your experience, what emotions emerged? Write down a few words or phrases to describe how you felt during any part of the exercise. Is this pattern familiar to you? Are there aspects of this pattern that you would prefer not to feel or express around others? If so, consider which of its physical aspects support the desire for seclusion or privacy. Then, take a good long break away from the practice of this pattern. Perhaps conduct another Step Out, take a long walk, or engage in another activity that will require you to express yourself in a different way.

When I was a young girl my mother used to place a finger on my forehead and gently wipe it back and forth, softly clucking to me, "You might want to release that pinched brow more. It will age you quickly." At the time, I was not quite sure what to do with that information, and certainly did not know how to release the forehead pinch. Her voice echoed in my mind many years later when I was a college professor taking my first Alba Emoting workshop. As soon as the 3b breath pattern and facial expression was coached, I found myself fully inducted in the emotion and sobbing away. As an actor and teacher of acting, I was thrilled to find that it was so easy to access this emotion so fully and with no personal or imaginary circumstances leading me there. I had nothing to cry about, but by simply applying the breath and face of this pattern, I felt truly sad.

As the other patterns were introduced, I soon learned from our instructor that I had the knitted brow tension entangled in most of the other patterns. I could not express anger, fear, happiness, or tenderness without the accompanying mark of sadness in my face, right up on my brow. I was surprised by this personal discovery and thought, "I'm not a sad person! People always say that I am so positive and happy. How can this be?"

As I learned more about the emotional effector patterns and basic emotion theory, I became aware of the many levels of emotion inherent in 3b and that my forehead entanglement did not necessarily mean that I was a sad person or that I came off to others as sad. I learned I was most likely carrying over the knitted brow into my way of expressing sympathy, empathy, caring, concentration, eagerness, and yearning. The knitted brow would come into my expressions of anger and fear because I was upset when I was mad or scared, and my entangled brow was an interpretation of how I felt about the situation. Unfortunately, I had used that knitted brow so much it became an expression habit, or entanglement.

Although we have an expansive emotional vocabulary to express these varying levels of emotional distinctions, our body's emotional vocabulary is limited to the basic emotions, like the ones covered in this book. When certain muscle triggers, like the knitted brow, are activated, it sends a signal of just one basic emotion (3b) to the brain, and with it comes all the chemical and energy shifts associated with that one emotion.

Once I trained more in the patterns, cleared my entanglements, and became a teacher of emotional effector patterns, I could often see this same habitual pattern in many others, and I would gently bring it to their attention and help them learn how to clear it as well.

Did you know...?

Chronic, or prolonged, states of negative emotions like sadness can compromise your immune system and reduce your body's ability to fight infections and heal wounds.[11] It can also aggravate skin conditions like psoriasis, eczema, hives, and acne. Loneliness, trauma, and anger can release higher levels of stress hormones like adrenaline and cortisol. If you are unable to shift from these high stress emotional states to more calming and relaxing emotions, the high levels of cortisol and adrenaline will eventually deplete the immune system and leave you more vulnerable to autoimmune diseases like arthritis or multiple sclerosis.[12] Chronic sadness can also eventually lead to depression, which is characterized by two symptom categories: emotional (apathy and sadness) and cognitive (deficits in memory and impaired brain plasticity).[13]

Expressing and purging our feelings of sadness, mourning, loss, and loneliness is an important part of being human, and there will be plenty of times in our lives when we need to give these emotions the attention they deserve. However, it is just as important for us to recognize when these emotions no longer serve us well. It is vital to our health and well-being to learn how to shift away from and fully release these high stress emotions.

Incorporating the Postural Attitudes

Once you have practiced the breathing patterns and facial aspects of 3a and 3b, you can experiment with the postural attitudes for each pattern. Since these become more complex as a person stands, walks, and then engages in activities, it is wise to begin their study in a sitting position and eventually move to standing and walking.

The following exercises will take you through gradual developments of the postural attitudes for 3a and 3b.

Preparing for the 3a Postural Attitude

The 3a pattern has a postural attitude that is floppy and loose, and does not have a specific pattern of movement or direction, unlike the other patterns. One of the most challenging aspects of this pattern for most people is reaching a level of relaxation and looseness that allows the muscles to truly let go of tension and flop. In order to help you acquire this physical attitude, let's try a short exercise as preparation.

1. Sit in the middle of a chair, so that your feet touch the floor and you have plenty of room between your back and the chair back.

2. Lift an arm up and out away from your body, no higher than shoulder height.

11. S. Cohen, et al., "Emotional Style and Susceptibility to the Common Cold" Psychosomatic Medicine 65 (July-August 2003): 652-7.

12. J. Marchant, "Immunology: The Pursuit of Happiness" Nature 503, 27 (November 2013): 458-60.

13. Marta Gómez-Galán, Dimitri De Bundel, Ann Van Eeckhaut, Ilse Smolders, Maria Lindskog, "Dysfunctional Astrocytic Regulation of Glutamate Transmission in a Rat Model of Depression," Molecular Psychiatry 18, 5 (May 2013) 582-94."

Then, let it drop down to your side. Did you feel parts of your body wanting to drop with the arm? You may have felt the instinct for your head, shoulder, and upper back to drop a little in that direction along with the arm. Repeat the arm raising and dropping again, and this time, see if you can encourage your head, shoulder, and upper back to flow along with the arm, as if the arm drop is causing a chain reaction in other nearby muscles. Repeat the same action on the other side.

3. Now, let's try a similar action with your legs. Pick your foot up to almost knee level off the floor and then let it drop back down. Don't stomp the foot, but instead let it loosely drop once your upper leg muscles release the tension it took to keep it raised. Encourage the rest of your body to move with the drop. You may feel your torso and head move forward in the direction of the foot drop. You may feel the arm on that side moving with the drop as well. Repeat the same action with the other foot, allowing the other side of the body to drop and flop.

4. Consider how you might lift your upper torso toward the ceiling, which will cause your back to arch, arms to swing back, and your head to tilt backward. Try lifting the torso up in this way and then drop back down, with arms flopping openly at your sides and head back. You might feel your back touch the back of the chair as you swing back. Try this torso lift-and-drop action a few times to get a sense of how it affects your entire body.

5. Let's see what happens when we combine some of these actions. Lift a leg and an arm on one side of the body, and drop and flop that side. Repeat on the other side as well. Try a diagonal action by lifting the right leg and left arm and dropping. Explore the other diagonal option as well. You may now start to feel that the entire body wants to drop in this loose, floppy way each time you lift a foot or hand.

6. Finally, while remaining seated in the chair, try lifting both feet and hands up and out, away from the body slightly, and then letting all four drop at the same time. Try it again and, this time, add the lifting of the torso as well. You will probably feel that your head and upper torso tilt back slightly as you lift all four and then tilt forward slightly as you drop all four. Essentially, you just created a full body flop while sitting.

7. Acquiring this full body flop may take big, broad actions. Once you feel the action is coordinated and affecting the entire body, try reducing its intensity a little. Get a sense of how this flop could be initiated by an inner impulse to be loose and relaxed, allowing the whole body to freely flop and gesture in any direction.

8. Let's see how this exercise applies to the sitting postural attitude of pattern 3a.

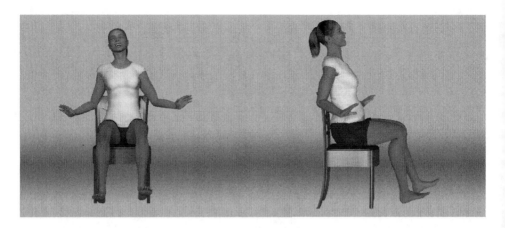

Sitting in 3a

1. While sitting in a chair, start in the zero sitting position and then begin the 3a breath pattern. That is, inhale through the nose in one quick and open inhale, and then go directly to a stepped exhale out the mouth with the stop-burst, stop-burst pattern. Add sound to the exhalation in the form of a ha-ha-ha. Be sure to use deep breathing throughout this pattern, engaging the abdominal muscles to create the bursts of air on the exhalation.

2. Add the 3a facial expression by forming a big smile on your face, starting with the muscles around your eyes abducting toward your ears. Then, encourage the cheek muscles and corners of your open mouth to pull up and back, forming a big smile that you keep throughout the pattern.

3. Then, invite the entire body to become loose and floppy such that various parts of the body may lift on the quick inhale through the nose and then drop with the first exhale burst. The whole body will lean in the direction of that initial flop while the step exhales are being emitted. Then, with the next inhale through the nose, the body will lift slightly in another direction and then drop in that new direction with the first exhale burst.

4. Explore this full pattern with the postural attitude. Eventually, allow the body to flop in various directions, including left, right, forward, and backward. Try not to plan which direction you will flop in next, and see if the movements can become impulsive, unpredictable, and lacking a sense of control or tension. Be sure to maintain the full smile throughout and check that your inhalation comes in through the nose.

5. Finish this exercise by returning to the zero pattern and then eventually completing a Step Out.

Pause & Reflect

Take a few moments to write about what it was like to practice the 3a pattern with its loose and floppy postural attitude. Could you feel the sense of a full-bodied laugh forming as you added each step of the pattern? Were you able to achieve a loose muscle tone throughout your whole body, or could you feel certain areas that had more tension than others? Muscle tension anywhere in the body can block embodiment of this pattern and full connection with the emotions it evokes. Don't worry if you were not able to achieve a loose and floppy body the first time you tried this. It may take many practice sessions to release areas of muscle tension. Simply raise your awareness of where the tension is and, as you continue your practice, try to release those areas a little at a time.

As you vocalize 3a, play with pitch and vocal tone and listen to the many versions of a laugh that is possible simply by playing with sound. Which laugh felt the most freeing, fun, and joyful to you?

I was working as an assistant teacher for a 9-day intensive workshop full of professional actors. The oldest participant was a 72-year-old professional actor with a strong, Clint Eastwood-style presence. His face had chiseled hard lines revealing a lifetime roadmap of expression, and he stood tall and strong but had a rigid posture full of muscular tension. I recall my own private, yet immediate, interpretation of his face and posture as angry, frustrated, and impatient. During our initial introductions, he shared that many people say he is intimidating and comes across as angry. He was mystified by these interpretations and wanted to see if he could learn more about his emotions both for himself and for his acting work.

As the workshop commenced, he struggled with the exercises, pushed hard, and tried to force the emotions to emerge. He frequently expressed frustration with not being given the emotion words in advance, disliking the discovery-oriented process of doing patterns and waiting for an induction. He wanted results and immediate application to his acting work. By the third day, he told our instructor that he was quitting the workshop, and it wasn't working for him. She gently coaxed him to give it a couple more days and offered some advice on how to let go of the need for results, trust the patterns, and enjoy the exploration process. She asked him to treat the next couple days as a short vacation of personal discovery.

The next couple days revealed remarkable changes. He was more relaxed and open to the exercises, and as a result his rigid posture slowly melted away as he welcomed the postural attitudes of the a-patterns. His face transformed before our very eyes as he practiced the facial expressions of 1a, 2a, and 3a. When we engaged in an exercise where the 3a pattern was shared across from a seated partner, his tall frame became so loose and floppy in the chair that he looked like a buoyant happy marionette, filling the room with joyous, spirited laughter.

The next day, during our morning check-in with the group, he shared a story of going to an audition for a TV commercial the night before and how he was supposed to play an adoring and happy grandfather in a tender moment. He had not played such a soft and nurturing role before and decided to use the a-patterns as his preparation before the audition. Afterward, the director remarked on how his acting was so genuine, warm, and friendly. He was cast on the spot. As he concluded his story, he shared that he now felt personally transformed and able to see how much tension and anger he had been unknowingly expressing all these years.

He completed the entire workshop and also offered a personal testimonial on the benefits of the technique for personal transformation as well as professional application. We all noticed that his face and posture had dramatically transformed in just nine days. The angry, impatient, frustrated man who had arrived nine days before, exited friendly, patient, and warm.

Managing the Desire for a Stimulus or Sharing

While practicing the 3a pattern, you may feel as if the laughter it expresses feels forced and unnatural. This is a common feeling, particularly when practicing the pattern alone. Many people are often moved to laughter after witnessing or thinking about something funny. However, our laughter can come from the simple desire to have fun and be joyous. This kind of laughter may actually produce a more pure state of joy, without any other emotions mixing in, as opposed to the kind brought on by external stimuli. For example, if we laugh at something like a funny event or joke, then our laughter expresses our interpretation of how we feel about the outcome of these events. The punch line of the joke may elicit surprise, disgust, or sarcasm, which would then mix aspects of 2b (fear), 1b (anger), and 3b (sadness) into the laugh. If our humor is derived from the unfortunate mishaps of another, then our laughter could be mixing in sympathy, ridicule, or pity (which have elements of 3b and 1b in them). Pure 3a has none of the other emotions mixed in.

Remember that laughter is an action, not an emotion, and that the act of laughing can have many different feelings associated with it. Pay close attention to your application of all three parts of the 3a pattern (breath, face, posture) and see if you can sense elements of any other patterns mixing in during your practice.

Laughter that emerges without a recognizable external stimulus or funny thought takes getting used to, but, with practice, this will become more acceptable to you. It may also be quite freeing to experience as it provides you with the opportunity to feel and express the emotion in its purest form.

Pure playful laughter can attract others and can be socially rewarding.[14] Laughter is also contagious and has a desire to be shared with others. Yet laughter that has mixes of 1b (anger) or 3b (sadness) patterns in it can have a menacing, vindictive, pitying, or demeaning quality to it and might repel those around you. Laughter that has 2b (fear) mixed in can look and sound hysterical, suspicious, and tense, causing you to look unstable or untrustworthy.

With all this in mind, you may feel that practicing 3a is challenging at first because of the need for a stimulus as well as the desire to share it with others. If this is true for you during your initial practice of this pattern, you may find you subconsciously start to modify the pattern in an attempt to make it feel or sound more like your own habitual laughter, or you might try to use imaginary stimuli as you begin the pattern in hopes of evoking an induction. You might also find that you attempt to push the pattern more forcefully in hopes of achieving a better result. All of these examples could end up mixing in other emotions.

As you practice the 3a pattern keep these guidelines in mind and use them as checkpoints during your practice:

- Trust the pattern and its ability to eventually evoke a pure emotion.

- Conduct regular checks during your practice, ensuring that you are actually applying all parts (breath, face, posture) of the 3a pattern as described in this book.

- Watch for any areas of muscle tension or attempts to push the pattern, and try to release muscle tension with each exhale. Common culprits of tension areas are the shoulders, neck, inside of the throat, lower back, pelvis, and upper legs.

- Don't rely on imaginative stimuli, like funny thoughts or images, to evoke the emotion.

- Don't think of this pattern as "Doing Laughter," but consider the goal to "Become the Laughter."

If you are practicing these patterns alone, you may want to eventually find someone else or, better yet, a group of people you can practice 3a with. This will allow you to

---

14. Jaak Panksepp, "Beyond a Joke: From Animal Laughter to Human Joy?" Science, New Series, 308 (April, 2005): 5718.

see how the pattern evolves as it is shared and expressed with others. However, keep the checklist above in mind and in practice as you share the pattern with others.

Every time I introduce the 3a pattern to a group, I look forward to the moment when the whole group catches on to the pattern, like a surfer catching a great wave. If I have teaching assistants working with me, I can see their anticipation of this moment as well, as their eyes search the room for signs of that first induction, which often acts like a surge flipping the entire room up and into a specific direction. It usually happens right at the time that I instruct the group to engage the voiced "ha" and add the big smiling facial expression. One person feels the induction and soon a systematic "ha, ha, ha" becomes peels of laughter. Since laughter is infectious, many others hear the familiar sound, and they find their pattern work soon becomes a laugh as well. Then, the room starts to roar as individuals catch the laughter wave and the room looks like a tumultuous sea of flopping, roaring laughter. The waves fluctuate up and down in various styles of expression from guffawing to giggling, and chuckling to roaring.

There are always a couple people in a group who struggle with their first few explorations of the pattern. Residual body tensions are often the culprit, and in these cases I see them stiffly applying the pattern, clearly struggling with tension in the shoulders, neck, and arms. As the room fills with laughter, I also see the struggling ones look around, wondering what they are missing while adding even more tension and frustration to their attempts to induct like everyone else. A room full of laughing people can cause those who are not laughing to feel isolated, frustrated, and intimidated. I softly side coach them to let go of tension, trust the pattern, and try not to be intimidated by how others are reacting. But it is not easy for them at this point, because they already feel as if they are missing something important, and those feelings start to block their ability to induce even more. In time, those individuals do find a way to connect with the pattern, often practicing it on their own or in a private session with an instructor, paying attention to residual tension areas before returning to the group environment.

In both cases, it is important to recognize how the infectious nature of laughter can work for induction of the 3a emotions, or against it.

Did you know…?

Laughter Yoga (Hasyayoga) is another form of "laughing for no reason." It emerged in the mid-1990s after Dr. Madan Kataria, a family physician from Mumbai, India, learned about the many health benefits of pure, joyous laughter. He formed the first Laughter Club devoted to teaching people to laugh regularly, and for no reason, as a means for promoting better health, happiness, and world peace.[15] At first, he used jokes and funny movies as ways to prompt the laughter but quickly realized that this did not produce a pure, joyous laugh due to individual interpretations of the subjective stimuli. So his wife, a yoga teacher, suggested physical methods for the laughter stimuli and developed a series of exercises for the clubs, which soon were called Laughter Yoga. The Laughter Yoga practice is based on deep breathing, a childlike playfulness, and physical exercises that help participants open up their bodies for loose and playful expressions, like open mouths, out-stretched arms, and heads leaning back with laughter (similar to the 3a postural attitude). The exercises also encourage increased energy and playfulness while reducing inhibitions and shyness.

There are hundreds of Laughter Clubs all over the world, including events sponsored by the World Laughter Tour (www.worldlaughtertour.com), which provide practical techniques to bring the benefits of laughter to any environment, without jokes or comedy. Their motto is "Think Globally, Laugh Locally."[16]

Since the emotions evoked by the 3a pattern want to be shared with others, you may benefit from attending a Laughter Club session, putting your practice of 3a into a social setting devoted to laughing for no reason.

Acquiring a 3b Postural Attitude

Now let's explore how the 3b postural attitude is significantly different from 3a. The 3b posture has a sinking and folding quality to it, as if your body is giving in to gravity by sinking downward while also wanting to fold inward, closing the body off to the rest of the world. Try the following steps to help you acquire this postural attitude.

Consider these three steps to acquiring the 3b posture:

1. Spinal Compression

2. Sinking

3. Folding Inward

---

15. www.laughteryoga.org, the official website of Dr. Madan Kataria, The Laughter Guru, an international global movement for health, happiness, and world peace.

16. www.worldlaughtertour.com, The Mission of World Laughter Tour, Inc. is to create and disseminate an adjunctive therapeutic modality called "laughter therapy," by properly applying laughter theories and practices into multi-generational, multi-cultural, systematic health and happiness programs.

Spinal Compression

Sit in the middle of a chair so that your feet touch the floor and you have plenty of room between your back and the chair back. Start by sitting in the zero position, and then place a hand on top of your head and gently push your hand downward, and sense what happens to your spine. Do you feel your spine press downward slightly, compressing? Then, by gently grabbing the top of your head, or a little bit of hair on top of your head, gently pull upward, encouraging your spine to decompress. Try this a few times until you get the sense of this compression and decompression movement. Then, take your hand away and try doing the same action without pressing and pulling your head.

Sinking

After practicing spinal compression, and getting to the point where you don't need to use a hand on top of your head, try full body sinking. Sit in zero and do a spinal compression, allowing your arms to hang at your sides. Now, relax your muscle tone enough that you can imagine gravity pulling your shoulders down more, moving them toward your hips, essentially decreasing the amount of space between your shoulders and hips. As you do this, you may feel that your pelvis rocks back or your low back presses back slightly to decrease the space between your shoulders and hips. This is the sinking element of the 3b posture. Now, go in the opposite direction and, working against gravity's pull, lift back up again. Decompress the spine and return to the zero posture.

Folding Inward

Once you have achieved spinal compression and sinking, add folding inward to the posture. To help find a place to initiate the fold in the torso, place a hand with your fingers pointing in toward your sternum, the vertical cartilage in the middle of your chest, and gently press inward, causing your shoulders and arms to curl forward. Then, angle your knees and toes inward toward the midline of your body, and let your hands rest on top of each other in your lap, or cross your arms over each other in the form of a self-hug. Look down at your arms or at the floor. This is a full body inward fold. To release this posture back to zero, unfold, lift up, and decompress.

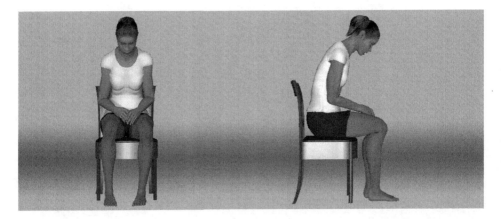

Throughout the last 15 years, I have noticed habitual slumping and curling posture increasing tremendously in my community. I often consider the influence of our technological advancements, particularly small, portable-sized technology, to be a big contributor. I look around and see children, teens, and adults constantly curling their bodies around cell phones and tablets. I see people slumped in front of laptop computers, everywhere. The more technology we tote around to coffee shops, waiting rooms, airports, and restaurants, the more we are encouraged to slump, curl in, and look down at tiny screens rather than engage with our surroundings through more open posture and lifted gaze.

Both the slumped, compressed, and curled posture and downcast eyes are strong triggers within the 3b pattern. They send signals to the brain that we are actually in this emotion, even if we are not consciously feeling it.

Even as I write this book, I am reminding myself to sit up, (or use a standing desk) uncurl, place my computer at eye level, and take regular breaks away to realign my posture and engage in some other activity that opens up my body and brings my eye gaze up and out.

Did You Know…?

Our modern, technology-centered lifestyles are contributing to the rise of depression. The rate of depression has increased tremendously across the entire industrialized world. In the United States, the rate of depression is 10 times higher today than it was two generations ago, and roughly one in four Americans will suffer from major depression at some point in their lives. In developing countries, clinical depression cases are much lower, and in hunter-gatherer communities, like the Kaluli people of the New Guinea highlands, depression is practically nonexistent.

Modern technology (computers, internet, social media, cell phones, televisions) have in one sense made our lives easier, but along with these conveniences also comes social isolation, less exercise, and limited exposure to sunlight and the natural world. We are spending most of our days and nights indoors and often curling our bodies around computer keyboards, tablets, and cellphones or slouching in soft furniture, watching television.[17]

Slumped, or sinking and folding, posture can affect self-esteem, decrease communication efforts, and increase the use of negative and brooding language. In a study comparing upright and slumped seated postures, researchers found that upright participants reported higher self-esteem, more

17. Ilardi, Stephen. *The Depression Cure: The 6-Step Program to Beat Depression Without Drugs* (Philadelphia, Da Capo Press, 2009), 4-18.

arousal, better mood, and lower fear, compared to slumped participants. Slumped participants used fewer words overall during speech, and the words they did use were made up of more negative emotion words, including sadness words. The study concluded that upright seated posture during stressful situations can help a person maintain self-esteem, reduce negative mood, and increase positive mood compared to a slumped posture. The investigators also note that sitting upright increases rate of speech and reduces self-focus, and they recommend the use of upright posture as a simple behavioral strategy for building resilience to stress.[18]

Be sure to keep this in mind as you practice the 3b pattern, and consider how you could shift away from the sinking and curling posture we are all so prone to doing when around technology. Then, get outside for regular sunlight, exercise, and socially engaging activities.

Sitting in 3b

Once you have practiced the full sequence of going from spinal compression, to sinking, and then adding folding, you are ready to combine this with the breathing pattern and facial expression.

1. Sit in the middle of a chair, so that your feet touch the floor and you have plenty of room between your back and the chair back. Start this exercise by sitting in the zero posture.

2. Then, begin the 3b breath pattern by taking short, quick sniffs in through the nose and then breathing out the mouth in one long, smooth, deflating exhale.

3. Add the facial expression by first creating the high forehead pinch with the eyebrows and then adding the pouting mouth with the corners of the mouth pulling down.

4. As you exhale out the mouth, compress your spine, imagining that a weight is pressing down on the top of your head, causing your entire body to sink down into the chair.

5. Then, also sink, reducing the space between your shoulders and hips and tilting the pelvis. Fold inward, toward the midline of your entire body. Allow shoulders to curl in and arms and legs to pull inward, possibly leading your feet and hands to point toward the center of your body. There is a heavy and private feeling to this posture.

18. S. Nair, M. Sagar, J. III Sollers, N. Consedine, and E. Broadbent, "Do Slumped and Upright Postures Affect Stress Responses? A Randomized Trial," *Health Psychology* 34, 6 (2015): 632-641.

6. The eyes look down at the floor or in toward the center of your body, around your navel.

7. Sound is emitted on the deflating exhale in the form of a long sigh or moan. Once your exhale is elongated enough with the long sigh, try a few abdominal pushes to expel a little more air at the very end of the exhalation. This might initiate some saccadic exhalations.

8. Explore this full pattern for a short while and then return to zero to complete this exercise. Be sure to regain the full embodiment of the zero posture by reminding yourself to elevate, decompress, and unfold into a position that sits tall and wide. Roll the shoulders up, back, and down to release the inward folding. Lift the back of the head toward the ceiling and stretch the spine gently upward to release the weighty compression feeling of 3b. Then, engage the zero breath pattern, making sure that your inhales are smooth and long, equal to the length of your exhales. Complete a full Step Out to fully release pattern 3b.

 Pause & Reflect

Take some time and write about your experience with sitting in 3b. What feelings were evoked by this posture of sinking and folding inward? Were aspects of this pattern difficult to release after you completed the lesson? Can you understand how the heavy deflating postural attitude could cause a sense of inertia and the inward folding could influence a sense of disinterest in engaging with the rest of the world? Recognizing how these postural attitudes affect our own abilities to interact with others can provide powerful personal discoveries.

Did you know…?

Negative emotions, like 3b, activate quick and decisive actions that can deliver immediate benefits. The emotion of 3b is often engaged when a person senses prospects are poor and they feel powerless and in need of support from others. The body reacts by activating its own internal risk management evaluation of the situation, and since the perception is that no available action is worth the risk of losing valuable resources, the body shuts down and prevents activity to conserve calories.[19] In these cases, we adopt a

---

19. M.C. Keller and R.M. Nesse, R. M, "Is Low Mood An Adaptation?: Evidence for Subtypes with Symptoms that Match Precipitants," *Journal of Affective Disorders* 86 (2005): 27-35.

"Why bother" or "It's useless" physical attitude until prospects improve, our perception of the situation changes, or we receive assistance from others. If we feel we need help from others, we tend to reveal these emotions more around those we trust and love, meaning we will likely cry more easily around friends and family than among strangers. That's because 3b also serves a social function as a call for support or comfort.[20]

Emotion Words for the Patterns

Now that you have had some time to explore the 3a and 3b patterns and assign your own words to the feelings that were evoked, let's look at some of the original words assigned to the patterns along with potential words for levels or degrees of intensity. Then, the chapter will conclude with exercises on standing and walking in the patterns.

Lexicon of Emotional States for the 3a Pattern

The words that follow are a form of lexicon of the emotional states associated with the 3a pattern. Each pattern has primary names associated with it that emerged during the initial research of these patterns. The additional words provided in the columns imply levels of intensity, or degrees, of this pure state. These degrees are represented by the terms Low, Mid, and High in the columns that follow. Keep in mind that the act of applying words to emotional states is highly subjective, and varies depending on individual interpretations of word meanings as well as life experiences. The words below are provided as guides to help you relate your experiences with the 3a pattern to familiar words used in our language.

Emotion Words for Pattern 3a
Primary Names: Happiness, Laughter, Pleasure, Joy[21]

Low Level	Mid Level	High Level
Amused	Boisterous	Ecstatic
Buoyant	Cheerful	Elated
Charmed	Effervescent	Euphoric
Lighthearted	Festive	Exhilarated
Optimistic	Gay	Jolly
Spirited	Jovial	Jubilant
	Merry	Rejoicing
	Mirthful	Reveling
	Playful	Vivacious

20. A.J.J.M. Vingerhoets and M.C. Becht, M.C., "*The ISAC Study: Some Preliminary Findings,*" Poster presented at the annual meeting of the American Psychosomatic Society, Santa Fe, NM (1997).

21. Susana Bloch, Pedro Orthous, and Guy Santibañez-H, "Effector Patterns of Basic Emotions: A Psychophysiological Method for Training Actors," *Journal of Social Biological Structure*10 (January 1987) 1-19. (Note: In this article, the original research team differentiated between the basic emotion's phasic [transient or stimulus bound] state, and its tonic [maintained-in-time] state and used these words to label the various states of this emotion. This article reveals that even the initial researchers used various words to describe one basic emotion.)

Mixed Emotions in Pattern 3a

When subtle elements of other patterns slip into pattern 3a, mixes are evident. Chronic postural tensions that you cannot easily release often cause a person to block this emotion or to create a mixed state. Remember that if you are practicing these patterns alone and without the aid of an instructor providing you with feedback, subtle mixes are most likely occurring.

The following words are offered to help you see how mixes can emerge in your practice of the 3a pattern. Potential mix-ins are labeled, but keep in mind that your interpretation of the word might mix in other patterns as well.

Mixed Emotion Words for Pattern 3a

3a with 1b	3a with 1b & 2a	3a with 2a
Devilish	Mischievous	Delighted
Sarcastic	Sly	Frivolous
Smug		

3a with 2a & 2b	3a with 2b	3a with 3b
Eager	Delirious	Grateful
Excited	Hysterical	Thankful
Enthusiastic		
Blissful		

Although you might recognize that these words can be conveyed with mixes, the selection of which basic emotions would mix in is quite individualized and determined by how a person interprets and expresses the word. For example, some might interpret *Blissful* as a subtle mix of 3a and 2b (fear), but others might interpret *Blissful* as having elements of 2a (sensuality) mixed in, and still others might have all three patterns mixed in. Whereas the word *Grateful* might be pure 3a for some, others might convey *Grateful* with 3a mixing into 3b, and yet others might have subtle mixes of 2a or 2b in their interpretation of this word. Once we apply a word to an emotion, the understanding of that emotion and how it is expressed is based on life experiences and individual interpretations.

I was teaching the basic emotion patterns to a group of ontological coaches and trainers. Their ontological training includes exploring the meanings, motivations, and behaviors associated with many different emotion words. They often use this lexicon of emotion words with clients to help identify and clarify situations and feelings. The coaches in my workshop were aware that an introductory training teaches the basic emotions and that higher levels of study address constructing and deconstructing emotional mixes.

The coaches were eager to understand how the basic emotions related to mixes, so during our last day of an introductory workshop, I created an exercise based on their own coaching lexicon of emotion words. I broke the coaches into small groups of three and had them select a few words from their coaching lexicon. Some of the words were admiration, contempt, envy, arrogance, pride, and shame. I then instructed them to discuss the words and assign what they believed were the basic emotions in the expression of each of those words. For example, Group One believed that admiration was a mix of 2a (sensuality) and 3a (happiness). Group Two believed that envy was a mix of 3b (sadness) and 2a (sensuality).

Then, I asked each group to combine with another group. Their task was to ask the other group members to model a word, not knowing how that group had intellectually deconstructed the word. For example, Group One asked Group Two to stand and physically express admiration. Group One soon realized that Group Two had very different physical interpretations of admiration, which some expressed with elements of 2b (fear), 1b (anger), and 1a (tenderness). Group Two then asked Group One to model envy, and they also saw some very different interpretations, including elements of 2b (fear) and 1b (anger).

They took pictures of each other modeling the different words, and soon the room was buzzing with excited observations of the various mixes and interpretations each of them had for the same words. It was an exciting lesson that illustrated how individual we truly are with our expressions of emotions.

For reference, here are the mixes the groups found in the other words:

Contempt: 1a, 1b, 2a, 3b
Arrogance: 1a, 1b, 2a, 2b, 3a
Pride: 1a, 1b, 2a, 3a
Shame: 1a, 1b, 2b, 3b

Exercise for Deconstructing Mixes

"Try on" a few of the mixed emotion words for any of the patterns in this book. First, choose several words from the mixed emotion list. For each one, stand up and, using a focal point, pretend that you are expressing that word to someone. Then, hold, or freeze, your physical interpretation of the word and sense what you are actually doing in terms of the emotional effector patterns. Ask yourself:

1. What am I doing with my breath, face, and posture?

2. What elements of the emotion patterns are evident in my expression of this word?

3. How many different emotion patterns are emerging in subtle ways (like a lift of the forehead muscles, eyes pushing forward, postural attitude shifts, or breathing adjustments)?

Write down what you did with your first interpretation of the word. Then, imagine a specific situation with your imaginary person. For example, if you are deconstructing being *thankful*, see if your expression changes if you are thankful for someone bringing you a cup of coffee, being your friend, or for having just saved your life. Can you feel different mixes with your interpretation of the word in the context of a specific situation? If so, then you can definitely see how mixes can be subjective from person to person, as well as within different situations.

Lexicon of Emotional States for the 3b Pattern
The words that follow are a form of lexicon of the emotional states associated with the 3b pattern. As with the list for 3a, the primary name associated with the pattern is provided at the top, and the additional words in the columns imply levels of intensity, or degrees, of this pure state. These degrees are again represented by the terms Low, Mid, and High. Use the words below as guides to help you relate your experiences with the 3b pattern to familiar words used in our language.

Emotion Words for Pattern 3b
Primary Names: Sadness, Crying, Sorrow, Grief, Depression[22]

Low Level	Mid Level	High Level
Brooding	Defeated	Anguished
Cheerless	Dejected	Crushed
Discouraged	Depressed	Desolate
Disappointed	Despairing	Inconsolable
Downcast	Despondent	Woeful
Downhearted	Heavyhearted	
Forlorn	Mournful	
Gloomy	Remorseful	
Glum	Powerless	
Solemn	Sulking	
Somber	Sorrowful	
Subdued	Tearful	
Sullen		

---

22. Susana Bloch, Pedro Orthous, and Guy Santibañez-H, "Effector Patterns of Basic Emotions: A Psychophysiological Method for Training Actors," *Journal of Social Biological Structure* 10 (January 1987) 1-19. (Note: In this article, the original research team differentiated between the basic emotion's phasic [transient or stimulus bound] state, and its tonic [maintained-in-time] state and used these words to label the various states of this emotion. This article reveals that even the initial researchers used various words to describe one basic emotion.)

Mixed Emotions in Pattern 3b

A very common mix into 3b is 2b (fear). It is particularly present in the eyes pressing forward and looking around quickly, searching to see if others are aware. Examples of this common mix are shame, embarrassment, guilt, loneliness, and humiliation. Sometimes 1b will mix in with pushing the jaw forward slightly, gritting teeth, or tensing the shoulders and neck as a protective measure against fully engaging true sadness. Watch for these potential mixes during your practice, and if you don't have an experienced instructor providing you with feedback, try video recording your practice so you can watch it later to check that these elements are not mixing into your practice.

Below are some words that imply mixes of 3b with other patterns, particularly with 1b (anger) and 2b (fear) but also including some examples where 1a (tenderness) and 2a (sensuality) mixes might be present as well. Keep in mind that your interpretation of any of these words, or the situation in which the word is being expressed, could make the emotional mix different from any provided here. These words and their categories are simply examples of potential mixes.

Mixed Emotion Words for Pattern 3b

3b with 2b	3b with 1b	3b with 2a	3b with 1a or 3a
Ashamed	Fretful	Melancholy	Apathetic
Desperate	Indifferent	Humbled	Cheerless
Dismayed	Morose	Yearning	Empathetic
Devastated	Mortified		Frivolous
Embarrassed	Pessimistic		Pitying
Guilty	Regretful		Sympathetic
Helpless	Tormented		Thankful
Hopeless	Uneasy		
Humiliated			
Lonely			
Overwhelmed			
Tortured			

Emotion Words Might Affect Pattern Practice

Notice if your understanding and practice of these patterns changes at all once you have subjective emotion titles in your mind. Keep checking that you are still applying all aspects of the pattern (breath, face, posture) and not subconsciously mixing in other pattern elements. This is very possible for two reasons: (1) using assigned emotion words for the pattern could lead you to behaving in the way you interpret each word to mean rather than doing the pattern and allowing the emotion to emerge through pattern application, and (2) once we stand and walk, we are required to control and keep track of so much more muscle movement that mixes naturally start coming into our initial explorations of the patterns. This is all part of the learning process, and with regular review of all three parts of the pattern, and through observing and sensing your application of the pattern to standing and walking, you will eventually clear the mixes over time. If you don't have the benefit of an instructor to provide you with feedback during this process, try a video recording of your practice sessions. You can learn a great deal about yourself, your habits, and your application of the patterns by watching yourself.

I was teaching an Emotional Body workshop in Montreal for professional performers and somatic practitioners. During my workshops, I sometimes offer private lessons in between our group sessions. The private lessons often help participants solidify their work on certain patterns, reach an emotional induction with a pattern that has been elusive to them, or clear away entanglements.

During this particular workshop, I had an unusual amount of men asking for a private lesson solely to help them reach a state of pure purging sadness—in essence, open weeping. The men expressed similar reasons for their request. They felt they could not truly reach an induction with 3b when they were in a room filled with others, particular with women present. Throughout their lives, they have received a multitude of messages that crying and sadness are unacceptable expressions, and certainly not to be indulged in around women. The men shared that hearing a room full of people crying also filled them with tension, almost to the point of anger, which they recognized was their armor for holding off sadness.

Throughout the rest of the week, I held private sessions with each of these men and helped them reach an induction with 3b, to the point where they were able to sob and weep away a lifetime of pent-up armoring. If anyone had witnessed their grateful hugs to me afterward and their exclaiming, "Thank you for making me cry" they certainly would not have understood the significance of this moment and the opportunity for these men to feel this level of emotional accessibility and acceptance.

Standing and Walking in the Patterns

Now that you have some of the emotion words in mind, let's explore standing and walking in patterns 3a and 3b. See if the emotion words help or hinder your practice of these patterns. In either case, be sure to review all three aspects of the pattern (breath, face, posture) as you practice and make sure that you are not mixing in other emotion elements.

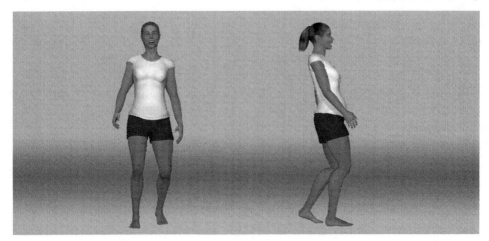

Standing and Walking in 3a

After practicing the 3a pattern in a sitting position, you may wonder how you can stand and walk in such a floppy postural attitude. Let's see how the 3a pattern moves through the world.

1. While sitting in a chair, begin the 3a breath pattern, by inhaling through the nose in one quick and open inhale and then going directly to a stepped exhale out the mouth.

2. Add the 3a facial expression by forming a big smile on your face, which you keep throughout the pattern.

3. Then, take on a loose and floppy postural attitude, in which various parts of the body may lift on the quick inhale through the nose and then flop with the first exhale burst. Let the flopped arms, legs, or torso affect the entire body and cause you to lean in the direction of the initial flop. Then, randomly flop in a different direction, including throwing your head back and lifting your arms up.

4. After allowing the body to flop in various directions a few times, use one of the inhalations through the nose to lift you up, leading with the torso, into a standing position. When you release the first exhale into a slight flop, allow your slightly bent legs to be the springs from which you flop, as if your knees were the shock absorbers of this flouncy stance. With the majority of your weight on the balls of your feet, feel the spring in this stance as you lightly flop and flounce in various directions while inhaling through the nose and exhaling out the mouth in steps.

5. Then, take a few steps forward, propelled by the inhalation and first floppy exhalation. The walk is loose and tends to zig-zag, or wander in various directions, led by the unpredictable floppiness of the postural attitude. Walk around for a while engaging this full 3a pattern. See if you can feel a lightness to

your walk coming from the spring in your step and the loose unpredictability of this flouncy attitude.

6. Finish this exercise by returning to the zero breath pattern, sitting or standing in zero, and then eventually completing a Step Out.

▌▌ Pause & Reflect

Take a few moments to write about your experience with walking in 3a. Write down any emotion words that came to mind as you stood and walked in this pattern. Were you able to feel buoyant? Sometimes, people describe standing and walking in this pattern as lightly bobbing in different directions, like a buoy marker on softly rolling sea waves. Others feel more like a silly, sloppy clown or an intoxicated person trying, and failing, to walk straight. If you were not able to feel the light, bouncy quality of this pattern in motion, could you sense any residual tension in your body that might have kept you from fully accessing this bouncy, flouncy posture? If so, with each future practice, notice where the tension is and see if you can find ways to release it.

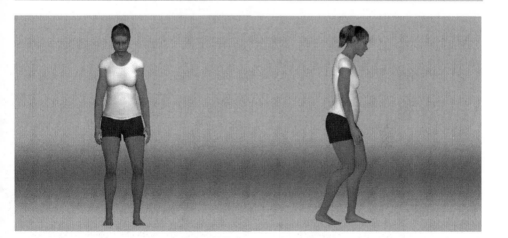

Standing and Walking in 3b

Like 3a, the 3b pattern has its challenges with standing and walking, but for different reasons. The weightiness of this pattern makes it difficult to contemplate even getting up, let alone walking. Let's examine how this pattern might be expressed when standing or walking.

1. Sit in the middle of a chair, and then begin the 3b breath pattern by taking short, quick sniffs in through the nose and then breathing out the mouth in one long, smooth, deflating exhale.

2. Add the facial expression with a high forehead pinch of the eyebrows and a downward pull on the corners of the mouth.

3. As you exhale out the mouth, imagine that a weight is pressing down on the top of your head, compressing your spine and causing your entire body to sink down into the chair. Then, also fold inward, toward the midline of your entire body.

4. With eyes looking at the floor, practice the full breath pattern and postural attitude for a few cycles. Then, use one of the sniffed inhales to initiate the movement to stand. Use the next exhale to deflate the standing posture into a sinking and folding stance, with the knees bending slightly and pointing inward so the toes point in slightly as well. Let the arms fold inward and the head hang down, with eyes looking at the floor.

5. Try to lift a foot and step forward. Depending on the level of the postural attitude, the weighty compression of the spine may make walking challenging, and you may feel as if your feet want to slide rather than lift and step. Try walking around with this compressed and inward attitude. The eyes will look downward and inward. If sound is emitted, it resembles a long sigh or moan.

6. Explore this full pattern for a short while, and then return to the zero standing position to complete this exercise. Remind yourself to adopt a tall and wide posture, rolling the shoulders up, back, and down to release the inward folding. Elevate the back of the head toward the ceiling and stretch the spine gently upward to release the weighty compression. Then, engage the zero breath pattern, and complete a full Step Out to fully release pattern 3b. You may need more than one Step Out to accomplish this.

▋▋ Pause & Reflect

As you explored standing and walking in 3b, could you feel the weightiness of this pattern? The deflating exhale combined with a sinking and curling of the entire body can make you feel like you don't want to do anything or go anywhere. Inertia is a resulting state of 3b and is felt profoundly when attempting to move in this pattern. It is as if walking forward, or doing anything, counters the 3b attitude. Take a moment to write about your experience with standing and walking in 3b.

Polarities Between the 3a and 3b Patterns

3a and 3b are mirror opposite patterns, with a stepped, or saccadic, breathing style on the exhalation of one pattern (3a) and on the inhalation of the other (3b). However, once 3b is engaged on a higher level of induction, saccades emerge at the end of the long, smooth exhale after having reached a below-empty level. These saccades at the end of the exhalation can easily evoke 3a, which is why many people find that they can laugh until they cry or cry until they laugh. If you approach someone from behind as they are practicing these patterns, you may not be able to tell if they are in 3a or 3b until you see their face. Let's explore what it feels like to shift between these two patterns in a polarity exercise.

3a ⟷ 3b

Shifting Between Polarities of 3a and 3b

Select an object or a picture of someone and place it a few paces away from your chair. It should be at eye level when sitting in the chair.

1. While sitting, look at your chosen object and start the 3a pattern. Breathe in through the nose with a quick, light inhale and out through your mouth in a long, saccadic exhale. Gradually allow the full 3a pattern to build to a floppy, unpredictable postural attitude accompanied by a big smile with your eyes and open mouth. Build the pattern slowly, and gradually allow yourself to get more floppy and loose while extending the exhaled saccades as long as you can. Stay in the chair and keep occasionally reconnecting with your focal point.

2. Do you feel degrees of laughter, joy, and giddiness as you build this pattern? Levels of 3a can vary from low to high: from amused, to cheerful, to festive, to happy, to jolly, to playful, to rejoicing. Can you sense your feelings about the object, or picture, changing as you slowly build this pattern?

3. On the next inhale through the nose, add the sniffs, or saccades, and then breathe out a long, smooth, sighing exhale that may end with a few saccades after you have begun to run out of breath.

4. Slowly invite the facial and postural aspects of the 3b pattern to shift you away from the 3a pattern, step by step bringing you toward 3b. Perhaps start by applying the knitted eyebrows and the mouth with the corners pulling down. Then, let the posture start to compress, then sink, then fold inward. Can you sense your feelings about the object you are looking at changing as you slowly move from 3a to 3b?

5. Can you feel degrees of sadness and tears forming as you explore this opposite direction, going from the buoyancy of 3a to the weightiness of 3b? Levels of sadness from low to high may move from gloomy, to brooding, to heavyhearted, to despondent, to mournful, to inconsolable. How do you feel about the object now?

6. Explore going back and forth between 3a and 3b while you look at your object or picture of a person. Can you sense the mixed emotions present in the transition between these two extreme poles? The mixed emotions occur when you are moving from one polarity to the other. The elements of both patterns are still present, creating mixes, until you fully release one pattern and settle into the pure state on the other side.

7. Finish this exercise by going into the zero pattern and then completing a Step Out.

Mixing 3a with 3b often brings about emotions like sympathy, empathy, pity, cheerlessness, thankfulness, frivolousness, and gratitude. If you find it difficult to see how 3a and 3b might be present in the expression of these words, try a little exercise where you stand with your back to a large floor-length mirror. Take one of the mixed-state words shared in this paragraph and embody the word, as if you were expressing that feeling to someone. Make sure you have committed your entire body to this word, and then turn and express it to the mirror. While holding onto this expression, see if you can identify subtle cues of either 3a or 3b within it. Check your breathing, face, and entire posture. Can you see any elements of these patterns in your own interpretation of the word? Then, try a few more words and see how they differ. Remember this: The interpretation and expression of emotion words is highly subjective and individualized. So, if you don't see aspects of 3a or 3b in one or two of the words you express, it does not mean that if someone else expressed that word that it would be the same for them.

Did you know…?

The saying, "Too much work and not enough play makes Jack a dull boy" now has plenty of scientific support. Joyful play is essential in childhood for building endurance, developing intellectual resources, and increasing creativity.[23] As people mature, play also fuels brain development.[24]
Joyful play is not just for children. Adults need their own kind of joyful play. Play reinforces the practice of pushing your limits, making you want to achieve your highest potential. Its influence crosses over into many areas of your life,

23. L.R. Sherrod and J.L. Singer, (1989). "The Development of Make-Believe Play," *Sports, Games and Play*, ed J. Goldstein (Hillsdale, Erlbaum,1989), 1-38.

24. J. Panksepp, "Attention Deficit Hyperactivity Disorders, Psychostimulants, and Intolerance of Childhood Playfulness: A Tragedy in the Making?" *Current Directions in Psychological Science* 7 (1998) 91-98.

including your intellectual, physical, and artistic behaviors.[25]

One particular theory, called broaden-and-build, reinforces these benefits of joyful play and contends that they lead to building enduring personal resources. The theory holds that when you play with loved ones or within a positive and supportive community, all the positive emotions begin to interplay and act as a cause-and-effect chain, resulting in a broader personal perspective and more flexible actions. For example, as you feel the joy in play, you push limits and develop interest in new things. You then explore new information and experiences, expanding yourself in the process. Then, as you grow from this broader view on life, there is the urge to sit back and savor your surroundings, finding more contentment and feelings of tenderness and love. The theory also suggests a recurring cycle and sustainability of these emotions, which allows them to become a constant. So, as you establish this new norm, there is more desire to regularly play, explore, savor, and love.[26]

Take a Break

Take a nice long break from pattern practice. Go engage in joyful play or something that feels openly energetic like aerobic activity, playing a sport, dancing, or taking an exhilarating walk. Prolonged practice of any emotion pattern can be exhausting and also makes it difficult to fully release the pattern from your muscles. Taking good long breaks away from the work is as important as engaging in short, attentive practice sessions. Additional pattern exploration can happen on another day, after some resting and releasing. For now, go out and engage with the world and see if you recognize some of the patterns you have practiced, both in your own behavior and in the actions of others. You have a new lens through which you can experience and look at the world around you. Go check it out!

Summary

By this point in the book, you have been introduced to all six basic emotion patterns. Practice all these patterns until you know each of them well enough to embody them while sitting, standing, and walking. Try to reach a practice level with each at which you can produce the pattern without looking at your notes or referring to the book for the details of how to do it. Once you have achieved that level of understanding for applying each pattern, you are ready to practice the exercises in the next chapter. These final exercises will teach you how to apply the patterns to speaking, singing, and various other activities and help you relate your newfound understanding of basic emotions to your personal life and professional practices.

---

25. B.L. Fredrickson, "What Good Are Positive Emotions?" *Review of General Psychology* 2 (1998), 300-319.

26. Ibid.

Practice & Application   8

Practicing the Patterns

The previous chapters provided you with somatic keys for accessing each of the basic emotions as well as a state of zero. Once you have practiced each of those patterns enough to remember how to produce them without looking at notes or requiring prompting, and have applied each pattern to lying prone, voicing, sitting, standing, and walking, then you are ready to practice the exercises in this chapter.

The Use of Drills for Practice

A pattern drill is a review of all six of the emotion patterns, often with the zero pattern after each emotion in order to clear before moving on to the next, and then finishing with a Step Out. The process takes ten to fifteen minutes, depending on how long you choose to stay in each pattern, and can be done in a sitting or standing position. The pattern drill serves two purposes: (1) as a reliable method for reviewing and practicing the emotional patterns and (2) as an emotional sweep of the six basic emotion patterns, which provides a purging of some chronic emotional states while also honoring the basic emotions in our system.

Reviewing and Practicing the Patterns

A pattern drill will help you refine the full embodiment of the emotion patterns and increase your body memory of them, making the patterns available to you more quickly and fully the more you practice. The drill helps you recognize where you are in your practice of the emotional effector patterns and understand which stage of learning you have reached for each: (1) mechanical, (2) inductive, or (3) integrative (see chapter 3 for review of these terms).

The inductive and mechanical stages of learning an emotional effector pattern can swing back and forth, depending on many factors. You may experience an inductive state with a pattern for part of one practice session, and then feel mechanical during another part of the same practice session because of a specific breath or muscle adjustment. The type of day you are having can also influence the learning stage you reach with each pattern. For example, if you are experiencing a day plagued with frustration or worry, you might have greater difficulty accessing some of the a-patterns. Or on a day where your ability to concentrate is challenged, you may not be able to achieve the same connections you made with certain patterns during previous drills. Residual body tension might also influence your practice experience, keeping you from fully embodying a pattern, particularly an a-pattern requiring great relaxation and loose muscle tone. During your drill practice, you will sometimes fully feel emotions emerging from the patterns. Other times, you may feel as if you are going through the motions, as if indicating the emotion but not actually feeling it. You can expect all that in the process of practice drills.

Practicing for Precision and Permanency

We use physical drills to attain precise and spontaneous actions. Athletes need their bodies to respond within seconds to conditioned triggers. The lap swimmer and runner both perfect their starting block launch by practicing drills to improve the quality and efficiency of a fully embodied action within a split second of hearing the starting shot. Watch any sports training session and you will see athletes engaged in a series of drills designed to ensure peak conditioning and spontaneous physical responsiveness upon demand. Individuals in other careers, like martial artists, soldiers, dancers, singers, typists, firefighters, and emergency medical responders, use drills for the same purpose.

Pattern drills are used to achieve a similar objective: to train your body to respond within seconds to a simple trigger with full embodiment of the pattern. You might find the trigger to be the initiation of the breath pattern, which leads you immediately into activation of the facial muscles and physical postural attitude of the pattern. Certain facial muscle movements tend to work well as a trigger into the pattern, and then the breath pattern follows, and so does the posture. Eventually, after reaching the integration stage with a pattern through regular practice, your body may respond to the mere thought of the emotion and not need a physical trigger at all. Regular practice of pattern drills will help you get to this point of fully integrated emotion pattern use. Once this level is achieved in your emotional expression, only occasional drills are needed to retain it.

Checking for Mixes

Drills will also help you perfect your embodiment of the emotion patterns and identify where any emotional mixes may be entering into your practice of each pattern. For example, as you practice 2b (fear) or 3a (joy), you may tear up or see 3b (sadness) entanglements in the forehead or corners of the mouth. Most people do experience mixes during their initial practice of the patterns. At first, these tend to be fairly obvious mixes you can identify on your own—if you regularly scan your body as you build the pattern and refer to the steps provided in this book for creating each pattern. However, as your practice continues and you are engaging more emotional inductions, you will need to find external methods for checking on your work and watching out for mixes and entanglements (see chapter 2 for explanation of entanglements). External sources of assessment and feedback will to help you advance your practice and clear up mixes and entanglements.

One external source is your instructor. When you practice the drills in front of an experienced instructor, the instructor can point out when and where those mixes appear and help you clear them. If you are practicing alone, a video can serve as an external source. You can record your practice and then watch and evaluate your replication of the patterns. If you notice mixes in your practice, try to address the following three questions:

1. **When does the mix first appear?** By asking this question you can pinpoint what might be triggering the mix. It might appear as you engage certain facial muscles or when you increase emotional intensity levels.

2. **Where does the mix occur?** The mix might occur in the breath pattern or only in the mouth muscles.

3. **Is the emotional mix present in other patterns?** If so, you are discovering a common entanglement.

Once you discover mixes, and determine the "when and where" of each mix, plan a separate practice session where you focus on one pattern only, with the purpose of addressing the mix or mixes discovered within your practice of that pattern. Use the steps that follow help you clear the mixes.

Clearing Mixes

1. Review the steps for the pattern. Prepare to rebuild your pattern application slowly, separating the parts of the pattern in your practice.

2. Start with the breath pattern alone (no face or postural attitude application). Practice until you can do the breath pattern exactly as written in this text.

3. Practice only the facial expression in the mirror (no breath pattern or postural attitude application). Practice until you can produce the facial expression exactly as written in this text.

4. Practice only the postural attitude in the mirror (no breath pattern or facial expression application), in sitting and standing positions. Practice until you can produce the postural attitude exactly as written in this text.

5. Then, while in front of the mirror, slowly build the full pattern, starting with the breath pattern alone. Once the breath pattern is established, add the facial expression. Watch for any mixes of other emotions coming into your practice. If you see a mix coming in, reduce the facial expression muscle activation slowly back down to a zero face, and go back to the breath pattern only. Then, start to build the facial expression again, very slowly. Watch carefully to see exactly when and where the emotional mixes enter into the facial expression. If they appear again, repeat the previous action, reduce the facial muscle intensity, and work your way back to a zero face, and then rebuild again. Eventually, with practice and attention, it is possible to control the emergence of the mixed emotion altogether.

6. Then, address any mixes in the postural attitude by starting with the breath pattern alone. Once the breath pattern is established, add the postural attitude. Watch for any mixes of other emotions coming into your practice. If you see a mix coming in, reduce the postural attitude muscle activation slowly back down to a zero posture, and go back to the breath pattern only. Then, start to build the postural attitude again, very slowly. Watch carefully to see exactly when and where the emotional mixes enter into the postural attitude. Be sure to address all areas of the full body, head to toe. Watch for subtle tension patterns in the neck, hands, feet, pelvis, and legs. If mixes appear, reduce the postural attitude intensity and work your way back to a zero posture, and then rebuild again, until you have mastered control of it altogether and the postural attitude mixes are gone.

7. The last step is to put all the pattern elements back together again. Build the pattern slowly, as if in slow motion, while standing in front of a full-length mirror. Start with the breath pattern. Then, add the facial expression, and

finally the postural attitude. Stay in the full pattern for at least five breath cycles and slowly increase intensity while you watch to see if any mixes come in. Then, slowly reduce intensity down to a low level, finish by going to zero, and then Step Out.

The "Clearing Mixes" exercise will refine your practice of the patterns and also help you address entanglements. Entanglements are when you have emotion patterns taking control of your ability to express yourself the way you desire. For example, you may discover there is some inherent 3b (sadness) mixing into your practice of 1a, 1b, and 3a. This may indicate an entanglement of sadness and the inability to express your own true tenderness, anger, or joy without tears. Practicing these patterns with the Clearing Mixes exercise and watching for this entanglement may eventually help you un-entangle the sadness from these expressions in your life and give you the ability to express these emotions in their purest sense again. It is a truly liberating prospect!

The Pattern Drill Provides an Emotional Sweep
Another purpose of the pattern drill is to provide all six of the basic emotions with the opportunity to be felt and expressed. It is a self-regulated way of honoring the basic emotions we were born with—and may need to reconnect with—on a regular basis. Some have related the pattern drill to sweeping out the corners of a dusty closet, as if reaching into the corners of our emotional recesses and breaking up the cobwebs that have developed over time. By taking the time to induct and express all of the basic emotions, in a safe and controlled drill environment, we can experience a feeling of emotional purging and cleansing.

The pattern drill can also help you purge any chronic emotional states lingering below the surface. Each of the six basic emotions has both a phasic, short-lived acute state and a tonic, low-level chronic state that can be sustained for long periods of time. For example, depression could be a tonic state of 3b (sadness), and crying may be its phasic, or acute, state. Hate could be considered a chronic, or tonic, state of 1b (anger), whereas showing aggression or attacking someone is the phasic state of 1b.[1] A tonic emotion is not always present, but is more like an attractor state, in which a person is habitually inclined to express this emotion. Susana Bloch states, "This does not mean that the emotion is present evenly all the time; rather it appears in waves, coloring the person's general mood, providing an emotional tonality that will impregnate his/her entire behavior."[2]

1. Susana Bloch, Pedro Orthous, and Guy Santibañez-H, "Effector Patterns of Basic Emotions: A Psychophysiological Method for Training Actors," *Journal of Social Biological Structure* 10 (January 1987) 1–19.

2. Susana Bloch, *The Alba of Emotions: Managing Emotions through Breathing* (Santiago: Grafhika, 2006), 58–61.

Examples of Emotional Effector Pattern Phasic and Tonic States[3]

	Acute Phasic State	**Tonic Chronic State**
1b	Aggression	Hate
1a	Maternal/Paternal Love	Friendship
2b	Panic	Anxiety
2a	Sex	Sensuality
3b	Crying	Depression
3a	Laughing	Joy

In these situations, like the person who has a tendency to be easily annoyed, the chronic emotional state of low-level anger is perpetuating hostility in their behavior. Conducting a full emotional sweep can help purge the chronic emotion while also giving attention to other emotions that have been suppressed.

Although zero and Step Out are used to help shift out of emotions, sometimes these practices do not fully release chronic emotional states. In these cases, the emotion may actually need to be engaged fully as a means of purging and releasing it before a person can achieve a zero state. Scientist and author of *Sentics: The Touch of Emotions,* Manfred Clynes, suggests if an emotion is not fully discharged it has the tendency to continue chronically until another episode that centers around the same emotion is strong enough to purge and fully release the emotion from the body.[4] For example, the person who is carrying chronic low-level anger and who is easily annoyed may exhibit behaviors of annoyance until an event triggers a stronger lever of anger. At that moment, the person would erupt, perhaps unexpectedly, as the body is finally given the opportunity to fully release all the pent-up anger held back within long-term chronic levels. With this theory in mind, a pattern drill conducted in a controlled and safe manner may provide the opportunity to engage and purge chronically maintained emotions, but in a somatic exercise that does not rely on cognitive triggers. In this case, a pattern drill may serve to sweep out any emotion that has persisted in a chronic, and possibly undetectable, state. The use of zero between the patterns and the completion of the entire drill with at least one full Step Out bring you back to zero and remind your system to calm down and let go of the various emotional states.

What to Expect After a Pattern Drill
After completing a pattern drill, you might have various reactions. Some feel

3. Susana Bloch, Pedro Orthous, and Guy Santibañez-H, "Effector Patterns of Basic Emotions: A Psychophysiological Method for Training Actors," *Journal of Social Biological Structure* 10 (January 1987) 1–19.

4. Manfred Clynes, *Sentics: The Touch of Emotions* (New York, Anchor Press, 1977) 169 – 171

rejuvenated, energized, alert, and eager to do something active. Others feel exhausted, numb, contemplative, or ready to lie down and take a nap for a while. The post-drill reactions are personal and circumstantial. They are directly influenced by such things as chronic emotional states, the intensity or level of practice within the drill, and personal situational influences. If you are having a day with emotional, physical, or concentration challenges, those personal challenges will affect the intensity, accuracy, and outcome of the drill. Likewise, if you are having a relaxed, centered, and inspiring day, this will also influence your pattern drill. Keep all of this in mind, and in practice. If you use the drill regularly, expect different results.

Pattern drills can be practiced on a daily basis, particularly in the beginning stages of learning the emotional effector patterns. Eventually, you may want to reduce your practice to weekly or monthly sessions, depending on what you want to achieve and what level of pattern learning (mechanical, inductive, integrative) you have reached in your practice. The pattern drills can also be used as an emotional sweep, applied as needed.

The Pattern Drill
Complete the following steps while sitting toward the front of a firm, straight-backed chair.

Zero

1. Start the zero breath pattern and focus your eyes straight ahead on a focal point so they are looking neither up nor down.

2. Relax the jaw with the mouth open slightly, the lips relaxed and parted just enough to exhale the air.

3. Engage deep diaphragmatic breathing supported by the abdomen muscles. Breathe in through the nose and out through the relaxed, slightly open mouth. Create a slow breathing pattern, with the inhalation length the same as the exhalation. Count the duration of each, in your mind, to ensure they are equal. Allow a gentle and soft turnaround between the inhalations and exhalations.

4. With each inhalation, remind yourself to empty your mind as the oxygen flows in through your nose, bringing a sense of lightness to your body and mind.

5. With each exhale through the relaxed open mouth, remind yourself to let go of tension in the muscles, releasing this tension as you release the breath.

1a

1. After a few breath cycles in zero, begin pattern 1a (tenderness). Change your breathing to nose breathing and engage an inhalation that is slightly shorter than the exhalation, allowing a small hold after the exhale, and acknowledging a gentle turnaround from inhale to exhale.

2. Gradually add the facial aspect of 1a by inviting the muscles on the outsides of the eyes and along the nasal ridge to abduct, back toward the ears. Allow the muscles in the cheeks and corners of your mouth to also abduct, up and back, completing the fully integrated smile.

3. Then, add the postural attitude. Start with the head tilting toward one side, keeping the front of the neck soft enough that the chin rests downward while the eyes continue to gaze at your focal point. Follow through with side bending and recognize how this affects your weight distribution all the way down to your feet. Remember to rotate your arms slightly so your palms open toward the ceiling.

4. Hold the side-bend toward one side for a few breath cycles and then try shifting slowly and gradually to the other side. Use the inhalation through the nose to bring your head to center, and then exhale through the nose as you settle into bending on the other side. Remain bent toward that side for a while as you engage the full pattern.

5. Then, gradually shift into zero breath. Bring your posture back up to sitting tall and wide, and breathe in through the nose and out through the mouth, with equal lengths of inhale and exhale. Relax the face and place your focus on the focal point for a couple of zero breath cycles.

1b

1. Change your breathing back to nose breathing and gradually engage the 1b (anger) breath pattern. Keep the inhalation and exhalation lengths equal to each other. Incorporate a clear, strong stop after the inhale and exhale (remember the ball-catching image used in chapter 5).

2. Gradually add the facial aspect of 1b by inviting the muscles on the outsides of the eyes and along the nasal ridge to adduct, moving in toward the midline of the face. Allow the muscles inside the nostrils to constrict, causing tension in the breath pattern. Add tension under the eyes, as if the lower eyelid is trying to cover your eye.

3. Engage the 1b postural attitude. Start with moving the entire torso forward, and then lift it up slightly. Make sure the arms and hands move forward as well and the face presses directly forward. The jaw may also press forward, staying true to this posture's intention to initiate forward movement.

4. Add a gripping tension in the toes and invite the muscle tension to follow all the way up the legs and through the arms, down to the hands. Practice the entire pattern for a few breath cycles.

5. Switch your breathing back to zero. Bring your posture and your facial expression back to zero. Remain in the zero pattern for as many cycles as it takes to feel as if you have fully released the 1b pattern.

2a

1. Change your breathing to mouth breathing and gradually engage the 2a (sensuality) breath pattern. Make the inhalation and exhalation of equal lengths to each other. The inhalation and exhalation have a soft, slow-motion turnaround with no holds or pauses.

2. Gradually add the facial aspect of 2a (Receptive) by forming a subtle upper lip smile. Then, allow your eyes to move back, deep into your eye sockets with your eyelids gently closing or almost closing.

3. Engage the postural attitude. The posture is openly receiving, with head resting back slightly. The torso has subtle spinal undulations that lead with the navel pressing forward, followed by the throat pressing forward, and then returning back to center, the neck movement following that of the navel. Continue with the full 2a pattern for a few breath cycles, allowing the spinal undulations to be a subtle spinal rocking, forward and back.

4. Gently switch from the receptive to the active mode by first dropping the upper lip smile and then placing your focus in the middle of your chin with the intention of a subtle exposure of the lower teeth. Then allow your eyes to move closer to zero eyes, but keep them slightly retracted and actively focused on a focal point.

5. Sit in a position of an openly receiving upright posture with the head lifted up and facing forward. Keep the gentle and subtle spinal undulation, but do not tilt the head back so much that you lose eye contact with your focal point.

6. Practice this pattern for a few breath cycles and then return to zero. Bring your posture and your facial expression back to zero. Remain in the zero pattern

for as many cycles as it takes to feel as if you have fully released the 2a pattern.

2b

1.   Change your breathing to mouth breathing and gradually engage the 2b (fear) breath pattern. Switch your breathing activation area to the high chest. Shorten the length of the inhalation and exhalation, creating shallow breathing, and add an occasional fairly long hold after the inhalation.

2.   Encourage your eyes to move forward, as if pushing out of their eye sockets and increasing peripheral vision. Allow the mouth to drop open, and stay open, creating an oval or circle shape.

3.   Fully embody this pattern by engaging the postural attitude. The upper back moves backward and lifts up, and other muscles in the body reflect this backward retreating action. The eyes and face remain aligned with the focal point.

4.   During the occasional breath holds after the inhale, activate the eye movement, with the eyes darting around the room while the head stays still and the body faces the focal point.

5.   Practice this pattern for a very short amount of time, and then return to zero breath. Switch your breathing back to deep diaphragmatic breathing, releasing upper chest tension as you bring your posture and your facial expression back to zero. Check that you have fully relaxed the eyes, upper chest, and back, and slow your deep breathing rate down to long, smooth inhales and exhales. Stay in zero breath until you have fully released the 2b pattern.

3a

1.   Begin the 3a (joy) breath pattern by inhaling through the nose in one quick and open inhale and then going directly to an exhalation out the mouth in steps, with the stop-burst, stop-burst pattern. Add sound to the exhale in the form of a ha-ha-ha, using the abdominal muscles to create the bursts of air on the exhale.

2.   Add the 3a facial expression by forming a big smile on your face, starting by abducting the muscles around your eyes toward your ears. Then, encourage the cheek muscles and corners of your open mouth to pull up and back, forming a

big smile that you will keep throughout the pattern.

3. Invite the entire body to be loose and floppy, in that various parts of the body may lift on the quick inhale through the nose and then drop with the first exhale burst. The whole body will lean in the direction of that initial drop while the step exhales are emitted. Then, with the next inhale through the nose, the body will lift slightly in another direction, and then drop in that new direction with the first exhale burst.

4. Explore this full pattern, allowing the body to flop in various directions including left, right, forward, and backward. Be sure to maintain the full smile throughout and check that your inhalation comes in through the nose. Then, return to zero breath, sitting tall and wide in the poised and centered zero posture.

3b

1. Begin the 3b (sadness) breath pattern by taking short, quick sniffs in through the nose and then exhaling out the mouth in one long, smooth deflating exhale.

2. Add the facial expression with the high forehead pinch of the eyebrows and the pouting mouth with the corners of the mouth pulling down.

3. As you exhale out the mouth, imagine that a weight is pressing down on the top of your head, compressing your spine and causing your entire body to sink down into the chair. Also let your body fold inward, toward the midline, allowing shoulders to curl in and arms and legs to pull inward. Even your feet and hands should point toward the center of your body.

4. Direct your eyes to look down at the floor or in toward the center of your body, around your navel.

5. On the deflating exhale, allow sound to be emitted in the form of a long sigh or moan.

6. Explore this full pattern for about five breath cycles, and then return to zero. Be sure to regain the full embodiment of the zero posture by reminding yourself to sit tall and wide, rolling the shoulders up, back, and down to release the inward folding. Elevate the back of the head toward the ceiling and stretch the spine gently upward to release the weighty compression feeling of 3b. Then, engage the zero breath pattern, making sure that your inhalations are smooth and long, equal to the length of your exhalations.

Step Out
Complete a full Step Out.

1. Stand in zero, engaging zero breath. Keep your eyes on the horizon line for the following sequence until you "shake out."

2. Bring your palms together in front of your hips and loosely interlace your fingers.

3. Inhale through your nose as you raise your arms up over your head and bend your elbows so your clasped hands end up hanging behind your head. Use this entire movement for your inhale.

4. Keeping your hands behind your head, gently squeeze the palms together as you complete the inhalation and then hold your breath for a short beat, to signify an ending point.

5. Exhale through your relaxed open mouth as you loosen your palm squeeze, raise your hands back over your head, and bring your clasped hands back down in front of your body. Use this entire movement for your exhale.

6. Repeat this calibrated arm movement with the inhalation and exhalation two more times to complete three cycles of zero breath.

7. After the third breath cycle, bring your hands up to gently massage your face and pat it lightly to release any residual tension.

8. Shake your body out much like you might see a wet dog shake his entire body. Spread your legs slightly and twist your whole body back and forth quickly, like a full body wiggle, while you stretch your arms and lift them over your head. Feel free to add a little hop, or lift yourself up and down as you wiggle and shake and stretch out at various angles, essentially "throwing off the axis" of symmetry.

9. Allow muscles to move freely and wildly in this shake out for a few seconds while you make an audible vocal sound like "ha!" to release any residual tensions that may still exist in the body.

Postural Points of View
In the emotional effector pattern research, the postures are described as having postural points of view, or body positions, reflecting how a person feels.[5] Susana

---

5. Susana Bloch, Pedro Orthous, and Guy Santibañez-H, "Effector Patterns of Basic Emotions: A Psychophysiological Method for Training Actors," *Journal of Social Biological Structure* 10 (January 1987) 1–19.

Bloch would later refer to these as directional attitudes.[6]

In 2011, Steven Porges explained in *The Polyvagal Theory* that these directional responses are the result of a right brain process. Within seconds we monitor our surroundings while also evaluating our own physical state and assign a simple behavioral response of approach or withdraw for the situation.[7]

As you continue your practice of the patterns and use them in the exercises that follow, it is important to understand postural points of view. Below is a chart showing how each postural point of view expresses by approaching or withdrawing, and high or low muscle tone response.

As you can see from the chart, 1b (anger) has both high muscle tone and the desire to approach the object of its anger. Its opposite is 3b (sadness), with low muscle tone and the desire to withdraw from others. In comparison, 2b (fear) has high muscle tone yet uses the muscle tension to withdraw rather than to approach.

Postural Points of View

6. Susana Bloch, *The Alba of Emotions: Managing Emotions through Breathing* (Santiago: Grafhika, 2006), 125–127.

7. Stephen W. Porges, *The Polyvagal Theory: Neurophysiological Foundations of Emotions, Attachment, Communication, Self-Regulation* (New York: Norton & Company, 2011) 139–143.

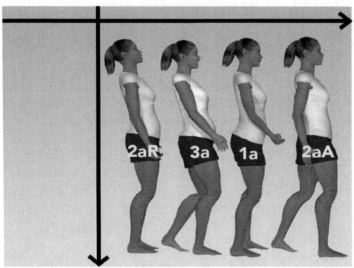

Interestingly enough, all the a-patterns fall in the lower right hand quadrant because all of them have some degree of low muscle tone and a desire to approach, or connect with others. If we try to distinguish between the a-patterns in terms of potential degrees of muscle activation, it is possible to look at these emotions in this way:

- 1a (tenderness) has slightly higher levels of muscle activation because of its greater desire to approach and connect with others, yet it still wants to bring others to the self.

- 2a /R (sensuality/Receptive) is an emotion more focused on receiving sensual pleasures and is less apt to approach or use much muscle tension for moving forward.

- 2a /A (sensuality/Active) is focused on approaching others and would be more prone to slightly higher levels of muscle activation in order to make these connections.

- 3a (joy) oscillates between personal enjoyment of pleasure and wanting to share happiness with others, and so this emotion often falls right in the middle ground between standing in place and wanting to approach others, with varying levels of muscle engagement.

Each emotion's postural point of view will also vary its placement within the quadrant, depending on the emotional intensity. For example, in the case of 2b (fear), someone may have very low-level fear, like shyness or uneasiness, and just a small internal feeling for the need to withdraw (2b/Level 1 in the graph below). As the level of fear rises in that person, their muscle tension rises and their need for withdraw increases, as with nervousness or anxiousness (2b/Level 2 in the graph below). A higher intensity of fear means more muscle tension and a strong need to retreat, like in situations of great shock or terror (2b/Level 3 in the graph below). These are just a few examples of emotional intensity and how it is manifested through the postural points of view. There are plenty of other emotion words for which fear is at the base of the named emotional experience. They could fill in all the spaces in between these three examples on the chart.

As you continue with the exercises in this chapter, keep these postural points of view in mind, particularly when exploring levels of intensity with the emotion patterns and making decisions on what movements you would make with your head, spine, arms, hands, legs, and feet. Consider how you may choose to approach and handle your chosen object when you are experiencing each emotion. Refer back to the Postural Points of View chart to help guide you.

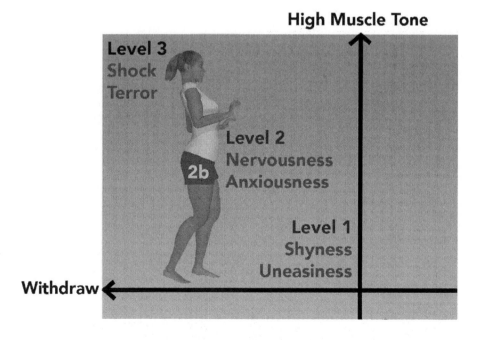

Expressing with Your Emotional Body

Once you have had the opportunity to practice with the pattern drills, and clear as many mixes as possible, it is a good time to experiment with applying the patterns to various modes of expression, including physical expression, speaking, and singing. This level of the practice can be highly rewarding, because you are able to see and feel how the emotion patterns relate to everyday expressions and interactions with your surroundings. To illustrate, let's start with a simple exercise where you can see how your emotional state influences how you feel about your space and the things around you.

Object Endowment

For this exercise, you will need a chair as well an object that you can handle in many different ways and not worry about damaging. An object to consider for the exercise might be a shawl, bath towel, coat, shoe, or book.

1. Place your chair in a space large enough that you have plenty of room to walk both around the chair and at least six paces from the chair. Then, select a place in the room where you will place your object, about six paces away from your chair. Then, go and sit in your chair.

2. To provide yourself with a baseline pattern of movement, stand and pick up the object. Hold it for a moment, and then put it back where you found it, and then return to your seat. This will now become your basic blocking, or pattern of movement, for the exercise.

3. This time, while seated and looking at a focal point (not at your object), start an emotion pattern of your choice. Perhaps it is the emotion pattern 1b (anger). Whichever pattern you choose to start with, build the entire pattern in the seated position, including breath, face, and postural point of view.

4. Once the emotion pattern is fully engaged, turn your focus to the object. Allow yourself to feel that emotion for the object.

5. Then, when you feel compelled to do so, and while maintaining the purity of this emotion pattern, stand and walk to the object and pick it up. Make sure that the way you approach, pick up and handle the object is true to the postural point of view. For example, if you are in pattern 1b (anger), you might advance aggressively and the tension in your arms and hands will cause you to use strong and jerky movements and handle the object firmly or possibly roughly.

6. After holding the object for about a minute, put the object back down in the same place again. Be true to your postural point of view with how you replace the object as well.

7. Then, return to your seat while maintaining the same emotion pattern, and then sit with the attitude of the emotion.

8. Once seated again and while still in the emotion, look back at your object one last time.

9. Then, turn your focus back to your focal point, slowly release the emotion by reducing the intensity of the muscle engagement of the pattern, and engage zero breath.

10. Finally, repeat all the previous steps with a different emotion pattern. Try this exercise with about three different emotion patterns.

 ## Pause & Reflect

How did your feelings for your object change with each new emotion choice? What differences did you notice in the way you handled your object, approached your object, and left your object, depending on which emotional state you were in? Did you notice any stories about the object emerging within the exercise? When context is aligned with emotions, you might feel the need to make sense of the situation. The imagination can quickly create stories or pretend circumstances in an attempt to justify the behavior. This is a natural and expected response when the emotion patterns are applied to activities in which you are interacting with objects and people as well as speaking or singing.

Non-Narrative Movement with the Patterns

After practicing the "Object Endowment" exercise, try exploring a non-narrative movement phrase with the patterns. A non-narrative movement phrase is a series of movements that are not trying to tell a story or provide any literal meaning. The result is an abstract representation comprised of movement.

For example, here is a series of three specific movements that may be considered a very small and simple non-narrative movement phrase:

(1) Stand with feet together and both arms held up in the shape of a Y.

(2) Bring your hands down and place them on your hips.

(3) and then lunge forward, by stepping one foot forward and bending that leg so you can place both hands on the floor on either side of the forward foot.

The actions of this movement phrase do not obviously tell a story or imply any specific meaning or emotion, so the phrase would be considered non-narrative, or abstract. For the following exercise, create a non-narrative movement phrase that consists of three to five specific movements. Make sure there is a clear stop or pause when one movement is complete before the next movement begins. Practice the movements in order until you have the series memorized.

1. Assign a basic emotion pattern to each of the movements in the series. For example, in the movement phrase given above, movement (1) with the arms in the Y might be assigned 3a (joy), movement (2) with arms on hips might be assigned 1b (anger), and movement (3) with the leg stepped forward in a lunge might be assigned 3b (sadness).

2. Practice doing the series of movements with these basic emotions. Do each movement to the best of your ability, but express each with the breath, face, and postural attitude elements of the pattern you have assigned to it.

    For example, in movement (1), with the arms up in a Y, during your initial practice you stood with your arms and legs stiff and rigid, but now this Y shape will be expressed as loose and floppy. In movement (2), where the hands are on hips, you may just need to push the chest up and forward to fully embody anger in this stance. You might have previously embodied the lunge position in movement (3) using taut muscles and an upward and outward gaze, but now with your choice of a sadness pattern application, the lunge will be expressed with some muscular collapse with head hanging down and eyes downcast as you exhale a sigh.

    Practice this series a few times with these emotion patterns and see how the emotions affect this non-narrative movement phrase. Do you feel any meanings emerging because emotions have been assigned to these movements?

3. Then, repeat all the previous steps with different emotion patterns assigned to the movements.

 Pause & Reflect

Take a moment and consider what it was like to explore non-narrative movement with the emotion patterns. Are some emotions more challenging to convey depending on the type of movement you are doing? Do you find mixes coming in as you attempt to retain the original movements you had planned? How much does the emotion affect the movement or gesture? Which is stronger, the emotion or the intent to the convey a particular movement sequence? Is it possible to obtain a balance? This is an important question many dancers, choreographers, actors, and singers consider all the time in their rehearsals and performances. Yet, we also conduct patterns of non-narrative movement every day, and they have the potential to convey emotions as well.

Speaking and Singing in the Emotion Patterns

The exercises up until this point in the book have been purely physical applications of the patterns. Once you begin to speak with the patterns, two things occur that make maintaining the pure emotional state more challenging: (1) the breathing required for speaking and singing will affect the emotional breathing pattern and may cause some level of emotional mixing, and (2) words create cognitive associations, tempting you to subjectively interpret what you are saying rather than simply speak text while staying true to the basic emotion pattern.

As you proceed with the following exercises, recognize that some level of mixing will most likely occur. With this in mind, approach these exercises with the intention of staying as consistent as possible with the application of the basic emotion patterns. For example, speaking or singing in the pure emotion patterns of 1a or 1b is impossible to do if you are staying absolutely true to the basic emotion pattern, since they both require an exhale out the nose. You can easily hum in those patterns and remain consistent with the pure states, but once you open your mouth to speak, some level of mixing is going to happen. When exploring how to speak in these particular patterns, place most of your focus on maintaining the other elements of the pattern (face, posture, voice, and inhalation through the nose), and allow those elements to affect the vocal and physical delivery of the text.

Speaking with the Emotion Patterns

In preparation for this exercise, you will need to choose and memorize a very short piece of text. The best text to work with contains one or two sentences stating something quite common and without inherent emotional content. This way the text will be transformed emotionally by the patterns applied, and not led by the subtext of the words. Selecting the text to fulfill this criterion is not always easy, so to help you, here are some examples:

- It looks like it's going to rain today. Should I bring my umbrella?
- Now where did I leave my book? I was just reading it yesterday.
- The new paint on the wall looks more yellow than white.
- I'm going shopping. Do you want me to pick up anything for you?
- I am going out for a walk. I should be back in about an hour.

1. Select, and memorize, a short piece of text.

2. Start the exercise in the zero pattern. You can do this exercise in either a sitting or standing position.

3. Then, begin an emotion pattern of choice.

4. Gradually add a touch of sound to the emotion pattern. If it is pattern 1a or 1b, this will be a touch of sound through the nose.

5. Allow the touch of sound to extend through the length of your exhale, and let the power of the air, the quality of the vocal source, and the shape of your vocal filters (see chapter 5) affect the sound of your voice as it essentially "rides the exhale." If you are in pattern 1a or 1b, eventually allow your mouth to open halfway through the exhale to let air and sound escape through the mouth as well, in preparation for speaking.

6. Once you have explored nonverbal sound on the exhale for at least three exhales, add the text to your exhale, and do your best to match the vocal quality you found in the nonverbal exploration as you apply the text.

7. While you practice text application for at least three exhales, focus on staying true to the pattern. Check that you are remaining consistent with the integrity of the pattern's basic breath pattern, facial muscle movements, and posture. Raise your awareness of sudden facial expression shifts caused by images evoked by certain words or phrases. If it takes more than one exhale to say your text, don't rush through the text simply to get it out. Some patterns will affect the text quite differently in tempo, rate, volume, pitch, and intensity than other patterns.

8. Return back to nonverbal voicing on the exhale for a couple breath cycles, then back to nonvoiced application, and then simply to experiencing the pattern silently.

9. Shift to the zero pattern.

10. Repeat steps 2–8, by selecting a different emotion pattern to practice with the same text. Continue this practice until you have practiced all the emotion patterns with the same text.

After you have explored this exercise with the short sentences, you are encouraged to try it with other longer pieces of text that you know well. Later in this chapter, in the "Performing Emotional Bodies" exercises, you can explore more levels of expressing text through delivering longer pieces, and with the intention of eventually speaking with emotional mixes.

Pause & Reflect

What was it like to speak the same text in each of the basic emotion patterns? How did the subtext, or meaning, of what you were saying change with each emotion? Did imaginary situations or scenarios emerge during your practice? If so, this is a common reaction to these kinds of exercises, as the brain tries to make sense of the feelings expressed along with language. Did this exploration of speaking text in the emotion patterns help you better understand the relationship between voice, text, and personal expression? What did you learn about yourself, and others, by exploring this exercise?

Singing Emotional Bodies

Singing in the emotion patterns is a great way to explore vocal expression because songs tend to extend vowel sounds longer than regular speech. Depending on the type of song, singing may also use more pitch inflection and provide greater expressive range. As you approach this exercise, consider singing as the next step in vocal expression after speaking. If you have not been comfortable with singing in the past or if you worry about your quality of sound when singing, try to let go of these concerns and focus on the purpose of this exercise as an exploration of vocal emotional expression. You may find it to be quite liberating to approach singing in this manner.

So often in modern cultures the practice of singing is approached as a technical skill or craft, and singing is considered an art only for those who are gifted or talented performers. But what if you were to consider singing as simply another form of human expression, and take away the culturally derived expectations for a specific quality of sound, style of presentation, rhythm, inflection, or pitch clarity?

Take a moment and look at the origins of the word *singing*, which provide clues about the original purpose of singing:[8]

- Singing in Old English was *singan* and meant "to chant, celebrate, or tell in song"

- The Welsh word for singing is *dehongli* and means "to explain, interpret."

- Ancient words meaning "sing" are derived from roots meaning "cry", "shout", and "seize".

---

8. Dictionary.com. Online Etymology Dictionary. Douglas Harper, Historian. http://www.dictionary.com/browse/sing (accessed: July 21, 2017).

Ancient languages remind us of the days when we were more connected with singing as a form of common human expression filled with emotion. Keep these ancient roots in mind during this next exercise, and see if you can fully embrace, from head to toe, the holistic expression of song.

Singing with the Emotion Patterns

In preparation for this exercise, you will need to choose and memorize a very short song. I like to work with short folk songs or nursery rhymes because they are common knowledge for many people and easily remembered, having been ingrained in memory since our youth. The practice of using childhood songs also lends itself well to exploring basic emotions since these songs were introduced to us when we were children, at a time when most of our expressive experiences were with basic emotions. Although cultural folk songs and nursery rhymes will vary depending on your country of origin (you are encouraged to select a song you know well), here are some examples of songs that are useful for this exercise:

> "Twinkle, Twinkle, Little Star"
> "Happy Birthday"
> "Itsy Bitsy Spider"
> "Edelweiss"
> "Baa, Baa, Black Sheep"
> "Jack and Jill"

1. Start the exercise in the zero pattern. You can do this exercise in either a sitting or standing position.

2. Then, begin an emotion pattern of choice.

3. Gradually add a touch of sound to the emotion pattern as you did in steps 2–4 in the "Speaking in the Patterns" exercise.

4. Once you have explored nonverbal sound on the exhale for at least three exhales, begin the song on your next exhale, and do your best to match the vocal quality you found in the nonverbal exploration as you deliver the song.

5. While you continue to deliver the song in this emotion pattern, focus on staying true to the pattern with your voice and your entire body. Check that you are remaining consistent with the integrity of the pattern's basic breath pattern, facial muscle movements, and postural point of view. Take your time singing the song and let the emotion pattern determine the song's tempo, rate, and volume. Give in to this singular emotional expression of the song, fully and with your entire body. Give yourself permission to explore the song as many times as you like in this one emotion, until you feel as if you have achieved a full body expression through voice, face, arms, legs, hands, feet, spine, and body gestures.

6. Return back to nonverbal voicing on the exhale for a couple breath cycles, then back to nonvoiced application, and then simply to experiencing the pattern silently.

7. Shift to the zero pattern.

8. Repeat steps 2–7, selecting a different emotion pattern to exercise with the same song. Continue this exercise with a couple other emotion patterns, using the same song.

After you have explored this exercise with the simple nursery rhymes, feel free to try it with other longer songs you know well. Later in this chapter, in the "Performing Emotional Bodies" exercises, you can explore more levels of expressing songs, with the intention of eventually singing them with emotional mixes.

 Pause & Reflect

What was your experience with singing the same song in different basic emotion patterns? Were you able to fully embody the expression of the song? Singers of all backgrounds and abilities often struggle with embodied expression of their songs, sometimes resorting to stiff, tense deliveries or attempting to express songs using only facial expressions. This exercise encourages the use of the entire body as an expressive instrument for singing and helps singers find greater degrees of expression in their songs.

How did the subtext, or meaning, of the song change with each emotion? Did imaginary situations or scenarios emerge? Did this exploration of singing in the emotion patterns help you become more comfortable with expressing emotion through song? Did you learn anything new about yourself and your relationship to singing by exploring this exercise?

Reevaluating and Revising Your Emotional Body

Learning the emotional effector patterns raises your awareness of your own habitual behaviors and gives you the opportunity to reevaluate and revise various aspects of your expressive behavior and daily habits to better support desired outcomes. This new knowledge and skill can be applied immediately to so many areas of your daily life. Let's first look at your daily breathing, posture, and facial expression habits. Then you can decide if some of these habits are causing unconscious and unnecessary chronic emotional stress on your system. If you do determine that your daily habits are inviting more fear, anger, or sadness into your behavior than you would prefer to experience or express to others, then you might want to consider adopting some of the recommended modifications provided.

Breathing Habits

Pay attention to your daily breathing habits. Spend a few days observing your habitual breathing tendencies. Is there any muscular tension in your upper chest, shoulders, or around your nose when you breathe? When you breathe without speaking, can you hear yourself breathing, as if the act of breathing causes a whooshing or raspy sound? See if you can sense times when you are holding your breath, as opposed to when your breath is flowing easily. Is there a regular pattern to the length of your inhale and exhale, and does one tend to be longer than the other? At least once a day during this period of observation, stop and time your resting breathing rate by counting the number of breath cycles per minute.

Then, consider which sentence (A or B) in each set below best describes the discoveries you made about your daily breathing habits.

> **A.** When breathing in through the nose, the muscles around my nose feel open and relaxed.
> **B.** When breathing in through the nose, the muscles around my nose feel tight and constricted.

> **A.** When breathing but not speaking, I don't hear the air flowing in and out of my body.
> **B.** When breathing but not speaking, I do hear the air flowing in and out of my body with a whooshing or raspy sound through my nose or throat.

> **A.** My resting breath cycles per minute (BCPM) average under 16.
> **B.** My resting breath cycles per minute (BCPM) average over 16.

> **A.** I breathe deeply, using abdominally supported breathing most of the time.
> **B.** I sense high chest muscle activation in my breathing periodically throughout the day.

> **A.** My breathing seems to flow evenly and easily most of the time.
> **B.** I have a tendency to hold my breath for at least a few counts at a time.

> **A.** When breathing out the mouth, the air flow is relaxed, open, and about equal in length to my inhale.
> **B.** When breathing out the mouth, the air flow is long and seeping, I tend to sigh often, and my inhales are shorter than my exhales.

If most of the sentences marked with an *A* describe your daily breathing habits, then your breathing habits support a-pattern emotions. However, if you recognize many of your breathing habits in the sentences with a *B*, then you have tendencies toward the b-pattern emotions. This is the first step in raising your awareness of these habits. Daily or weekly practice of the a-patterns will help reinforce healthier long-term emotional breathing practices and provide options for a new default breathing method. As you regularly tune your awareness into your daily breathing habits, you can also consciously shift your breathing practices in the moment if you notice you are not in an emotional state that is supportive of the immediate situation.

Postural and Gestural Habits

Select three days to observe just your habitual postures and gestures. Is there any muscular tension in your body pulling your body backward or downward? At first, you might bring your awareness to the core of your posture and movement, noticing if your spine has a tendency to tilt or curl in one direction more than the other. Gradually expand your sensing out through your limbs, and pay attention to your gestures as well. Become aware of any postural and gestural tendencies you have when you sit at a desk, eat meals, or interact with others (as opposed to when you are alone). See if you can sense times when your postural point of view changes significantly, and try to recognize what might influence these changes.

Then, after three days of observing, consider which sentence (*A* or *B*) in each set below best describes the discoveries you made about your daily postural and gestural habits.

A. When walking from place to place, I feel my posture is open and flows easily with low muscle tension.
B. When walking from place to place, I feel my posture is rigid with high muscle tension; or my posture tends to be closed off, with arms crossed or hands in pockets, or I tend to hold objects in front of me.

A. When sitting at a desk or table, I tend to sit with upright, open posture.
B. When sitting at a desk or table, I tend to sit with sinking, curling posture.

A. When reading off of a digital device (phone, e-reader, tablet), I hold the device up so my posture is more upright and open.
B. When reading off of a digital device (phone, e-reader, tablet), I hold the device closer to chest level, and my posture tends to sink and curl around the device.

A. When standing around talking with other people, I tend to use open, relaxed posture with inviting arm and hand gestures.
B. When standing around talking with other people, I tend to use closed posture, with arms crossed or in my pockets and closed hand gestures.

A. When I am sitting in a casual setting with other people, I tend to keep my body and my eyes turned to those around me and use open, relaxed posture and gestures that invite conversation.

B. When I am sitting in a casual setting with other people, I tend to keep objects between myself and others (such as a pillow in my lap), or I fold my arms, cross my legs, or look at my cell phone, preferring not to draw attention to myself.

A. When I speak to people, I use direct eye contact and keep my eyes on them most of the time, including after I have spoken with them and while listening to what they are saying.

B. When I speak to people, I don't use a lot of direct eye contact and prefer to let my eyes move around most of the time, especially after I have spoken, to see how my words have been received by others.

If most of the sentences marked with an *A* describe your daily postural and gestural habits, then your habits support a-pattern emotions. However, if you recognize many of your habits in the sentences with a *B*, then you have tendencies toward the b-pattern emotions.

Raising your awareness of these tendencies, and what might be causing them in your daily life, will help you recognize changes you can make to shift to more beneficial practices. For example, if you found your use of digital devices was causing you to have a sinking and curling posture for many hours during your day, then there are easy adjustments you can make to change this habit right away. You can hold your digital device up higher to read texts, use the speaker option on your phone and hold it just in front of your chin, or purchase an e-reader cover with a built-in stand and place it at eye level so you don't need to hold the reader.

If you noticed you were sinking and slouching when sitting at your desk, set up your monitor so it is at eye level. Even if you work from a laptop, purchase a separate keyboard and place the laptop up higher on a box so the screen is at eye level. Choose a chair that allows you to sit toward the front of the chair seat and place your feet flat on the floor, and keep reminding yourself to sit upright. If you find yourself continually slouching and need an extra physical reminder, sit on a yoga ball or get a standing desk.

Be aware of how personal accessories might influence your posture. Carrying heavy backpacks force us to pull our posture forward and curl our shoulders inward to counterbalance the weight. Over time, purses and computer bags hanging from one shoulder cause muscle tension to build up on one side of the body more than the other, making it difficult for us to fully access certain a-pattern emotions.

The next time you sense you are sitting or standing with a lot of muscular tension or in a closed or sinking posture, try shifting to an a-pattern postural attitude right there in the moment and see what happens.

Facial Expression Habits

Recognizing our facial expression habits is more challenging than observing our own breathing and postural habits. Since the face contains our eyes, nose, mouth, and ears, it is central to our sensory perception. We are constantly using these facial aspects to sense our surroundings and, at the same time, to express how we feel. Attempting to evaluate our facial expression habits throughout the course of a few days is highly challenging and unlikely to result in accurate observations. If you don't have the benefit of working with an experienced instructor to provide you with feedback, you might find it helpful to video record yourself in action or find a few video clips others have taken of you and observe. Observing lots of candid photographs is also helpful in recognizing your facial expression habits.

After observing your facial expression habits, either in live behavior or in video recordings or photographed snapshots, consider which sentence (*A* or *B*) in each set below best describes the discoveries you made about your facial expression habits.

A. I tend to have relaxed muscles around my eyes or just a little activation on the outsides of the eyes that causes crow's feet.
B. I tend to have muscle tension around my eyes, particularly under my eyes, causing them to narrow and my brow to furrow low, near the bridge of my nose.

A. My forehead muscles are fairly relaxed and disengaged.
B. My forehead muscles are actively engaged, either pinching together or lifting up, causing vertical or horizontal lines.

A. My eyes appear to sit comfortably and easily in their sockets.
B. My eyes appear to strain forward out of their sockets, as if bulging at times.

A. The corners of my mouth easily pull up and back toward my ears, bringing my cheek muscles with them into a comfortable smile.
B. The corners of my mouth seem to strain or tighten when I attempt to smile, and I can't seem to give a full, cheeky smile.

A. When my mouth forms a smile, my eyes also look like they are smiling.
B. When my mouth forms a smile, my eyes do not look like they are involved in the smile or are showing a different emotion altogether.

A. I find I can open my mouth easily and without feeling excessive jaw tension.
B. I find I can't open my mouth easily, and almost always feel some level of excessive jaw tension.

If most of the sentences marked with an *A* describe your facial habits, then your facial habits support a-pattern emotions. However, if you recognize many of your facial habits in the sentences with a *B*, then you have tendencies toward the b-pattern emotions.

Making changes in your facial expression habits may take some time and require a lot of practice, but it is possible. One of the best ways to make changes here is by doing facial muscle isolation exercises. For example, if you discovered your eyes have a tendency to push forward out of their sockets, then practice the eye muscle movement exercises found in chapter 6, where you bring the eyes deeper into their sockets, to help train the muscles to move in that direction more often. Likewise, if you noticed the muscles on the outsides of your eyes tend not to engage when you form a smile with your mouth, then practice the eye muscle movements in chapter 5, where you encourage the muscles to move out toward the ears in pattern 1a, to help you integrate this facial expression more fully. Practicing in front of a mirror is also helpful because it provides you with immediate feedback on how you are doing with these muscle isolations.

Consciously shifting facial expressions in the moment is possible. The next time you notice you are using a facial expression habit you are working to modify, try shifting to a different expression or do a slight muscle isolation movement right there in the moment and see how you feel.

Self-Regulating Your Emotional Body

Learning the emotional effector patterns is like conditioning your body to become more open and accessible to emotions while you gain clarity on how to physically express them. I often relate this process to that of studying a martial art. Both of these methods rely on an initial developmental process of repetitive exercises and movements designed to build a physical vocabulary foundation. Eventually, this basic physical vocabulary is used to create more detailed movements and elaborate combinations and can be applied to many different types of situations. For example, the martial artist practices basic movements and sequences repeatedly until they are engrained as an auto-response to be deployed when needed within any real-life threatening situation. The emotional effector patterns can be used for self-regulation of emotion as a way of better preparing for personal life interactions and situations that may feel challenging. To better understand how to use the patterns in these situations, let's first look at some general emotion regulation strategies.

In a given situation, where you are consciously aware of the need to regulate your emotions, you might find you tend to use these emotion regulation strategies:[9]

---

9. James J. Gross, "Emotion Regulation," in *Handbook of Emotions*, 3rd ed., eds. Michael Lewis, Jeannette M. Haviland-Jones, and Lisa Feldman Barrett (New York: Guilford Press, 2008), 500–508.

1. Place yourself in a situation that is more likely to elicit emotions you would like to have and/or less likely to elicit those you would prefer not to have

2. Emotionally prepare for a situation by changing your thinking or feeling about it ahead of time

3. Adapt while in a situation in order to achieve a better emotional outcome

4. Change your emotional response from moment to moment

5. Imbue a situation with a new meaning by altering its emotional significance

These strategies could use cognitive methods, like changing your thinking about the situation or changing the topics being discussed during an event. They may also use somatic methods, which involve adjusting your physical and emotional interaction with the event, often resulting in cognitive changes as well. The exercises that follow will expand on how you can use the emotional effector patterns with these strategies.

The Emotional Lens

The saying "The best laid plans of mice and men often go awry" comes to mind when considering how knowing different kinds of emotion regulation strategies can help navigate unexpected challenges. For example, what if the following three occurrences were situations you had planned in order to elicit emotions you would like to have?

(1) walking in your favorite quiet park to help you de-stress from a long, hard day at work

(2) meeting a date at a restaurant where your ex-husband or ex-wife never goes, to avoid an awkward encounter

(3) going to a social gathering where you know a few friends will be as well, to help make socializing a little easier

However, these best-laid plans could go awry if (1) the park is crowded with noisy people, (2) that ex happens to show up for lunch with a friend, or (3) you attend the social gathering and learn your friends were not able to make it and you are now in a group of strangers attempting to socialize on your own. In these cases, although you had carefully planned for each, to achieve a desirable emotional outcome, you will need to employ additional emotion regulation strategies in the moment as well. Here is where you adapt to the environment and change your thinking or feeling about the situation so that your experience is different. To do so, with consideration of how to apply the emotional effector patterns, I recommend putting on a different emotional lens.

To understand how to apply an emotional lens to a situation, it is best to have experienced the emotional lens in an exercise a few times, separate from a stressful situation so you can see and feel how it affects you and your environment. Then, once you have an understanding of how it can be used, you are better equipped to adopt an emotional lens spontaneously or in more challenging occasions. Here is the basic "Emotional Lens" exercise:

1. Find a space outside where you can walk around in nature and not be approached by other people who might interrupt your exercise. Some good examples of appropriate spaces might be your backyard, a park, garden, empty schoolyard, or wooded path.

2. Stand at a selected starting point, and close your eyes. Take in your environment through your other senses. Listen, feel, and even smell your surroundings. Awaken your senses to every nuance of this place, but without using your eyes. Can you feel the presence of a recognizable emotional pattern emerging as you respond to this place? Welcome a pattern in, and allow your whole self to begin a basic emotion pattern that seems to match how you feel in this space right now.

3. Slowly open your eyes and see your surroundings through the lens of this emotion. How does it look to you? How does it feel to you as you take it all in?

4. Slowly move through this place with the postural attitude of the basic emotion you are in, walking a desired path anywhere this emotional lens leads you. Take in this path through your senses. Touch, interact, and pause wherever it makes sense.

5. After about three minutes of exploration, bring your journey back to the starting point and, once back to this "home position," slowly release the emotion pattern and shift into the zero pattern.

6. While standing in the zero pattern, slowly open your eyes and look around the space by simply turning around in a small, slow circle and looking out at your surroundings. "How does this place look and feel to you now?"

7. Close your eyes again. Now, gradually take on a different pattern from the one you just experienced. Pick any of the emotion patterns you would like to explore.

8. Once you feel you have fully embodied the new pattern of choice, slowly open your eyes, and take in your environment through this new emotional lens. How does it look to you now? When you are ready, walk the same path you made in

steps 4 and 5. Interact with the same objects; however, stay true to the perspective and attitude of the new pattern. Does the space feel any different? Are your interactions any different?

9. After exploring the second emotion pattern for about three minutes and returning to your "home position," pick yet another pattern you have not explored so far in this exercise and follow steps 3–5.

10. Complete the exercise with a final Step Out.

 ## Pause & Reflect

What was your experience with the "Emotional Lens" exercise? Did your experience on the path change with each new emotional lens? How did the new emotion affect what you saw, what you heard, how you interacted with the space, and the pace at which you decided to walk your chosen path? This exercise helps us see that we can be on the same journey in the same space with the exact same surroundings, but have a completely different experience depending on our emotional lens. There is an ancient saying, "You cannot step into the same river twice because the river is forever flowing and changing, and so are you." Can you relate this saying to your experience with this exercise?

How might this exercise translate to the life situations mentioned previously? How would you react if you had planned to walk in the park for a moment of solitude, but it was crowded and noisy? What if you were at a restaurant where your ex showed up unexpectedly? And what would you do now if you went to a party, hoping friends would be there to help you socialize, but found yourself on your own? How might adopting a certain emotional lens as a situation modification strategy for each of these examples help you adapt to the new developments in the environment and steer yourself toward a more pleasant outcome?

Although the Emotional Lens practice is not limited to outdoor experiences, it is most beneficial to conduct this initial exercise outdoors where you have more natural stimulation to respond to during the exercise. This helps you recognize how the emotional lens changes how you feel about things you hear, taste, smell, touch, and see. The personal understanding and practice gained during the Emotional Lens exercise in nature can translate to human social interactions as well. Sayings like "Looking at the world through rose colored glasses" and the Thich Nhat Hanh quote "Sometimes your joy is the source of your smile, but sometimes your smile can be the source of your joy" come to mind when I watch people practice the Emotional Lens exercise. It can be transformative to realize how much our own choices in emotional embodiment can dramatically change our experience within an environment.

Variations on the Emotional Lens Exercise

Once you have experienced the basic Emotional Lens exercise, try some of these variations for more advanced practice and application of the basic emotion patterns and their relationship to emotion regulation.

Recognizing Emotional Responses – Begin the Emotional Lens exercise. Follow steps 1–4 and, while you are exploring your space, instead of maintaining one emotion pattern throughout your journey, become aware of how the environment is influencing your feelings, and then adapt your emotion pattern accordingly. For example, maybe you start the exercise in 2a (Receptive), and are walking down a path and investigating the flowers, but then a bee buzzes by your ear, and you recognize a subtle level of 2b as you hear that sound. Instead of maintaining the 2a, switch to 2b and redirect your attention to the source of your fear. Stay in 2b as you investigate the path until something else you see, feel, or hear initiates an emotional change. Perhaps you then see in the distance a child running with a kite and feel some 1a at that sight. Allow that shift to come in as well, and so on. Follow these instinctive emotional shifts throughout your chosen path until you return to the "home position," and then clear to zero. In this exercise, you are building self-awareness of emotional reactions to your environment and recognizing how the slightest sound, movement, smell, or image can shift how you feel.

Transforming Emotional Responses – Follow the instructions for the "Recognizing Emotional Responses" exercises, but with each new emotional response, ask yourself if you would like to try to transform that reaction into a more desirable emotional lens than what your initial impulse was. If so, then transform the response into a new choice. For example, imagine your instinct is to respond to the sound of the buzzing bee with a 2b emotional lens. As a result, you find yourself in an undesirable reaction. You want to see what it would be like to transform your experience with the bee into 1a (tenderness), so you shift into 1a, and explore what it is like to experience the situation through that lens. Continue down the path, allowing yourself to respond instinctively to the environment, but then question the instinctive response and choose different emotion patterns in the moment. In doing so, you are practicing attentional deployment, immediately shifting away from unwanted feelings and focusing on a new choice.

Vocalized Emotional Responses – Follow the directions for any of the Emotional Lens exercises and their variations listed previously, and add vocalized sound to your patterns, as well as a spoken common sentence or phrase. This will help you explore how your voice sounds in these situations as well.

Interacting with Others – If you have the opportunity to do this exercise with other people who have practiced the emotional effector patterns, then you can also add a level of human interaction to the exercise. Have each person select their own starting point fairly close to the other participants, but when they begin their walking path they can go in any direction they choose. This way, people are somewhere within the area and may possibly cross paths, be seen or heard by others, and provide even more stimulus for this exercise.

Managing Emotional Hangover

We are complex emotional beings. We not only develop the basic emotions with which we were born into mixed emotions, but we also manage to acquire emotional entanglements, have emotions about our emotions, and carry our emotions with us well beyond the events that initiated those emotions. We may do this by ruminating on feelings about something that occurred, thereby perpetuating the duration of the emotions around that occurrence. We may also attempt to suppress our feelings about an event, believing it will go away if we don't express the emotion outright. However, the emotion just ends up existing at a chronic low level of intensity with the potential of emerging later on, and most unexpectedly.

How often have you felt a strong emotion about an event and found that you carried it in your body, not just for hours, but for days? Have you ever suppressed an emotional outburst, but found that the emotion stayed with you, feeling like some kind of heavy baggage you were carrying around, until something occurred days or weeks later that triggered a release? You are not alone, and we have all been there at one time or another. In situations like these, learning how to modify your emotional response after an event has occurred can help you influence its impact on your life. Here are some strategies for using the emotional patterns as a somatic approach for response modulation.

Zero Pattern or Step Out – Both the zero pattern and Step Out are excellent transitional measures to take as a practice for clearing away emotion. Whether you are leaving an intense conversation or witnessing an event that stirred unwanted emotions, these two techniques can be used immediately and take a small amount of time. The zero pattern can be accomplished anywhere, often without anyone even knowing you are doing it. If you can get to a quiet private space, you can also complete a Step Out until you feel the emotion has cleared to neutral.

A Pattern Drill or Emotion Purge – There are plenty of times when the zero pattern or Step Out are not enough to clear an emotion, and the emotion may need to be felt, expressed, and essentially purged. This is where conducting a full pattern drill may help. Another option is to use an emotion purge in a case where a certain emotion keeps surfacing and does not clear. In this case you may try to start the emotional effector pattern of the resurfacing emotion, as a way to purge it. We often suppress certain emotions, denying their release and expression. Some emotional theorists have found that if the suppressed emotions are not felt or expressed in a controlled and safe manner, the emotion may stay with us in a low level and may cause more damage in the future.[10]

If you are working with a trained therapist or emotional effector pattern teacher, the pattern drill or emotion purge exercise is recommended as a guided practice, where the instructor or therapist can ensure your clear return to a neutral state at the end. If practicing these patterns on your own, and you are confident that you don't need professional guidance at this time, keep these practice guidelines in mind:The pattern drill or emotion purge is best done in a private, quiet space

- Schedule a practice session that is long enough so you can take your time with each pattern, as needed, and which provides time to fully clear to a neutral state.

- Practice in a place where the emotions expressed are not affecting others, and make sure that you have returned to a neutral state before interacting with others to avoid emotional hangover affecting your life and relationships.

- It is best to use the zero pattern as a transition in between emotional patterns in a pattern drill and to finish the entire exercise with at least one full Step Out.

Select a New Emotional Choice – If the zero pattern, Step Out, pattern drill, and emotion purge are not working, then sometimes a new emotional choice is helpful in reducing the effects of some forms of emotional hangover. For example, if you cannot seem to let go of heavy 3b (sadness), perhaps shifting to the light and bouncy 3a (joy) will help take the heaviness away from your posture and lighten your mood. Additionally, the act of laughter has a wonderful purging quality and may help you release some of the stress associated with 3b. Another example might be if you are feeling nervous or intimidated and need to stand in your power. Adopting low-level 1b (anger) might be beneficial in acquiring aspects of courage or pride because it can pull your posture up and forward and deepen your breathing. Selecting a new emotional choice can be done anywhere and anytime, and when applied on low levels, can even be accomplished without anyone knowing what you are doing.

---

10. E.A. Butler, B. Egloff, F.W. Wilhelm, N.C. Smith, E.A. Erickson, and J.J. Gross, "The Social Consequences of Expressive Suppression," *Emotion* 3 (2003): 48–67.

Not Everything Can Be Self-Regulated

If at any time during your practice of the exercises in this book you feel as if you are still emotionally stuck, or unable to shift out a difficult emotional state, it is advisable to seek the assistance of a licensed therapist, and perhaps one that specializes in a somatic approach. Life can challenge us in so many complicated ways, and sometimes we can't self-regulate our way through these challenging moments. Seeking the aid of a professional who is trained to assist you during these times is a wise direction to take for yourself, as well as for those around you. Remember, not everything can be solved with these patterns or self-regulation of emotion methods.

Performing Emotional Bodies

The emotional effector patterns can be used for any type of performance practice. Whether you are an actor, singer, dancer, storyteller, or musician, you are using your body to express ideas and emotions, and the emotional effector patterns are an excellent somatic approach for this purpose. Before a performer begins to apply the patterns directly to performance practices, they need to first use them for self-awareness, since their own body is their expressive instrument. All the exercises listed so far in this chapter can be used for this purpose. The exercises that follow, however, are more specific to performance practices and applications.

Step Out for Transitioning In and Out of Performances

So often, performance techniques train artists on how to acquire emotional states but do not necessarily provide the tools to get out of those emotions. Additionally, many performance practices provide warm-ups and ways into the work but do not offer cool-downs or ways out of the dramatic world of the performance. The Step Out is an excellent technique to apply regularly to rehearsal and performance practices, as a way of assisting the performer in preparing for the performance as well as in letting it go. Use Step Out as a regular preparation before beginning and ending your rehearsals and performances. This way, you can clear away any potential emotional hangover from outside the rehearsal hall as well as leave the emotions of the performance behind before going home. Step Out can also be used backstage, in between scenes or performance segments, and before going out on stage for a curtain call or talk-back with the audience. Film actors can use Step Out to clear emotions in between lengthy shot setups, and musicians or soloists can use it as a way to center and focus before going on stage for a particularly challenging performance.

Step Out is a private moment during which someone is to be left alone until they clear and re-engage socially with others. When you adopt Step Out as a regular personal practice for performance, select a place off to the side, not in the middle of a public area, where you won't be disturbed. If others have not trained in this method, just ask that you be given the space to complete your exercise until you return to the group. Eventually your practice will be respected and you will be given the space you need to take care of yourself.

Applying Emotions to Performance Texts

Most performance practices use some type of text. Whether it is a script, story, or song with lyrics, the text of a performance conveys meaning in some form. A performer ultimately expresses these meanings with their emotions. The emotional patterns can be applied to text performance in a number of different ways, and the approach you use depends on your preferred performance practices as well as the type of performance you are engaged in. The following exercises provide a few ways to employ the emotional effector patterns with text and explain how these exercises might be applied to performance practices.

Applying Emotions to Text Beats

This is a basic text analysis approach used in rehearsal for connecting the emotion patterns with text. It can be used for any type of script, story, or song. To prepare for this exercise, you will need a short piece of text. It can be a monologue, song, poem, or story that takes no longer than two minutes to perform. The text must be well memorized. To complete this exercise, you will need a hard copy of the piece so you can write notes on and around the text.

1. Break the text into beats. A beat is the smallest unit for which a beginning, middle, and end to a subject or action are implied. A script can be broken down into scenes, and those scenes can be broken into beats. A story is composed of a collection of paragraphs, which can be further delineated by beats. A song is written in verses, and those too can be broken into smaller meaningful beats. A poem is often a collection of stanzas, and those stanzas may have individual beats in them as well. This analytical breaking down to the smallest expressive unit of text is referred to as "beating a script" or "scoring the text," for it resembles the process of breaking down music into measures. However, a beat in a theatrical script cannot be measured by beats per minute or beats per measure, like in music. The beats in a script are measured by identifying shifts in subject matter tactics or minor actions.

    Scoring the text requires identifying shifting beats, and each new beat is identified by placing a line between the beats, or if typing out the text, placing the next beat on a new line. A new beat is signified when the text implies the introduction of a new subject, action, or emotion. Let's use a simple nursery rhyme to demonstrate breaking a text into beats:

    > Jack and Jill went up the hill
    > To fetch a pail of water. *(Beat #1 – Intro of subject/action)*
    > Jack fell down *(Beat #2 – new action)*
    > And broke his crown, *(Beat #3 – new action/emotion)*
    > And Jill came tumbling after. *(Beat #4 – new subject/action)*

2. Assign a basic emotion to each of the beats identified in the text. Selection of

basic emotions is quite subjective and depends on your interpretation of the text and what you are hoping to express with it. For your first time exploring the text, assign basic emotions that seem to match with your own interpretation of each beat. The assignments might look like those noted below:

> Jack and Jill went up the hill
> To fetch a pail of water. *(Beat #1 – 1a, Feeling tender toward Jack and Jill.)*
> Jack fell down *(Beat #2 – 2b, Feeling surprised and scared for Jack falling.)*
> And broke his crown, *(Beat #3 – 3b, Feeling sad that Jack was hurt.)*
> And Jill came tumbling after. *(Beat #4 – 2b, Feeling scared for Jill falling down the hill.)*

3. Rehearse the text with the basic emotions you selected for each beat. Make sure you embody the basic emotion patterns clearly from head to toe and with your breathing as you move from one beat to the next. This is a particularly challenging exercise at first, and most likely if you go too fast or attempt to "act the text," you will immediately start mixing emotions rather than actually applying the basic emotions to the text. If you find this is happening, and clear to zero between each beat so you can remain in control of the pattern application throughout the text. Practice the text with the zero pattern between beats a couple times. Then, remove the zero pattern, and see if you can move from one emotion pattern to the next without mixing emotions. Once you feel you are able to control the ability to shift from one pattern to the next, without mixing, and with full embodiment of each emotion pattern, you are ready to move to the next step.

4. Take one last practice of the text with the basic emotion patterns applied to each beat, and as soon as you finish the last word of the text, go to zero. While in zero, take a moment to consider the story you are telling with this text. Note: "you" can be either the character you are playing or you as the interpreter of the song, depending on the type of text you are performing. Think about the following:

- What is it you are trying to say with this text? Essentially, what is your perspective on or point of view about the text?

- Who are you talking to when conveying this text? Try to see them now, and imagine where they could be if you were to start talking to them.

- What do you hope to gain by sharing the story of this text?

- Can you imagine yourself in a place and a circumstance where all this could be happening? If so, imagine yourself there now.

5.   And when you are ready, start your text again, but this time, do not try to do any of the emotional patterns, but instead let your body memory take you back through the experience of conveying the messages contained in the text, and just focus on sharing your story. The emotions will come up on their own, as they are needed, and in support of the text you have been practicing. This is called, "bubbling up," like little bubbles slowly emerging from a pot of water simmering on a stovetop.

When in the bubbling up stage of this exercise, allow the emotions to bubble up as they wish to appear and however they manifest in your behavior. The hint of a basic emotion may now appear in your posture, gestures, or subtle facial expression. Don't force the expressions. If you have practiced the basic emotion patterns with your text enough, there will be subtle aspects of each of those basic emotions expressed in each beat because of body memory associated with the text. You will find now, unless you are still attempting to consciously control the patterns, that you will naturally start to convey emotional mixes, and the basic emotions you practiced in each beat will make subtle appearances on certain words or phrases.

This is the basic exercise for applying emotion patterns to beats in a text. It can be used as a performance training method, in which you practice the application of emotions to performance, or it can be used as a regular rehearsal method for preparing text pieces for performance. The basic emotion application to beats is a process, but not a product, since most adult humans behave and express in mixed emotional states. This does not mean that you would not use basic emotion patterns here and there in your performance, but the overall expressive product would more often be a collection of mixed emotions and occasional pure states of expressions.

Variations on Applying Emotions to Beats

At first, you may find you assign basic emotions to the beats that are obvious expressions of those beats. However, as you explore the text more, you might want to change the emotions you initially assigned and select new perspectives on the events.

Try some of these approaches for assigning basic emotions to the beats:

- Select a basic emotion that would give you a unique or novel perspective on the action in that beat.

- Consider the opposite of the basic emotion you chose before, to provide you with a completely different reaction to the events in that beat.

- If you consider the text to be on the serious side, try choosing basic emotions that help reveal a humorous perspective, and vice versa.

- If you consider the text to be dark and scary, try choosing basic emotions that tell a light and sensual story, and vice versa.

For example, here is "Jack and Jill" again, but this time with the application of one of these variations. Can you tell which variation is being attempted here? How does it affect the interpretation of the story?

> Jack and Jill went up the hill
> To fetch a pail of water. *(Beat #1 – 2aR)*
> Jack fell down *(Beat #2 – 2aA)*
> And broke his crown, *(Beat #3 – 3a)*
> And Jill came tumbling after. *(Beat #4 – 1a)*

The emotion patterns applied to this Jack and Jill story give it a unique or novel perspective by applying sensual, lusty, and humorous emotions to the first three beats of the story. Exercising some of these variations in emotions with beats helps us break out of our own rigid patterns when interpreting text and provides us with new insights into the text's expressive potential. Try a few different variations of patterns with beats and see what new perspectives you can gain on the text and your expression of it. Eventually you will determine the combination that feels like the best fit for this particular performance text. That is the final combination you will want to practice until you have it well known and ready to bring to the point of bubbling up. The results can be absolutely exhilarating to feel, and riveting to watch in others!

Drop-in

After you have practiced applying emotions to text beats, you are ready to explore the "Drop-in" exercise. Drop-in helps you see how the basic emotion patterns can be applied to your performance practices in the moment, without the need to rehearse the emotion patterns in advance. This exercise explores your own abilities to sense emotional subtext and invite your entire body to feel and express those emotions. This exercise also helps you progress toward the integrative stage of using this technique, where you can simply think of an emotion and allow it to emerge rather than consciously applying the emotional effector patterns to evoke the emotion.

To prepare for this exercise, you will need a short piece of text that you have memorized well. It can be a monologue, song, poem, or story that takes no longer than two minutes to perform.

1. Begin the exercise with your eyes closed and visualize the given circumstances of the text. Consider some of these questions in your visualization:

    • What is my perspective on or point of view about the text?

    • Where am I within the story of this text?

- Who am I talking to? Why am I conveying this to them?

- What do I hope to gain by sharing this with them?

- How do I feel about each and every person or detail within the story of the text?

Take your time mentally answering these questions. Go through the text slowly in your mind as you ask yourself how you feel about every word, phrase, image, or action.

2. When you feel you have a clear sense of the answers to all the visualization questions, open your eyes. Looking out into the space in front of you, imagine the person you are talking to is there and you are in the environment you had imagined.

3. With that first realization of these imaginings, allow a basic emotion to emerge that matches how you feel about what you "see." Then, with this emotion present, begin slowly speaking your text.

4. As you sense a new beat, or shift in feeling about what you are saying, allow a new emotion pattern to shift in as well, and express this with the text, until another new beat is felt, and a new emotion pattern emerges with it, and so on until you complete the delivery of the text.

Here is an example of how this might go with a text as simple as "Jack and Jill":

Performer Visualization of "Jack and Jill" Text:

What is my perspective on or point of view about the text? I want to have fun creating my own whimsical version of the story where Jill is less to blame for Jack's fall.

Where am I within the story of this text? I am at a restaurant.

Who am I talking to? Why am I conveying this to them? I am talking to my good friend, sharing a cocktail before dinner.

What do I hope to gain or get by sharing this with them? I am hoping my friend will see that even a short classic nursery rhyme can have a fun, mysterious back story.

How do I feel about each and every person or detail within the story of the text? I think Jack offers to help Jill get the pail of water so he can attempt to sneak a kiss from her, but he underestimates her reaction. She leans way back

. from his attempt and her move ends up flipping him over her, which because
they are on a hill, throws him and her off balance and they both come rolling
down the hill.

With this visualization in mind, the resulting Drop-in might end up something like
this:

> Jack *(Beat #1 – 2aA, Who is feeling lusty toward Jill)*
> and Jill *(Beat #2 – 1a, He has fond feelings for Jill)*
> went up the hill *(Beat #3 – 2aA, Foreshadows his desires as they go up the hill)*
> To fetch a pail of water. *(Beat #4 – 2aR, This statement becomes a euphemism
> for "to get a kiss")*
> Jack fell down, And broke his crown, *(Beat #5 – 3a, Reacting to the funny
> scene of flipping over Jill's back)*
> And Jill came tumbling after. *(Beat #6 – 1a, Feeling empathy for Jill getting
> caught up in Jack's plan)*

At first, you will need to practice the Drop-in exercise very slowly, to the extent that
it is like speaking and acting in slow motion. Take your time, and allow pauses to
occur while you take on the emotion fully, from head to toe, before speaking. This
will help you condition your body to respond fully and align your embodiment with
text. Gradually, you will increase the speed of this process, and before long, you will
find you can do this instantaneously. But, at first, give yourself the time you need to
develop this ability; don't rush the process. The results will be so much better in the
end if you take your time with this part of your emotional expression development.

Rehearsal and Performance Uses

All the exercises provided in this chapter can be used in preparation for
many different types of performances. With this in mind, in the following
recommendations, the word *rehearsal* refers to any type of practice session you
may have for your performance, whether informal, in-home preparation or more
formal, scheduled rehearsals with a company of performers. The word *performer*
denotes all types of performers, including singers, actors, dancers, storytellers,
performance artists, and public speakers. You can use this method as your own
personal approach and process, or if others in a performance company have
trained in the method, you can share this exciting process with them. Below is
a list of possible uses of the emotional effector patterns, zero, and Step Out in
rehearsals and performances.

1. Utilize Step Out as a ritual for beginning and ending rehearsals or for
    managing challenging moments in rehearsals or performances.

2. Construct the embodiment of your character or your stage persona by using one or two basic emotions as the primary mode for expression and behavior.

3. Explore various perspectives or points of view on the text by changing your initial interpretation of the text with new basic emotion motivations and reactions.

4. Score the text (or dance) with basic emotions in advance of rehearsals and, if practicing the technique on your own, rehearse in the basic emotions at home until you reach the bubble-up phase. If you have the opportunity to rehearse with others who use the method or are open to a rehearsal process using basic emotions, practice for a while using only basic emotions, and then one day in rehearsal make the decision for everyone to shift to bubbling up. It is an exciting moment to see this transition in the rehearsal process.

5. Use Drop-in as a rehearsal tool to help you constantly stay connected to the feelings and meanings of what you are saying and doing. This will then translate into your performance practices and help you stay connected and in the moment with your performance as well.

6. Use a basic emotion pattern (or combination of patterns) to help you access or work through a challenging moment in your rehearsal process. This can be particularly helpful for highly emotional scenes or are emotionally complex. It may take a couple rehearsals exploring the best basic emotion pattern (or patterns) to use to help you find what is needed for the moment, but once you have discovered this and embodied it, your emotional muscle memory will help you reconnect with it more easily in the next rehearsal and in the performance.

Continued Development

When you have practiced the emotion patterns enough that you can apply them from memory to practice drills and exercises in this chapter, they have essentially become a new vocabulary for you. Like any new knowledge or skill, you now have this available to apply to your life, wherever and whenever you find you need it. As with any skill learned, there is a certain amount of practice necessary to maintain it, or to keep it fresh and readily available. Here are a few recommendations for continued practice of the method and for personal development of your new expressive vocabulary:

1. Conduct a pattern practice drill weekly at first, and then after a few months move your practice drills to once a month to serve as a physical reminder of all the emotion patterns, zero and Step Out.

2.   Use the supportive resources provided on www.emotionalbody.co.

3.   Video record yourself occasionally conducting an emotion pattern drill or completing one of the exercises in this chapter, and look for any possible mixes or entanglement habits in your patterns.

4.   If you know someone else who is studying the emotional effector patterns, set up regular practice sessions with them so you can observe each other doing exercises in the patterns and receive feedback on any possible mixes or areas in your body where you are not fully committing to the patterns.

5.   The best way to continue your practice of emotional effector patterns is to attend a workshop or course taught by an Emotional Body instructor. This way you will gain a full understanding of the emotional effector patterns, receive the benefit of personalized feedback, and have the opportunity to do exercises and activities along with others, learning how to share and interact with the emotional effector patterns. Visit www.emotionalbody.co to learn about upcoming workshops and courses.

Meet Your New Emotional Body

You have had the opportunity to learn about emotions, acquire a physical method for accessing their primary states, and practice techniques for embodying them, releasing them, and shifting these states at will. You have acquired a more holistic understanding and clearer sense of your own emotions as well as the expressions of others. This will affect how you think, feel, see, sense, and move through the world. Essentially, you have acquired a new emotional body.

You will find you have gained a new level of respect for all emotions. As you increase the time you spend practicing these patterns and experiencing emotions free from context, the less mysterious these emotions will become. You will learn to sense subtle emotional levels both in yourself and in the behaviors of others. You may find you are able to give more space to others, allowing them to experience their emotions without interfering with that experience.

As you navigate through your days and interact with others, allow your emotions to serve you well in life. Enjoy using your new emotional body!

Made in the USA
San Bernardino, CA
05 March 2020